THE EMERGENCE OF THE MODERN MIDDLE EAST

THE EMERGENCE OF THE MODERN MIDDLE EAST

Albert Hourani

University of California Press
Berkeley and Los Angeles

© Albert Hourani 1981

All rights reserved. No part of this publication may be reproduced or transmitted in any form or by any means, without permission.

First published 1981 by
UNIVERSITY OF CALIFORNIA PRESS
Berkeley and Los Angeles, California
ISBN: 0-520-03862-6
Library of Congress Catalog Card Number: 78-66071

Printed in Great Britain

TO ELIZABETH MONROE
in gratitude for many
years of friendship

Contents

Acknowledgments ix

Introduction xi

1 The Ottoman Background of the Modern Middle East 1

2 The Islamic City 19

3 Ottoman Reform and the Politics of Notables 36

4 A Note on Revolutions in the Arab World 67

5 Sufism and Modern Islam: Mawlana Khalid and the Naqshbandi Order 75

6 Sufism and Modern Islam: Rashid Rida 90

7 The Middleman in a Changing Society: Syrians in Egypt in the Eighteenth and Nineteenth Centuries 103

8 Lebanon: the Development of a Political Society 124

9 Lebanon from Feudalism to Nation-State 142

10 Lebanon: Historians and the Formation of a National Image 149

11 Ideologies of the Mountain and the City: Reflections on the Lebanese Civil War 170

12 Middle Eastern Nationalism Yesterday and Today 179

13 'The Arab Awakening Forty Years After' 193

Notes 217

Index 235

Acknowledgments

Of the essays in this collection, *'The Arab Awakening* Forty Years After'* has not previously been published; it was given as the second George Antonius Memorial Lecture at St Antony's College, Oxford, on 15 June 1977. I am grateful to the editors and publishers who have given permission to reprint the others:

The Ottoman Background of the Arab Middle East: Carreras Arab Lecture, delivered at the University of Essex on 25 November 1969, and published by Longman for the University of Essex, 1970.

The Islamic City: A.H. Hourani and S.M. Stern (eds), *The Islamic City* (Oxford: Bruno Cassirer Ltd, 1970).

Ottoman Reform and the Politics of Notables: William R. Polk and Richard L. Chambers (eds), *Beginnings of Modernisation in the Middle East: The Nineteenth Century* (Chicago: University of Chicago Press, 1968). © 1968 by the University of Chicago.

A Note on Revolutions in the Arab World: P.J. Vatikiotis (ed.), *Revolution in the Middle East* (London: George Allen & Unwin Ltd, and Totowa, New Jersey: Rowman and Littlefield, 1972).

Sufism and Modern Islam: Mawlana Khalid and the Naqshbandi Order: S.M. Stern, A.H. Hourani and V. Brown (eds), *Islamic Philosophy and the Classical Tradition* (Oxford: Bruno Cassirer Ltd, 1972).

Sufism and Modern Islam: Rashid Rida. Bulletin d'Etudes Orientales, vol. 29 (Institut Français de Damas, 1977).

The Middleman in a Changing Society: Syrians in Egypt in the Eighteenth and Nineteenth Centuries. Colloque internationale sur l'histoire du Caire (Cairo: General Egyptian Book Organisation, Ministry of Culture, n.d.).

Acknowledgments

Lebanon: the Development of a Political Society (New York: John Wiley and Sons, 1966). ©1966 John Wiley and Sons.

Lebanon from Feudalism to Nation-State: Middle Eastern Studies, vol. 2 (1966).

Lebanon: Historians and the Formation of a National Image: B. Lewis and P.M. Holt (eds), *Historians of the Middle East* (London: Oxford University Press, 1962). © 1962 by the School of Oriental and African Studies.

Ideologies of the Mountain and the City: Reflections on the Lebanese Civil War: Roger Owen (ed.), *Essays on the Crisis in Lebanon* (London: Ithaca Press, 1976).

Middle Eastern Nationalism Yesterday and Today: reprinted with permission from *Foreign Affairs* (October 1963). © 1963 by Council on Foreign Relations Inc.

I must also thank the following for permission to publish quotations:

Oxford University Press, for the quotation from Albert Hourani, *Arabic Thought in the Liberal Age 1798-1919* (1962).

The Institute of Current World Affairs, New York, for three quotations from George Antonius, *The Arab Awakening* (London: Hamish Hamilton Ltd, 1938).

The Hogarth Press Ltd and Deborah Rogers Ltd for the quotation from *The Poems of C.P. Cafavy,* trans. by John Mavrogordato (London: 1951). © by John Mavrogordato.

I am deeply indebted and grateful to those who helped in various ways towards the publication of this book: Sarah Graham-Brown for her editorial work, Patrick Seale, my literary agent, and John Winckler and the late Allan Aslett of Macmillan.

The essays, together with those for another volume, *Europe and the Middle East,* were prepared for publication during a month spent at the Villa Serbelloni on Lake Como in 1975. Once more I must thank the Rockefeller Foundation for its generosity, and Bill and Betsy Olsen for the care and understanding with which they looked after my wife and myself.

Introduction

The essays in this collection were written at different times and are of different kinds. Some are long, some short; some deal with very general subjects, others with more limited ones; some are summaries of the work of other people, others are based on my own thought and work; some have footnotes, others omit them, either because the subjects they deal with are not of a kind which allows for full documentation, or because the purpose for which they were written made it inappropriate to provide detailed references.

Nevertheless, I think they have two different strands of unity. They all deal with the Near or Middle East, and almost all of them were written as part of a single process of thought and research. They are products of an attempt both to write about the modern history of the region and at the same time to discover *how* to write about it and explain to myself why I have not been more successful in doing so.

There was a time when I believed that I knew how to do it. Some early books and articles, which I now think to have little value, dealt with current problems of Near Eastern politics in a way which was then more or less familiar. They were concerned primarily with the relations between the imperial powers, France and England, and the nationalist movements of the Near East (movements which could not be very clearly defined because their aim was not to defend or justify existing political entities but to bring new ones into existence). The explicit problem of these works was that of the relations which existed or might exist between the European powers and the nations of the Near East, but this problem was seen within a broader framework, that of the 'impact' of western civilisation upon the old civilisations of Asia.

This way of looking at history I learnt, I suppose, at school and university. At school, the detailed study of British political and constitutional history—that is, the study of the development of the oldest unbroken institution in Europe except the papacy—was a

Introduction

subject of compelling interest. At Oxford, one of the historical processes which concerned me was the development of the European states-system, and the relations between the great powers in the nineteenth and early twentieth centuries. I remember in particular the works of W.L. Langer[1] as giving me a sense of the almost mathematical precision which could be attained in the study of changes in political relationships within a system of generally accepted rules.

That I should have tried to write about the Near East in ways derived from these studies can be explained partly in terms of certain personal factors which can be of no interest to anyone except myself, and partly in terms of some books which moved my imagination at a time when I was looking for subjects to think and write about. Two books by Arnold Toynbee played a part: his *Study of History*,[2] and the 1925 volume of the *Survey of International Affairs*,[3] which dealt with the Islamic world at the moment of British and French predominance after World War I, and contained by implication a whole theory about the 'impact of the west'. In George Antonius's *Arab Awakening*,[4] the speed, clarity and elegance of the narrative, and the understanding of men and governments, much impressed me, although after a time I became aware of certain complexities which had been omitted from his analysis of the nature of the Arab movement.

I was able to publish two books of this kind under the aegis of the Royal Institute of International Affairs,[5] to which I shall always be grateful for having encouraged me to attempt a kind of writing by no means easy: that which deals with contemporary or nearly contemporary history, in which men's passions are engaged, with as much precision and detachment as one can muster. After some time, however, I was no longer satisfied with this. I more or less ceased to write on contemporary subjects many years ago, and I have included only a few pieces of this kind in the present volume, and these only because they seem to me to contain a few ideas which I still find to be valid, or some phrases which please me.

I found this type of writing difficult because I was not so successful as others in drawing a line between analysis undertaken for its own sake and advocacy of a particular policy. The Institute had been established after the Peace Conference of 1919 in order to provide for those active in politics, and for a wider and educated public, full and accurate information about other countries, and so

Introduction

help to prevent another disaster such as World War I. It did not as such express opinions, but it naturally attracted to itself those who had a deep concern with policy and strong views about it. I do not think it is correct to say that those who published under the aegis of the Institute had the same views or formed a school, or that all of them failed to prevent their own opinions from intruding. For me at least, however, what is now called 'policy-oriented' writing led to a confusion between two types of discourse, the expository and the moral.

Moreover, since the Institute was British, and books it published were aimed in the first place at a British audience, there was a tendency to address one's advocacy to the British government, and in so doing to overrate the extent to which its policy could be changed. It took me a long time to understand the delicacy of the statesman's art: the interrelations of foreign policy and domestic politics, the need to set policy towards one country or region within a broader framework, the limits within which it is possible to affect the policy of other countries, even of weaker ones, in ways short of invasion and occupation, which themselves set in motion new and unpredictable processes. I tended perhaps to ignore the limits on any government's freedom of action, and in particular to exaggerate the extent to which the imperial governments could impose a form on the matter of Near Eastern society.

It was with some such considerations in mind that, after a time, I began to concern myself more with that 'matter': with the nature and inner movements of the Near Eastern world on which Europe had tried to impose a new form. The Toynbeean concept of contact between separate civilisations still underlay what I wrote, but I was beginning to have a greater sense of the complexity of the process called 'westernisation'. It could not simply be a transfer of ideas and institutions; the civilisation receiving the 'impact' could to some extent determine what it should accept, and adapt it to its own purposes, although in the process it might lose its own purposes and have to rediscover them.

The influence of which I was most conscious at this time was that of H.A.R. Gibb, in particular that of his systematic writings on Islam, the products of his creative period in Oxford of the 1940s and early 1950s, when I was his junior colleague.[6] I was moved by his vision of the Islamic *umma*, formed by a perpetual tension between 'church' and 'congregation', persisting throughout history, resisting the ideas and passions of the world not so much

Introduction

by rejection as by taking what was of value in them and refining it. (I should now place greater emphasis than he did, however, on the Shi'i tradition and the later developments of metaphysical and mystical thought in Iran and India.) What I now wished to do was to study one aspect of this process: the way in which certain new ideas from nineteenth-century Europe were taken into the thought about politics and society which was expressed in Arabic. I did this in a book, *Arabic Thought in the Liberal Age*,[7] which I now consider to have been an extended footnote to Gibb's *Modern Trends in Islam*.

The book took the shape it did because of two concerns, neither of which had any essential connection with the Near East. The first was an interest in the history of thought for its own sake: in taking an idea, showing how it grew, was linked with others within a system, answered certain questions and gave rise to others. This had been the main direction of my studies at Oxford. I belonged to the last generation of those for whom the study of philosophy was essentially the study of its history. In a sense my mind was formed by the careful reading, which then lay at the heart of the syllabus for the Honour School of Philosophy, Politics and Economics, of the movement of epistemological thought from Descartes onwards; Kant was the culmination of the process for most teachers of the time, but I am pleased to have learnt something about Hegel from the last Hegelian in Oxford, before the interest in him died out there, to be revived with different emphases a generation later. Along with this I learnt something about two other lines of intellectual history: the movement of speculation about the origins and nature of civil society, from Plato to Marx, and the history of economic thought.

The development of Arabic social and political thought in modern times offered a special interest but presented special difficulties. It involved tracing two lines of influence: one which ran from medieval Islamic thought to the modern age, and the other which came from outside the Arab and Muslim world, from western Europe and in particular from England and France. Looking at the book now, I think I was unduly concerned with the second line and neglected the first. I had not been trained as an Islamic scholar, although I had lived and worked with some who knew far more than I (apart from Gibb, I think with special gratitude of Richard Walzer and Samuel Stern); I could not so

Introduction

easily hear echoes of Islamic thought in the authors I was studying as those of Comte or Spencer.

The other factor which gave the book its shape was a concern with the problem of belief in the modern world: with the relationship and tension between the attempts of the individual mind and conscience to articulate the truth, and the great cumulative traditions of human thought and spirituality. I had thought much about the nature of a society in which the individual no longer had the support of an accepted tradition, and in particular about the problems which would arise in the second and third generations, when those who had thought themselves out of a tradition were succeeded by those who were indifferent or unaware of it, or for whom it was at most a focus of feeling or a source of social cohesion. What interested me most as I wrote the book was to place moments of thought in relation to each other, to trace the sequence of the generations, from one which was still thinking within an Islamic tradition to one which was near to secularism, and for which even Islam had become a kind of secular heritage, what the Arabs had done in history.

I must confess that I found the later generations less interesting than the earlier ones. In the nineteenth century there had been some thinkers, not indeed of the first order, but of great interest because one could see in them both an inherited sense of responsibility to their own tradition, however they may have interpreted it, and a mixture of curiosity, wonder and anxiety when they found themselves inescapably confronted by the civilisation of Europe. There was a certain excitement in tracing the first attempts of those brought up in this tradition to say new things and to decide how far they could legitimately go in accepting something new into it; this process could be regarded as a new phase in that unending movement in which Gibb had found the inner history of Islam. The later thinkers, writing of nationalism or socialism in terms which did not much differ from those current elsewhere in the 'third world', were doing something which was important within a certain social and political process, but to expound their ideas was not a task which could excite my mind.

A perceptive American historian of a younger generation once told me that, if the purpose of my book were to find out 'what had gone wrong' with the Arab nationalist movement, then I had chosen the wrong subject and the wrong method: such a question could not be answered by a study of what had been written by a

Introduction

few writers for a limited reading public. This was not in fact what I had tried to do, but the point was a valid one. I had said little in the book about the connection between the movements of thought which were its subject and the movements of social and political change with which they were connected. In an essay on Middle Eastern nationalism (Chapter 12), I made an attempt to trace some of the connections, and later I spent some years doing preliminary work for a study of the changes which had taken place in Near Eastern society, and particularly in Syria, during the era of 'Westernisation'. Some of these essays are fragments or by-products of this unwritten study. Some of them are the result of detailed investigation; they are the raw material from which I might have made chapters of a book. Others represent an attempt to think out the categories in terms of which the modern history of the Near East might be understood.

Such an attempt had already been made by H.A.R. Gibb and H. Bowen in *Islamic Society and the West*.[8] This was my starting point, and indeed my book was at first intended as a continuation of theirs. At some points, however, I did not find their framework of ideas suitable for what I wished to write.

Islamic Society and the West had owed its origin to Toynbee's concern for the relations between civilisations; it had been commissioned by the Royal Institute of International Affairs as part of a series dealing with 'the impact of the West'. As time went on, I became more doubtful of the concept of a 'civilisation' as an intelligible field of study: was it possible to think of an entity called a society or culture, spread over many centuries and a large part of the world, but having a unity which in the end could be defined in terms of a single factor? Could human societies and cultures be regarded as the outward embodiment of ideas? These doubts were increased by a colloquium on the 'Islamic city', organised together with Samuel Stern and other colleagues in 1965:[9] what emerged from the discussions was a sense of a continuum of medieval cities, and of the complex ways in which Islamic beliefs and laws were absorbed by urban societies which had a life of their own, determined in part by their own separate histories, and more fundamentally by geographical and economic factors. The work of some sociologists and anthropologists gave me suggestions for a more adequate formulation. I had read something of Max Weber as a student, but only began to feel the impact of his work, and see the relevance of his concept of 'ideal types',

Introduction

when I heard it being discussed by colleagues during a brief period at the University of Chicago in 1963. Later, C. Geertz's *Islam Observed*[10] formulated some of the ideas which ran through these discussions: 'Islam', 'Islamic society', and so on were not embodied realities but 'ideal types' in Weber's sense, that is to say, logically coherent systems of concepts which, if used with care, and in association with others, might help us to understand an individual entity or process in the human world.

The concept of 'Westernisation' or 'the impact of the West' also needed revision. It seemed to imply that certain ideas and techniques which were essentially 'Western' had been imported into, or forced upon, other societies, which to the extent to which they accepted them would become societies of a 'Western' type. Such a statement however was too simple in more than one way. Ideas and institutions which had first developed in western Europe and North America, for historical reasons which could be analysed, might not be essentially 'Western': they might in course of time become culturally 'neutral', so to speak, the common property of all societies in the modern age. When they came into a society, they would not necessarily change it into something other than itself; they might be absorbed into and adapted by a society which still continued to exist and to move in its own way. J. Berque's *Egypt, Imperialism and Revolution*[11] left on me when I read it the indelible impression of a delicate interplay between two rhythms of change, one which foreign rulers tried to impose from outside and one coming from within an ancient society. This would, among much else, throw a different light on the process I had tried to describe in my book on Arabic thought. Intermingled with the movement of acceptance of new ideas were other movements, of thinkers who still lived within one or other of the ancient traditions of Islamic piety and learning and tried to preserve them, although those traditions too were undergoing subtle and sometimes unnoticed changes. At least throughout the nineteenth century, the movements of thought in which social and political change was reflected had to be seen in terms not only of the tension between 'Islam and the West', but also of an older tension between different Muslim ideals, those of personal devotion and legal correctness. Two of the essays (Chapters 5 and 6) say something about this other tension.

The explicit subject of the book then would have been a certain region of the Near East, Syria in the broad sense, with social and cultural traditions which could partly be explained in terms of Islam, during a period when those traditions were undergoing a process of change, of which the pace and direction were determined both by external and by internal factors. This was a region which had social divisions as well as unity, and had no single political embodiment, and to that extent it was more difficult to write about it than, for example, about the Egypt of Berque's book. In thinking about it I became more aware than before of the significance of the four hundred years' experience of Ottoman rule. The Ottomans had brought to Syria as to so many other countries a certain organisation of political and military power, a system of law, methods of administration and taxation, which had deeply affected the nature of society; they had provided also a focus for the political and social imagination of their subjects, who had defined themselves in reference to the Ottoman state and looked on it as the stable basis of the world order. An attempt to write the history of a number of Ottoman provinces would involve seeing them at all times in their relations with the centre. Those relations, however, varied from one time or place to another: Ottoman rule too was in a sense an 'ideal type', to be used in different ways as a principle of explanation, and one of the essays (Chapter 1) tried to explore some of these ways.

The core of the book would have been a study of subjects in their relations with their rulers, of imperial and provincial élites, of imperial cultures and provincial cultures. The dynamics of Ottoman society, however, were more difficult to describe than the statics. To break down society into its constituent units—quarters of cities, religious groups, villages, pastoral groups and so on—was easier than to show how they interacted with each other, and how the modes of interaction changed. In certain kinds of society such questions could be answered partly, although not wholly, in terms of formal institutions: the struggle for power and the uses of power within formally existing and generally recognised institutions provided a field of interaction and a way of studying and describing it. When there are no such institutions, how does the interaction take place and how can it be described? One way of answering these questions would be to say that where there were no institutions there was no significant action, and the history of such a society could only be the history of an all-powerful government. It seemed clear to me, however, that even societies without formal institutions had implicit ones, that is to say, habitual modes of

Introduction

social action, and that the history of the Near East showed not just the imposition of the will of rulers, whether indigenous or foreign, but an interaction between it and the feelings, convictions and collective aspirations of the various social groups. The kind of analysis undertaken by social anthropologists, and more recently by a new type of political sociologist, provided certain tools of explanation: such concepts as those of access, of political manipulation as an alternative to bureaucratic control, of informal alliances and relations of patronage and clientage, suggested a distinction between different modes of politics, those of courts, bureaucracies and 'notables'. A book which appeared at the time when I was thinking about these ideas, I.M. Lapidus's *Muslim Cities in the Later Middle Ages*,[12] helped me to clarify them in a number of essays (Chapters 2, 3 and 4).

By the time I had made these studies I had a fairly clear idea of the kind of framework into which such a book as I intended to write could be fitted, but doubted whether I could write it. It was too ambitious for the resources at our disposal; the detailed monographic work on which it should be based was lacking. Of the three ideas around which a work of social history could be organised—wealth, power and truth—I had by now some idea of how to deal with the second and third, but the first posed more difficult problems. In particular, we did not yet know much about the wealth generated in the countryside and the ways in which it was appropriated by the city. There was not lacking the material on which a study of it could be based, in Ottoman archives, judicial records, business papers and consular reports, but I did not think I possessed the techniques necessary to exploit them. I am pleased to see that younger historians trained in a number of different traditions are now beginning to work on such problems in a way conforming to the highest standards of modern historiography.[13]

Certain words which recur again and again in these essays may need some explanation. I write sometimes of the 'Near East', sometimes of the 'Middle East'. When I use the term 'Near East', I intend to refer to the countries lying around the eastern end of the Mediterranean: Turkey, Syria (in a sense to be explained later), Egypt, sometimes the Balkan countries, sometimes the Sudan and western Arabia, of which the history is linked with those of Egypt and Syria. I use the term 'Middle East' to refer more generally to countries of Arabic speech or Islamic faith. The two terms cannot be sharply distinguished from each other, and I hope the context will make it clear to which region I am referring.

The other word which needs explanation is 'Syria'. When I am writing of the last fifty years or so, I use the term to refer to the Syrian Republic which was established by the French during the period of the Mandate and became independent in 1946. When I write of earlier periods, however, I use the term to refer to an area which extends further to the north and south, and stretches from the foothills of the Taurus mountains to the Sinai desert. This larger area can be regarded as having a certain unity, both cultural and social, throughout most of its history. English writers of the nineteenth century normally called it 'Syria', and I have thought myself justified in doing so too. Its human unity has rarely found a political embodiment, and when I write of 'Syria' in this broader sense I should not be regarded as making an implicit judgement about whether or not it should be politically united.

Wherever a precise transliteration of Arabic is necessary, I have adopted the system used in the second edition of the *Encyclopaedia of Islam* with certain changes; diacritical marks have been omitted in the text but inserted in the footnotes. When a word or name can be regarded as having been anglicised, I have used the familiar English form, and sometimes when a word or name of Arabic origin is used in an Ottoman context I have used the standard modern Turkish form.

While preparing the essays for publication in this book, I have tried to improve them in various ways. I have added a few references in the footnotes and bibliographies, not exhaustively but so as to draw attention to some recent work dealing in a significant way with the subjects of the essays. Every now and then, when I have come across a statement of fact or a generalisation which now seems to me so untrue as to be likely to mislead the reader, I have omitted or changed it. I have tried, however, not to make changes of such a kind as to appear to be claiming greater foresight than in fact I possessed. In the historical essays I have not claimed for myself the results of research done by others since those essays were first written; in those of more political relevance at the end of the book, I have not eliminated predictions which have turned out to be incorrect, or inserted others in the light of what has happened since I wrote.

1 The Ottoman Background of the Modern Middle East

I want to talk this evening about some 400 years of history, stretching from the beginning of the sixteenth to the beginning of the twentieth century (or, to be more precise, from 1516 to 1918) when most of the Arab countries were ruled by the Ottoman Turks from their capital at Istanbul. In older books about the history of the Arabs, you will not find much said about this period. I once asked the author of one of the best-known of them why he had virtually omitted this period; he replied, it was because there was really no Arab history during these centuries. *A priori* it is a little difficult to believe that nothing important happened for four centuries in a region of ancient civilisation, and among peoples who had once created so much, but what he meant, I think, is clear: first, that politically the Arabs played only a minor part in this period, and therefore, the central theme of history is missing (for, although most of us have given up the old conception of purely political history for something broader, even social history cannot be understood if we leave out of account the *struggle* for power in which all social forces express themselves, and the *use* of power in order to maintain, destroy, change or impose a social order); and secondly, that the rule of the Ottoman Turks over Arab society prevented Arab and Muslim civilisation from developing further, or even killed the life it had.

This indeed is a fairly common view of Islamic history, and one held not only by Arab writers. In a sense it is very much of a nationalist view. Those who wish to replace the old political order of the Middle East, based on religious adherence, by a new one based on national loyalty, like other revolutionaries at other times, have used the image of some more distant past as a way of condemning the immediate past. At some time or other the Arabs have appealed against the Ottomans to early Islamic history, the Egyptians to the Pharaohs, the Lebanese Christians to the

Phoenicians, the Turks themselves have looked back beyond Ottomans and Arabs to the Hittites, the Persians to their imperial past, the Jews from the Diaspora to an earlier history in Palestine. Like so many other factors in Middle Eastern nationalism, this is a reflection of certain ideas common in nineteenth-century Europe: the romantic cult of a distant past, blended with the revolutionary idea that man is free to break and remould his social world; more specifically, the idea that the coming of the Turks ended the brilliance of early Muslim civilisation, and prevented it developing further and along lines similar to those on which modern Europe has progressed. Thus Rousseau deplored the domination of the Arabs by the Turkish barbarians,[1] and John Henry Newman, in his *Lectures on the History of the Turks*, allowed them only the virtues of the barbarian (valour, truthfulness, sobriety), denied them the civilised virtues of rational discipline, and accused them of having extinguished an earlier Islamic state, the Caliphate, which had been truly civilised.[2]

So simple and sweeping a view will not stand up to close examination. Anyone who has travelled in the lands which the Turks once ruled—not only what we now call Turkey, but the Balkans, the Arab Middle East and the North African coast—must have noticed how deep the Ottoman impress went and how lasting is the unity it has imposed on many different countries and peoples: the buildings, from the domes and graceful slender minarets of mosques in the Ottoman style, to the solid barracks and government houses of a later period; the formal and elaborate manners of the old families of Istanbul and the provincial capitals, so different from the manners—no less good but in a different mode—of mountain villagers or Beduin; a certain style of government and politics, difficult to describe but which continued almost until our time, not only among Turkish politicians but in the palaces in Baghdad, Amman, Cairo and Tunis, among the older statesmen of Egypt before the revolution, and the older nationalist leaders of Syria, Iraq and some Balkan countries—patient, cautious, carefully balancing one force against another in order to neutralise them all, giving your enemy time and scope to ruin himself, seeing how far you can go but always leaving a way of escape if you have gone too far.

If the traveller finds these relics of the Ottoman past, historians also of the present generation—using the vast Ottoman archives in Istanbul, and being less under the influence of the final disintegration of the Empire into hostile and bad-tempered nation-states than their predecessors—have given us a new picture of the way in which Turkish tribesmen came into the Muslim world and what they did for it. They did not come as alien conquerors into a world which tried to resist them or which could protect, rule and develop itself without them; and they themselves contributed something positive to it, something without which it might not have survived, or at least would not have taken the shape it did.

They first came into the Muslim world from central Asia by one of those movements of nomads which occur from time to time, because of over-population, changes in vegetation or water-supply, tribal wars, or changes in pattern of trade, urban production or government in the settled areas surrounding the nomadic world: in this instance, perhaps, something which happened in China, for Bernard Lewis has suggested that it was 'the consolidation of the Sung régime in China after an interregnum of disorder (which) cut off the route of expansion into China and forced the central Asian nomads to expand westwards.'[3]

But that is only half the story. As Turkish tribesmen came into the eastern regions of the 'Abbasid caliphate of Baghdad, they found a role waiting for them: first of all as mercenary soldiers, but then as something else, as defenders and rulers of Islamic society and civilisation. Here once more there is an ancient fallacy which stands in our way: that Islam was a religion of the desert, and its society was dominated by the interests and values of the nomads. The Arabs may have been, to quote a phrase current in their early history, the 'raw material' of Islam, but once Muslim society and the caliphate were well-established they conformed to the pattern of all Middle Eastern civilisations, at the heart of which have always been the great cities drawing their food supply from a dependent rural hinterland and linked to one another along the trade-routes. It was in such cities that high Islamic culture grew up and the great Muslim governments were rooted, and the main purpose of the governments was to defend the life, society and civilisation of the cities and their hinterland. Settled life was always precarious in the Middle East: if the rural hinterland and the trade routes were to produce the surplus without which large-scale urban life would have been impossible, they had to be protected against nomads and mountaineers, against foreign invaders, and against all those forces, natural and human, which could cause the irrigation system to decay. (There is a very important recent book by Robert Adams, *Land behind Baghdad,* in which he has used all kinds of methods—those of the geographer and archaeologist as well as the historian—to study the use of water and land in a certain district of Iraq from the beginning of history until today, and shown how closely it has been connected with the policies and strength of governments.)[4]

The great Muslim cities needed a political order, and they could not produce it for themselves: as the power of the 'Abbasid caliphs declined, in the tenth and eleventh centuries, there did not emerge—as there did in some parts of medieval Europe—some countervailing power in society itself, which could in the end produce its own self-perpetuating order. The answer of Islamic society to this problem was to produce a new kind of autocracy with a military basis. Within the framework of the caliphate there grew up a succession of states known collectively as 'sultanates'. The sultan ruled within territorial limits and did not claim universal rule over the Muslim world. In general, so long as there was a caliph in Baghdad he acknowledged his formal authority. His power originated not in divine choice but in the sword, it was maintained and handed on to his successors by the sword, but it was turned into legitimate authority by being exercised within the limits of the religious law, the *shari'a* and by being used for the greater purposes of Islam—to extend the bounds of Islam, to protect it against attacks from outside, to maintain orthodox belief and law, to organise and protect the pilgrimage and the other ritual acts.

It is here that the historic role of the Turks is to be found. By and large it was they, and for a time the Mongols with whom their history is closely linked, who provided the politico-military groups which founded and maintained these sultanates. This was true not only of the western or 'Turco-Arab' half of the Muslim world but also of the eastern or 'Turco-Iranian' half. The Safavi Shahs, who virtually created what we now call Persia or Iran, were of Turkish origin, and the language of their court was Turkish for a century or so; the Mogul emperors of India also were of Turco-Mongol origin. That the Turks could play this part they owed partly to their military talents and solidarity, but also to a kind of natural authority and skill as organisers of governments and administrators (I shall return to this later). This was understood and accepted by the Muslim world of their time. Thus the greatest of Arab historians and thinkers about history,

Ibn Khaldun, had no doubt that the Turks deserved well of Islam. To quote Bernard Lewis again,

> he saw in their coming a proof of God's continuing concern for the welfare of Islam and the Muslims. At a time when the Muslim Caliphate had become weak and degenerate, incapable of resisting its enemies, God in His wisdom and benevolence had brought new rulers and defenders, from among the great and numerous tribes of the Turks, to revive the dying breath of Islam and restore the unity of the Muslims.[5]

But it was not an unconditional acceptance on the part of devout and serious Muslims. For the Muslim city populations and for their leaders, the families of urban 'notables' with an inherited social influence and a tradition of religious culture, the welfare of Islamic society demanded a kind of balance or alliance: the sword was in the hands of the Turkish sultans, of their households of high officials and commanders, and of their armies, but they should use it in alliance with the *'ulama,* that is to say, those who were learned in religion and the religious law, who taught, interpreted and administered it. By and large, the sultans accepted this alliance: they respected the *'ulama,* consulted and used them in matters of state, supported the judges who administered the law, the *muftis* who interpreted it and the schools where it was taught; more generally, they used their power in the interests of urban stability and wealth—to keep trade flowing, to proect the cultivator from the nomad. In return, the notables and *'ulama* on the whole supported them: they had common interests, and besides the main tradition of later Islam (or at least of Sunni Islam) is Hobbesian—any government is better than anarchy. But there was often an underlying tension between men of the sword, ethnically different from those they ruled, and not far removed from the nomadic life with its tribal solidarity, and the Persian or Arab sedentary populations. The city notables could bring some pressure to bear on their rulers: they held the keys of legitimacy, they could give the rule of a sultan a kind of Islamic sanction; and they also controlled the machinery of urban politics, they could—within limits—raise or prevent movements of protest and revolt among the craftsmen or proletariat of the popular quarters. On the whole, however, the balance was in favour of the men of the sword, not only *because* they had the sword, but because in most states of this type they added social to political power: the sultan, his officials and his commanders dominated the land, took the rural surplus, and in this way controlled economic exchanges between countryside and city, the food-supply of the urban masses, and the work of the craftsmen. But this also in another way worked in favour of urban civilisation: it gave the Turkish political and military élite their own interest in keeping the city and its hinterland stable and prosperous.

II

It is in this context that we should look at the Ottoman Turks. In its early phases, the Ottoman state was one of a number of Turkish sultanates, growing up in the disintegrating body of the first of the great Turkish empires, that of the Seljuqs, and on the frontier with Byzantium. Then came two events which changed its nature. One is well-known: the capture in 1453 of Constantinople, which became the sultan's new capital, Istanbul. From now onwards the state was one of the greatest in the western part of the Muslim world. It had a large trade with the Italian cities, and became a naval power in the Mediterranean: thus it had close contacts with western Europe and was a factor in the European balance of power. Its own nature also was changed. With Istanbul it acquired for the first time a great cosmopolitan city; the society it ruled was no longer that of hill-valleys and market towns, and it needed a more complex kind of administration. With Istanbul and the Balkans also it acquired a large non-Muslim population, Christian and Jewish, and this too posed new problems of administration.

The other event is less well-known but was no less important. In 1516-17 the Ottomans turned southwards and occupied the territory of the other great state of the western half of the Muslim world, the Mamluk state of Egypt and Syria. From this there followed the occupation of the province of Hijaz in western Arabia, including the holy cities of Mecca and Medina; the occupation of Iraq, disputed for a time by the Safavis of Iran but confirmed in 1638; and the occupation of North Africa as far as Algeria, but not of Morocco, by sea-forces in Ottoman service, in order to prevent the Catholic reconquest of Spain from spilling over into Africa.

This expansion into the Arab countries made the Ottomans the greatest rulers in the Muslim world west of Iran. What was still more important, it brought the Ottoman government into contact with the most ancient Muslim urban civilisation: with the great schools of Cairo, Damascus and Aleppo, with the main stream of Islamic theology and law, and with an urban class which would bring into the new universal Islamic state its own tradition of social leadership and of a balance between government and the forces of society. What was perhaps most important of all, from now onwards the Ottomans were rulers of the holy cities: of Jerusalem; of the Shi'i holy cities in Iraq, Najaf, Karbala and Kazimayn; and of Mecca and Medina, and the main routes of pilgrimage to them. Every year pilgrims from Egypt and Africa gathered in Cairo, pilgrims from Turkey and the Caucasus, Syria, Iraq and Iran in Damascus; they had to be led and defended on the way to Mecca, the holy cities and their inhabitants had to be protected and nourished, the orthodoxy of the religion in the name of which the pilgrimage was made had to be preserved.

From this time until it ended, the Ottoman empire had a distinctive and complex nature. In the first place, it was a family state: one where loyalty focused upon a family, the descendants of Osman, rather than any individual member of it, and where the family as a whole claimed sovereignty. Secondly, it was a Turkish state, in some senses although not in others. The family was Turkish, claiming descent (with or without reason) from the Oğuz tribe from which the Seljuqs also had come. It used all through its history certain forms and symbols of Turkish tribal origin: for example, the horses' tails which were marks of rank in government service. The language of the court, of command in the army, and of the government offices was Turkish. But it was not Turkish in any exclusive racial sense. Throughout Islamic history there was always a consciousness of the differences among Arabs, Persians and Turks, the three peoples who between them had borne the main burden of Islamic history. But it was never a distinction so deep as to destroy the sense of what they had in common as Muslims; and effectively it was a linguistic and cultural rather than a racial distinction. A servant of the Ottoman sultan who used Turkish would not necessarily have thought of himself as a Turk; a subject of the sultan who did not speak Turkish would not until the very last years of the empire have thought of himself as being shut out of the political community.

Thirdly, it was a Muslim state. That does not mean that the sultan thought of himself as caliph or successor of the caliphs. The Ottomans sometimes used the title of 'caliph', but they did so without attaching much weight to it, in the later sense in which it could be used of any powerful just sultan who maintained the ordinances of the Faith. They sometimes used it as a term of praise for other Muslim rulers, and sometimes omitted it from their own titles.

Here for example is a list of titles given in a collection of Ottoman diplomatic correspondence: '. . . the Padshah whose glory is high as heaven, King of Kings who are like stars, crown of the royal head, the shadow of the Provider, culmination of kingship, quintessence of the book of fortune, equinoctial line of justice, perfection of the spring-tide of majesty, sea of benevolence and humanity, mine of the jewels of generosity, source of the memorials of valour . . .' writer of justice on the pages of time, Sultan of two continents and of the two seas, Khaqan of the two easts and of the two wests, servant of the two holy sanctuaries . . .⁶

The title of caliph is missing from this litany, and it was not in fact until the nineteenth century that the sultan began to put forward a serious claim to be caliph of all Islam, as a way of rallying support from Muslims both inside and outside the empire, and of warning the European powers against pressing too hard on him. Until then, the pattern to which the state conformed was that which I have already sketched: it was a sultanate ruling within the bounds of the *shari'a* and devoted to the greater purposes of Islam. It was consciously Sunni, with a consciousness sharpened by the long conflict with the Safavis who were Shi'is. With the Turkish talent for clarity and order, it formed the *'ulama* into a hierarchy with fixed ranks, official appointments and regular salaries. The heads of the hierarchy, the *shaykh al-islam* and the chief justices, were consulted in the highest matters of state, and the provincial judges, the *qadis*, were the main channels of contact between the central government and the Muslim public opinion of the great cities. The government gave patronage and protection to the Islamic schools of the Arab cities, and itself founded new ones in Istanbul to educate those who would fill the highest posts in the religious service. It also subsidised and favoured some of the great Sufi orders, or at least the more orthodox of them: that is to say, the brotherhoods of those following a path to mystical knowledge of God laid down by some master of the spiritual life and under the guidance of his successors.

But, fourthly, the Ottoman empire was yet another kind of state: it was a universal empire holding together in a single framework of order and administration, and a single loyalty to a ruling family, many different regions—the Balkans, Asia Minor, the countries of western Asia, Egypt, the North African coast; many different ethnic groups—Greeks, Serbs, Bulgars and Rumanians, Turks and Arabs, Kurds and Armenians; different religious communities—Orthodox, Armenian, Coptic, Maronite and other Christians, and Jews of more than one kind; and different social orders—people of the cities, peasants of the plains and river-valleys, villagers of the mountains (Albania, eastern Anatolia, Kurdistan and Lebanon), nomads of the steppe and desert. In its dealings with these groups and communities, we can see it approaching an ideal of rule common in later Islamic history, derived in some ways from an ancient Persian theory of kingship, in others from the thought of Plato: that is to say, the ideal of the absolute ruler, standing apart from the society he rules, responsible only to God or his own highest self; regulating the different orders of that society in the light of principles of justice, so as to enable each to act in accordance with its own nature, to live in harmony with others, and to contribute its share to the general good.

It was in accordance with this ideal that final and almost unlimited power lay in the hands of the sultan, living secluded in the inner court of his palace, surrounded by an elaborate household, and with a disciplined army and a carefully organised civil service to carry out his will. In the earlier phases of the empire at least, a clear distinction was maintained between *'askar* and *ra'aya,* those who wielded power and the subjects, and not only the army, but the officials of the household and many of the high officers of state, were drawn not from Turks or other Muslim peoples but from men of Christian origin, from the Balkans or the Caucasus, recruited or conscripted in their teens, trained in military schools or the Palace, and from there sent into the army, the household or the government. They were 'slaves,' but in the Islamic sense, which does not carry with it an implication of human indignity, but means rather bondmen who sink their personality into that of their master, have no loyalty except to him, can therefore build up no dangerous independent power, and whose wealth reverts to him by confiscation at their death.

It was in accordance with this ideal also that the Ottoman government preserved the customs and laws of various communities and gave them the backing of the state. In their collections of administrative regulations *(kanun-name)* they formulated and reformed the customs of various regions in regard to taxation, and therefore to land-use and ownership. The local lords of the mountain valleys, like those of Lebanon and Kurdistan, were fitted into the administrative system by being recognised as governors, fief-holders, or chief tax-collectors of their districts; so long as they delivered the taxes and refrained from troubling the trade-routes, their local rule was recognised. In the same way, some of the nomadic chiefs—like the chiefs of the Mawali in the Syrian desert—were given investiture and subsidies so long as they kept the desert trade-routes open. The non-Muslims posed a more difficult problem: they formed a large part of the population of the empire and owned much of its wealth. Here once more we see the Ottomans using their talent for order and giving logical and formal expression to practices which had long existed in Muslim states. After the conquest of Constantinople, the Greek Patriarch of the city was formally recognised as head of the Eastern Orthodox Christians of the empire, an Armenian Patriarch as head of the Armenian Orthodox, and a Grand Rabbi as head of the Jewish community. They were not only religious but civil heads: their decisions and orders had the force of the government to back them up; they were responsible to the government for the obedience of their communities, and for collecting the poll-tax which non-Muslims had to pay; in return, they and their communities were given freedom of worship and a broad tolerance and protection. (This combination of religious and civil authority is still to be found in places where the Ottomans ruled: for example in Cyprus, where the Greek Archbishop was Ethnarch or head of the nation, and by being so became leader of the nationalist movement and then President of the Republic.)

If we look at the Ottoman state in these different ways, as a Turkish, an Islamic and a universal state, we shall find that there were no lines of exclusion which kept the Arabs out (at least, the great majority of Arabic-speaking peoples who were Muslims). As I have said, the ruling group was 'Turkish', but not in a racial sense; the highest offices were open to all Muslims. But in fact very few men of Arab origin seem to have filled them. There are some exceptions: for example, a son of the famous prince of

Lebanon in the seventeenth century, Fakhr al-Din, drawn into the palace service after his father had revolted and been killed, became a famous official of the household and the ambassador of the sultan to the Mogul emperor in India. We hear also of a few provincial governors of local origin: for example, the Jalili family, who ruled Mosul throughout most of the eighteenth and the early nineteenth century, and who belonged perhaps to a local Christian family converted to Islam. By and large, however, Arabs did not exercise direct political power in the Ottoman service.

The religious hierarchy gave them more scope and served as a channel of social mobility, for the language of theology and law was Arabic, and in principle learning and piety were the only passports needed for religious office. In fact matters were not quite so simple: the highest positions in the religious service tended to be held by graduates of the imperial schools in Istanbul, and members of families with a tradition of office. Even the provincial *qadis* were sent out from Istanbul for a limited period and drawn from this privileged group: here once more we find the Ottoman instinct for preventing any subject obtaining too much power or keeping it too long. But beneath the *qadi* lay other offices in the provincial capitals; his deputy judges, the *muftis* of the various schools of law, the *naqib al-ashraf*, a kind of doyen of the *sharifs* or descendants of the Prophet, the only recognised aristocracy of blood. These were for the most part local men, and in the Arab cities they were drawn largely from ancient Arab families of 'notables' with a tradition of learning and leadership, a kind of *noblesse de robe:* families some of which went back to a period before the Ottomans, and some of which have played a leading role until modern times—the Bakris in Cairo, Khalidis and 'Alamis in Jerusalem, Jabiris in Aleppo, Gaylanis in Baghdad. Under the Ottomans as before, these notables acted as intermediaries between the 'men of the sword' and the local Muslim population. Basically they were loyal to the sultan, but they were also leaders of their cities and heirs of the urban civilisation of Islam. At times they tried to curb Ottoman power or the use of it, and they had the means of doing so: they could mobilise public opinion by making use of preachers, heads of quarters, leaders of popular organisations; and they had some influence through their links with the religious hierarchy throughout the empire, and with its heads in Istanbul. What they did in the cities local Arab chieftains could do in the countryside: *shaykhs* of beduin tribes, hereditary rulers of mountain communities, lords of castles, like those who took over the Crusaders' castles in Syria after the Crusaders left, and dominated the surrounding districts from them. As with the city notables, we find them playing an ambiguous part: recognised by the Ottoman government in one way or another, fitted into the administrative or fiscal system, not usually trying to throw off Ottoman sovereignty, but resisting too much interference in their districts or their rule of it. Here too we find names still familiar: Shihabs and Jumblats in Lebanon; Tuqans in the Nablus district; the *sharifs* of Mecca, a family of descendants of the Prophet whose local power in the Hijaz had some recognition from Istanbul, and who were the ancestors of the Hashimite family.

III

Those of us who are old enough to remember World War II perhaps find it easier than scholars of an earlier generation to understand the swift rise and fall of Islamic states: the rush of armies from one to another of the chain of cities with their fragile hinterlands, spread along the trade routes and divided by steppe or desert. The wonder is not that these mushroom creations for the most part vanished so soon, but that some like the Ottoman state lasted for so long. But sooner or later the impulse which had won and kept an empire weakened, and disintegration began, usually along two lines: first by a fragmentation inside the system of government, the ruler ceasing to control his army or government, and the central government losing control over the provinces; secondly, by the forces of society bursting out of the framework imposed by the government, instruments of order becoming leaders of discontent or revolt, the lords of the mountains and steppes eating away the hinterland of the cities.

Such a process of disintegration can be seen in the Ottoman Empire at least from the seventeenth century onwards. At the centre, the Sultan's power weakened, different groups struggled in the Palace and government; then there came a certain revival by a shift of power to the Grand Vezir and the higher bureaucracy, but a partial and fragile one. In the provinces, there was a growing decentralisation: some provincial rulers, in particular those of the North African 'regencies' of Tripoli, Tunis and Algiers, became virtually independent, giving little more than nominal obedience to

Istanbul; in others, a balance between central and local governments was maintained. Some of these local governments, for example Cairo and Baghdad, were in the hands of groups of Mamluks, self-perpetuating military élites; others, in those of local families who had made their rule hereditary, like the Jalilis of Mosul or the 'Lords of the Valleys' in Asia Minor. In the cities, the Janissary army, which had once maintained order, became a popular political organisation, and sometimes a danger to order. In the mountains, the feudal lords of Lebanon extended their control eastwards over the Biqa' plain lying between them and Damascus, and the lords of Kurdistan moved down towards the Euphrates. In the steppe, pastoral groups crystallised into 'tribes' or 'federations' around new shaykhly families. Large units of this kind ('Anaza, Shammar, Bani Sakhr) threatened established patterns of control over the trade routes in the Syrian desert: in 1757 even the Pilgrimage from Damascus was pillaged by the Bani Sakhr. In central Arabia itself, there arose one of those movements which recur from time to time in Islamic history, products of an alliance between a religious reformer and a dynasty, and aiming at the creation of a virtuous Islamic state: the new state, that of the Wahhabis, occupied the holy cities, rejected Ottoman sovereignty, and rejected also the kind of orthodoxy for which the Ottomans stood. In some places, the countryside no longer produced the surplus to maintain large cities and strong governments, either because of a shrinking of the agricultural hinterland or because the cultivators were under the control of tribal *shaykhs,* no longer under that of urban landlords. In Iraq this process had reached the point, by the end of the eighteenth century, where urban civilisation was threatened, but not yet in Syria and Egypt: eighteenth-century Cairo, Damascus and Aleppo were still splendid and well-built cities.

This was in a sense a natural process, such as had been repeated again and again in the history of the eastern and southern Mediterranean, but with it there was intertwined another and a new process, the growth of the power and influence of the great European states. First of all, military power: the last great Ottoman conquest was the island of Crete in 1669. There followed a long war with a combination of European states which ended in an unfavourable peace in 1699. Then in the 1760s another war with Russia showed that the Turks could not stand up to a major European power: a Russo-Greek fleet sailed the eastern Mediterranean and made landings in Greece and at Beirut. A generation later, in 1798, Bonaparte occupied Egypt for a brief period. With the change in the military balance there went a growth of European influence: the Ottoman government had to make alliances with England and Russia to drive the French out of Egypt, and European ambassadors began to play a part in the politics of Istanbul.

The history of the Ottoman empire in its last phase was woven out of the interaction of these two processes. To begin with, the growth of European influence helped to stop the disintegration. Fear of Europe, and pressure from Europe, gave the Ottoman government an incentive to reform itself; the new military and administrative methods gave it the instruments of reform. For roughly fifty years from the 1820s there was a period of rapid change, known as the *tanzimat* or reorganisation. Brought about by a combination between a reforming sultan and some high officials with a direct knowledge of Europe, its aim was first of all to create a modern army, then to use it to restore the power of the central government over the provinces, and to create a new framework of centralised administration and secular law. Behind these aims lay to some extent a revival of the ancient ideal of kingship: of a ruler governing not by caprice but by natural justice embodied in regulations, and both helped and restrained by a bureaucracy. Mingled with this were certain new ideals: that of citizenship—of all subjects of the sultan having guaranteed rights, and all of them having equal rights and a direct relationship with the government; and the idea of 'civilisation,' of a rational, active, progressive, self-determining, modern way of life, brought into existence by western Europe but open to the whole world.

We should not under-estimate the success of the reforms. If we compare the empire of 1870 with what it had been in 1820, there is no doubt that methods of administration and justice had changed; the non-Muslims were freer; provinces as far away as the Hijaz and Tripoli of Africa were once more controlled from Istanbul; the provincial administration had been reformed and the area of cultivation was growing; a certain idea of Ottoman 'nationhood' was spreading; the amenities of life at least in the larger cities and sea-ports had been improved; the Ottoman community was dragging itself in a cumbersome, half-reluctant way into the modern world. There were visible signs of this, not so trivial as they might seem: in government offices, the frock-coat and fez had replaced robes and turbans; merchants and notables were moving from houses in the old cities to Italianate villas on the Bosphorus, in the new quarters stretching from old Cairo to the Nile, in Smyrna and Beirut; the sultan himself had moved from the old Saray to a smart new Palace on the water-front with chandeliers, gilt mirrors and plush upholstery; he no longer looked like an oriental despot, but like one of that chain of benevolent autocrats, with epaulettes and decorations and careful beards, stretching from St Petersburg, Vienna and Paris to Dom Pedro of Brazil, the Emperor Maximilian of Mexico, and King Kamehameha of Hawaii.

But the process of reform contained in itself weaknesses and contradictions which were to carry the disintegration to its logical end. The reforming combination itself was a fragile one: a sultan who wanted absolute power and a bureaucracy which wanted power restrained by principle and regulation could not in the end agree, and the split came under Abdülhamid II at the end of the century; the *'ulama'*, some of whom had accepted and justified the earlier reform, grew hostile as it went further and threatened the rule of Islamic law; some of the officials put forward the idea of constitutional rule, and an Ottoman constitution was indeed granted for a few years in the 1870s. In the provinces, some of the stronger local governors were able to carry out their own version of the *tanzimat*, and—since the areas they were dealing with were smaller and more compact—with greater success: Tunisia under the Beys and Egypt under Muhammad 'Ali became virtually independent.

Underlying these changes in forms of government were two important changes in the social order, each with results which continued after the empire itself had vanished. First, there was an economic change, in some countries at least: the Middle East became attached to the European trading system as a 'plantation economy,' producing the raw materials of European industry and importing manufactured goods; in particular, the whole economy of Egypt was geared to the intensive cultivation of high-grade cotton on irrigated land for the mills of Lancashire. The result was a change in the relative strength and prosperity of different social groups. The old Muslim merchant class and the craftsmen facing the competition of machine-made goods declined; so did the nomads, whose economy, based on the rearing of camels for transport, was shaken by the coming of new methods of transport. On the other hand, there rose a new group of landowners, through grants of land by the ruler, or the registration of state land in their names, or lending money to the cultivators, or bringing new land into cultivation; and also a new type of merchant living on the import-export trade with Europe—a group largely European in the upper ranks, mainly oriental Christian and Jewish in the lower.

Secondly, there was an intellectual change, produced by new schools, the coming of the printing press and newspapers, the translation of books from English or French, travel, and the experience of living in a world dominated by Europe. Among officials, officers, teachers and merchants, there spread new ideas about how society should be organised: in particular, the idea that it should be organised on a basis of nationalism, of a sentiment of national loyalty and unity in which members of different religious or social communities should join; a nationalism explicitly secular but having, like everything in the Middle East, a concealed religious element. It was because of this perhaps that the idea of an 'Ottoman' nation proved too fragile to resist more limited and robust national ideas: first Serbs and Greeks, then Rumanians and Bulgarians created their own nation-states, then the idea spread to the Armenians, then to the Turks themselves, and to the other Muslim peoples, Arabs, Albanians and Kurds.

In this process of fission too we can see the expansion of Europe as a complicating factor. In some of the outlying provinces, direct European rule was established: by the French in Algeria in 1830 and in Tunisia in 1881, by the British in Egypt in 1882, by the Italians in Libya in 1912. Even in those parts which remained Ottoman until the end, European influence was all-pervading. European banks and merchants controlled the growing sector of the economy, and European concessionary companies built the public utilities. Oriental Christian and Jewish merchants mostly had foreign protection, and whole communities had links with one or other power—the Catholics with France, the Orthodox with Russia. Muslims as well as Christians and Jews sent their sons and daughters to mission schools. Not only the embassies in Istanbul but the consulates in provincial cities were centres of social cohesion and political life. In some parts, spheres of influence had been defined by 1914: the French in coastal Syria, the British in southern Iraq. When the empire fell to pieces after 1918, it did so partly along lines already marked out.

I do not intend to follow the process of collapse in detail, but let me make one last point. Many of the things Middle Eastern countries have in common can be explained by their having been ruled for so long by the Ottomans; many of the things which differentiate them can be explained by the different ways in which they emerged from the Ottoman empire. In Tunisia and Algeria, the Ottoman connection had grown distant and weak before the French came, and European colonisation changed the social structure so forcibly and deeply that little was left of the Ottoman imprint. In Tripoli, the Italian conquest took place at a moment when improved communications and the revival of the constitution in 1908 were strengthening the links with Istanbul; a certain pro-Ottoman feeling lingered in Tripoli during the first decades of Italian rule. In Egypt, the situation was more complicated. Muhammad 'Ali in a sense was a provincial ruler in the Ottoman tradition, gathering all power into his own hands, forming around him a largely Turkish household of officials and officers, turning political into social power by seizing control of the land. Later, much of the land fell into the hands of a new class of large landowners, many of them 'Turco-Egyptians'. Their social power was counterbalanced by that of the European and Levantine merchants and bankers, and the British occupation of 1882 was in some ways a victory for this second group. But not a total victory: the British ruled in uneasy alliance with a Palace and court still largely Turkish; and Egyptian nationalism, directed as it was mainly against the British presence, had undertones of hostility to the Turkish ruler and landowners. Until 1952 the three-cornered struggle of British, Palace and nationalists continued in various forms, and the Palace was a focus for the continuing power and influence of the 'Turco-Egyptians'.

The nation-state of Turkey itself emerged from the ruins of the empire by conscious rejection of the Ottoman past: the Turkish people, the nationalists believed, had wasted their strength trying to hold down an empire; the Islamic autocracy of the sultans had prevented progress. But the break with the past was not so deep as it seemed. The new Turkish state was built round the framework of the Ottoman bureaucracy and army, and this perhaps was why Turkey was able to remain independent of European tutelage. Many of the early leaders (although not Atatürk himself) came from the families of the officers and bureaucrats who had been at the centre of Ottoman government and reform. To have created and maintained the Ottoman empire was the great achievement of the Turks, and the historic imagination of things done in common, on which nationalist states depend, could not for long reject it.

The position of the Arabs in Syria, Iraq and the surrounding regions is perhaps the most complex. The natural leaders of the Arab provinces, the notable families of the great cities, were drawn more closely into the Ottoman system in the later nineteenth century. Their sons went into the imperial civil or military service through the professional schools; after the restoration of the constitution in 1908 they played an important part in Ottoman politics—once the Balkan provinces had gone, the empire became mainly a Turco-Arab state. Moreover, they could not be indifferent to the claim of the sultan to be the last embodiment of the greatness of Islam. But the growth of the Turkish national element in the Ottoman government estranged them from it, and the idea of Arab nationalism gave them a new way of expressing their discontent. It happened that World War I broke out just at the point when relations between Turkish and Arab Ottomans were most strained. Hence the Arab revolt against the Ottoman rule; but most Arabs who joined the revolt did so with misgivings about breaking up the unity of the empire and the Muslim peoples, many of them later regretted having done so, and even after the final separation, the Ottoman legacy remained. In the first generation the Arab nationalist movement was led by members of these same notable families and former officials and officers of the sultan; they brought to the movement a certain style of political action, and a memory of Ottoman unity. At the meetings which founded the Arab League in 1944-5, many observers must have been struck by the Ottoman as well as the Arab links between those who spoke for the various Arab states east of Egypt: they had been at school together in Istanbul, they had been in the same army or served the same government, they had a common way of looking at the world; behind the vision of Arab unity lay memories of a lost imperial grandeur.

2 The Islamic City[1]

When we speak of the 'Islamic city' we can mean several different things, and it is best therefore to begin by making some distinctions. A town or city comes into existence when a countryside produces enough food beyond its requirements to enable a group of people to live without growing their own crops or rearing their own livestock, and devote themselves to manufacturing articles for sale or performing other services for a hinterland. When these goods and services are relatively simple or are sold to the region lying immediately around the town, it is a market town. But it may produce a wider range of goods and sell them to a wider market, or perform more than the simplest services, and if so we may call it a city. But here also we must make distinctions. There are cities with a special function: desert or river or sea ports, for example, which devote themselves to the carrying rather than the making of goods; or holy cities, centres of worship, pilgrimage or religious learning. But there are also cities with many functions: which both make and transport many types of goods, which are centres of secular as well as religious activities, and so on. Among these again we may distinguish some which are centres of administration, the collection of taxes, the control of armies and the dispensing of justice; some of these are dependent or provincial centres, but others are metropolitan, the seats of autonomous or independent governments.

This is one type of division, but of course it is possible to think of others. One which has sometimes been made in recent years is that between 'spontaneous' and 'created' cities: those which have grown up over a long period, because of a particularly fertile hinterland, good natural communications, or some quality of enterprise in their people; and those which have been founded by deliberate act of a ruler or dynasty, to be royal residences or pleasances or centres of government. But an essay by Pauty[2] has shown that this distinction is more apparent than real. However a city comes into existence, it can only survive by taking on some permanent social or economic function. Created cities must become 'spontaneous' if they are to remain alive. Political power by itself will not maintain them: it must be used to create a permanent economic activity (for example, by diverting trade routes), so that, once the power vanishes through a change of dynasty or the destruction of a state, the citizens will be able to maintain themselves. For similar reasons, the distinction which might be made between cities created in Islamic times and those which have survived from an earlier period does not signify much; it may be, as we shall see, that some traces of an earlier time can still be found in the street plan of some Islamic cities, and it is not impossible (although this is more doubtful) that there is some continuity of institutions, but if so the reason is not simply that streets or institutions were inherited from the pre-Islamic past, but that they still performed some function in the Islamic age, and it is this function which will most concern us.

There is however another type of distinction which must not be left out of sight: that based on differences of time and place. What we might call the 'Islamic city' existed in some sense from the seventh century AD until the emergence of a single world-wide society in our own times. Even allowing for the slow pace of change in what we regard as 'traditional societies', it is clear that change did take place, and in the life of cities which existed throughout most or all of this long period several phases must be distinguished, in each of which the city, whether we look at it as a group of buildings or a community of people, had a rather different form. In his book on Aleppo Sauvaget distinguishes five main periods: those of the early caliphate, the anarchy which came when it disintegrated, the 'Turkish' dynasties, the Mamluks, and the Ottomans.[3] Such distinctions will vary from one city to another, but we must always make them; and we must be careful not to think of the Islamic culture and society of the last period, that of the great empires—Ottoman, Safavi and Mogul—as being the 'traditional' Islamic society or culture, that which it has always been.

Again, what we call 'Islamic cities' are to be found in different parts of the world: in Spain and North Africa, Egypt, Syria and Asia Minor, Iraq, Iran, Central Asia, and the Indian sub-continent. We cannot expect that urban life should have taken the same form in all these regions, not so much because of supposed differences of 'national character' as because of varying soils and climates, different inheritances, and involvement in various commercial systems. We might perhaps distinguish the cities in the western half of the Islamic world, with their common heritage from Greece, Rome and Byzantium, and their life passed between the Mediterranean and the steppe or desert where the Arab tribesmen lived, from those in the area of Iranian culture, lying between the Indian Ocean and the steppe or desert where Turkic tribesmen lived; and those again from the cities of the Indian subcontinent. But within each area we should again have to make sub-divisions: between cities of North Africa, the Nile valley, and the Levant; and between cities of Mesopotamia, the Persian plateau and Transoxiana. The danger of not making such divisions is the greater because research has not been evenly distributed. Most study in depth has been done by French scholars in North Africa; there are a few works on Egypt, Syria and Turkey some of them dealing with a later period; on Iran there is less still.[4] Until some of these gaps have been filled, we should beware of applying a North African or Syrian model to Egypt, or one drawn from the region of Arabo-Turkish culture to that of Irano-Turkish culture.

II

By a tacit agreement, most of the papers in this volume are confined to certain among these various types of city, and so will our introduction be. We shall be concerned more with large cities than local market towns, more with the western than the eastern Islamic world, more with the period before the rise of the three great empires than with the period after, and (because the sources are more readily available) more with the second half of that period—the age of the Fatimids, Seljuqs and Ayyubids, the Mongols and the Mamluks—than with the first, the age of the Islamic conquests and the undivided caliphate. Even as thus defined our field is a broad one, and it is the very breadth and variety which give rise to the problem with which our colloquium was most concerned. Over this wide area of the world and these many centuries, can we really speak of something called the 'Islamic city'? Did cities in the Muslim world have any important features in common, and if so can they be explained in terms of Islam, or must we look for other types of explanation?

A generation ago the answer to these questions seemed clearer perhaps than it does today. A number of scholars, who combined vast knowledge of detail with imaginative power and artistic sensibility, had put forward various ideas in the light of which it appeared that cities in the world of Islam did have a common character. Georges and William Marçais, both working in North Africa, suggested that the shape of the Islamic city was determined only in part by the exigencies of power (which decided, for example, where the citadel, the walls and the gates should be), but in part also by their being Islamic; or, in other words, by the fact that the city is necessary for Islam, since it is only there that the virtuous life as Islam conceives it can be fully lived. The congregational mosque in the centre of the city, the religious schools beneath its shadow, the hierarchy of *suqs,* whose position in relation to mosque and schools was determined by the religious role of the goods they sold or the attitude of the *shari'a* towards them, the residential quarters with their ethnic or religious solidarity, the cemeteries and shrines of saints outside the walls: all these, they suggested, existed and were where they were because the city was a Muslim city.[5] Massignon, going a stage further, asserted that there was one type of socio-religious institution above all which dominated the life of the Islamic city: the professional corporation or guild, going back beyond Islamic times into the Sasanian empire, encouraged by the Isma'ilis, having a religious basis and sanction expressed in rites of initiation and the cult of patron saints. Such corporations created within the framework of the *turuq,* the brotherhoods of mystics, provided (Massignon believed) the basis of urban society in the Muslim world: of solidarity between man and man, and of individual self-respect, the craftsman's belief in the worth of his own labour.[6] Yet another French scholar, Sauvaget, studying first the physical shape of cities and through it the human community, showed by close research in Syria that the physical shape of what we usually call the Islamic city was that of the Greco-Roman city which had preceded it, but somewhat changed by the dynamic forces of Islamic society. The classical cities planned by the Seleucids and embellished by the Romans, with their broad colonnaded avenues, temples, market-places, and rectangles of streets, were slowly transformed but kept traces of their first state. When the Arabs came, mosques and palaces gradually took the place of temples and cathedrals or were built on the *agora;* a certain lack of grandeur in the Islamic conception of the city, and the emphasis of

Islamic law on the individual, led to the gradual encroachment of shops and dwellings onto the broad avenues, and when the period of anarchy succeeded that of the early caliphate, the insecurity of life caused the population to withdraw into the city-quarters, small units where the ties of neighbourhood were reinforced by those of common religious allegiance or ethnic origin. With this, the city ceased to exist as a moral unity.[7]

The very clarity and precision with which such theories were stated revealed the problems inherent in them. From the writings of a Marçais or a Sauvaget there emerged a vivid sense of the 'personality' of an Islamic city, of the continuous tradition of civic life in Damascus or Aleppo or Fez, of a 'spirit' which had made it possible for the city to assert itself again and again as a force in Islamic history. In those of Massignon one could find an explanation of how this spirit had persisted and expressed itself: for him, Islamic society was essentially corporate, and urban Muslims had some special power of organising themselves, maintaining their communal existence in the face of political power, and giving it a religious sanction. But if we compare the Muslim cities with those of western Europe in the same period, a different and even a contrasting impression emerges. Max Weber suggested that there were five distinguishing marks of the city in the full sense: fortifications, markets, a court administering a partly autonomous law, distinctively urban forms of association, and at least partial autonomy. In this sense, Weber maintained, the city had fully existed in Europe, never in Asia, only in part and for short periods in the Middle East.[8] His definition does more or less correspond to what Europeans would think of as a city, and if we accept it then we must accept his conclusion that Middle Eastern cities are not cities in the full sense. Of his five marks two at least are missing in the Islamic city. It would usually have a market and a wall; if Massignon were right, it would have distinctively urban forms of association; but it had no legal privileges conferred by the state, for the *shari'a* recognised no privileges for one group of believers above others; nor, apart from some rare exceptions (some short-lived municipal bodies in Spain and North Africa), did it possess autonomy.

Thus we seem to be faced with a paradox. How was it that the 'Islamic city' was able to maintain its personality, its power of collective action, throughout Islamic history, when it never possessed municipal institutions in which that personality could be formally embodied, or a municipal law which would at once express and legitimise it? How was it that urban Muslims showed—once more, if Massignon is to be believed—such a power of corporate organisation in other ways, but were unable to create this kind of institution?

III

In the light of recent research as revealed in the papers published here, it is clear that in some respects the problem has been falsely presented. So far as the physical shape of the Syrian city is concerned, Sauvaget's work stands in principle unshaken, although Elisséeff's paper corrects it in certain important ways.[9] But Massignon's view of the corporate nature of Islamic society can scarcely be maintained. The exact opposite indeed might be nearer the truth: in the Islamic view of the world there was the individual believer and there was the whole community of believers, but in between there was no stable grouping regarded as legitimate and permanent. Islamic law did not recognise corporate personality except in a limited sense, and the whole spirit of Islamic social thought went against the formation of limited groups within which there might grow up an exclusive natural solidarity hostile to the all-inclusive solidarity of an *umma* based on common obedience to God's commands. Not only did corporations have no moral or religious basis, it is not certain that they ever existed. Cahen's paper throws doubt on Massignon's theory of the professional corporations and shows that they were not 'guilds' in the medieval European sense, but as they existed, were instruments of state control.[10] It was only at a later period, he suggests, that they acquired a life of their own. (Here we may carry his doubts further and ask whether even the 'guilds' of Ottoman times had so much of an independent life as we may be tempted to think. Except in a few specialised occupations did they exist in a fully articulated and autonomous form? Can we find more than a chief—*shaykh, amin*—whom the government recognised as responsible for his fellow-craftsmen, but whose independence and authority may have been limited; a certain community of feeling and interest among those who practised the same craft, often in the same part of the bazaar; and certain ceremonies, in particular at the moment when an apprenticeship was completed, of which the importance is difficult to assess?) More generally, Stern suggests that the absence of professional organisations is only one example of the absence of organisations in Islamic society.[11] Seen in this light, the lack of municipal institutions is not an exception which needs to be explained, but a further example of this general rule, and to be explained in the same way as other examples, by those features of Islamic law and theory already mentioned, and also by the fact that the power of the state was rooted in the city and this made it difficult for autonomous institutions to grow up.

It is clear moreover that the autonomous cities of the classical world and of medieval Europe, privileged corporations within a larger state, or city-states themselves, are not the norm which all cities at all times have tended to approach, but an exception which itself needs to be explained. Here as in other matters we may be misled by Weber's insistence that his ideal types were 'value-free'. His main problem was always to explain the emergence of the rational, bureaucratic, industrial society of modern Europe; he himself was conscious that special conditions had been present which enabled Europe to develop in such a different way from other societies, but it is easy to draw the inference from his writings that this unique society is the norm and others have been arrested or diverted in their natural development towards it. Very special conditions were needed to produce the chartered city of medieval England or the urban republics of northern Italy: in Italy, for example, the disintegration of Roman authority while urban life and trade continued, and in northern Europe the growth of monarchies based on a rural economy and society. These conditions did not exist in medieval Europe before the eleventh century; they ceased to exist fully in Europe when the nation-state and the modern bureaucratic government developed; they never existed in most of Asia and the Muslim world.

It would not however be true to say that, because municipal privileges never existed, urban life never existed. As Aubin points out, the city in the Islamic world resembled other Asian cities in its lack of formal institutions.[12] This lesson is driven home by Gernet's paper from which it appears that, at least until the growth of a commercial bourgeoisie in the Sung period, the urban conglomeration had no recognised existence at all in China.[13] In the vast sedentary empire, where the hand of the imperial government lay equally on all, a city was simply a piece of land where the population was particularly thick (and not always even that); it had no special government or administration, no special function in Chinese society. In one way the picture is like that of the city in the Muslim world, but in others very unlike; they are alike in the absence of municipal institutions and autonomy, but unlike in the quality and volume of public life. The Chinese city is passive beneath imperial rule, but the Islamic city is active, even disturbingly so, whether its activity takes place within the confines of a political system willingly or unwillingly accepted or tries to break out of it. It is this positive feature of public activity, rather than the negative one of not possessing what European cities possessed from the eleventh century onwards, which poses our real problem. How did this activity express itself? Why was it that Islamic cities were able to maintain it so continuously? To what extent, in this respect, did they differ from the cities of China, India, the Byzantine Empire and western Europe in the same period?

IV

If we are to understand this or any other aspect of the Islamic city, it may be best to begin not with the city in isolation but with the settled area of which it forms a part. The fact from which Middle Eastern history starts (or started before the technological revolution of our age) is the fragility of settled life. West of the Indian sub-continent, the regions in which Islam took root were those in which scarcity of water or the threat of the nomadic pastor made agriculture precarious (but we should not of course build on this fact any general theory about Islam being a faith specially adapted to such regions). The peasant could not maintain himself unless such water as existed could be stored and canalised, or unless there were some natural or human obstacle against the coming in of the nomad. For both these purposes a division of labour was needed. The village needed the town; but the town could not exist without the food produced by the peasant and delivered to the urban market, whether for sale or in payment of taxes. The basic unit of Middle Eastern society was what some social scientists have called the 'agro-city', the urban conglomeration together with the rural hinterland from which it drew its food and to which it sold part at least of its manufactures.

This basic unit can be analysed in one way, into town and

countryside, but also in another, into two mutually dependent components, government and society. The countryside needed a ruler, with an army and administration, to hold back the nomads; the town too needed him to maintain its hold over the countryside and thus ensure its food-supply, and to maintain also the system of laws which harmonised private interests and without which a complex urban life would not have been possible. But the government needed the wealth of the 'agro-city'; it could only exist, on any but the smallest scale, in an area where the production of food and manufactures was so far in excess of what the producers needed as to carry the burden of a palace, an administration, and an army.

There existed then a basic harmony between government and 'agro-city', or at least those elements in it which had an interest in a prosperous and settled life: craftsmen and merchants, scholars, those cultivators who had a safe tenure of their lands, and those who, although not themselves cultivators, had been able to establish a claim to part of the produce of the land and whom we call (by an analogy with western Europe which may be misleading) the 'landowners'. The mutual dependence was all the closer as the city grew in size and the government in strength. A large city had to have not only an immediate agricultural hinterland, but a larger commercial hinterland as well; it had to be an organising centre, a stage, or a terminus of trade-routes, and this would make possible a diversification of products, a division of labour, a standard of living and a growth of population such as could not otherwise exist. For all this too the city needed the power of the government, not only in order to protect existing trade-routes against pirates, nomads, mountaineers, foreign governments and mercenary armies, but even to create new trade-routes; as Aubin remarks, the power of the government could be used in various ways to draw towards its capital or provincial centres trade and wealth which formerly had followed other courses. On the other hand, the bankers, merchants and craftsmen of a great city, producing goods for a wide market and financing or organising international trade, would bring in revenue and enable the government to maintain a more complex administration and a more powerful army.

Such a relationship between government and settled urban society had existed in the Middle East before the rise of Islam. In the Islamic period it was given a distinctive shape by two factors:

first, the virtual monopoly of political power over most of the Muslim world, after the 'Abbasid caliphate disintegrated, by politico-military groups of mainly Turkic origin, Islamised but not always deeply so, and standing at a certain distance from the Arabic or Persian-speaking peoples whom they ruled; and secondly, the close connection between the commercial bourgeoisie and the *'ulama,* those learned in the law and other religious sciences, belonging to or grouped around the mosques and schools. This connection had several aspects: members of bourgeois families took to learning, men of learning married into such families, the *'ulama* possessed a certain economic and social power through their control of the *awqaf,* and both groups shared an interest in a stable, prosperous and cultivated urban life. Members of the great bourgeois families and of the *'ulama* together provided an urban leadership: their wealth, piety, culture and ancient names gave them social prestige and the patronage of quarters, ethnic or religious groups, crafts, or the city as a whole.[14]

This relation between government and urban society may help to explain the forms and limits of activity in the Islamic city. If we look at the city from above, from the point of view of the ruler, we may have the impression of a passive society on which a hierarchy of control has been imposed. At the apex stood the ruler and his 'household', a group closely identified with him, almost in fact an extension of his personality: this included his family, his harem, his palace officials, his personal army, whether 'slave' or 'free', with a professional *'asabiyya* oriented towards maintaining him in power. Beneath the ruler lay a whole system of control: the governor and his household, the secretaries in the government offices, the *sahib al-shurta* or *muhtasib* who maintained order, the *qadi* who administered justice, other functionaries who supervised public acts of worship, the heads of quarters, of villages, of crafts, and of non-Muslim communities, whom the government held responsible for the payment of taxes and the maintenance of order and obedience. All these could be regarded as emanations of the ruler's personality, possessing an authority derived from his and existing to carry out his orders and wishes. But on the other hand they had a connection, which could be a close one, with the urban society they controlled, and this not only exposed them to pressures from it, but also made it possible for them to have a social power and influence independent of the ruler. Some of those exercising functions in or for the government might themselves be drawn from the urban population. This would be true of the *shaykhs* of quarters, villages or crafts; it might be true of higher officials also—as Ashtor-Strauss has shown, a *ra'is al-balad,* responsible for police and order in the whole city, was often found in Syria before the Ayyubid period.[15] In the same way, many of the holders of posts connected with law or worship would be drawn from the local *'ulama,* and so too might be the *qadi.* Even those who were not by origin from the local urban society might be drawn into it. They had at least the tie of religious faith; they might be closely connected, by the necessities of their work if not by blood or marriage, with leading families of the city; the holders of religious posts would have some connection with the local *'ulama*; officials or soldiers who were given land-grants or held tax-farms would be drawn into the economic life of society and might partially control the exchanges between town and countryside. More generally, the ruler and his subordinates could not lightly ignore the wishes of those groups in the city with which their interests were bound up.

When formal institutions do not exist and the exercise of power is not defined, political roles tend to be ambiguous. The 'notables', the leaders of the bourgeoisie and the *'ulama,* obeyed the government not only from fear or self-interest, but from concern for peace and security, from that preference for social peace at almost any price which was the principle of later Islamic society, and from the final need of the city for political power and authority, to bring in the food-supply from the rural hinterland and to keep the trade-routes open. But they were also 'leaders' responsible to the urban population. At times they could use their independent power over it to mobilise urban forces and put pressure on the ruler. This mobilisation was carried out through an ancient machinery of contacts between notables of the city and leaders of quarters, popular preachers, *shaykhs* or *turuq,* leaders of certain crafts, and leaders of organisations of the under-employed unskilled workers, or of the peasants whom economic chance drew backwards and forwards between the rural and urban parts of the 'agro-city'. In this process even those who held posts under the ruler might take part: the *qadi* could become a spokesman for the local *'ulama,* the *shaykhs* of quarters or villages could act as clients of local leaders rather than servants of the ruler.

Circumstances would decide whereabouts on the spectrum between obedience and rebellion the local leaders and their followers would be found. There were times and places when a relatively stable balance existed, when a strong government ruled in close partnership with the bourgeoisie and their leaders, and the influence of the leaders was thrown on the side of the existing order. But there were other times when the balance was shaken, and, because of a weakening of authority or the widening of the gap between the interests of the ruler and those of the townspeople, the urban leaders and notables would emerge as organisers of protest or even of rebellion. But it did not often happen that such a movement was taken to the point of an overturning of authority. Throughout most of our period, the social norm remained that of close cooperation between men of the sword and notables of the city. As Stern points out, it was in general only at moments of interregnum, when a dynasty or state had collapsed or been defeated, that the local leaders came forward as a provisional government: they would administer the city for a time, until one of them emerged as ruler, or until they had to hand it over to its new master. Lapidus explains why it was that, such rare exceptions apart, the local leaders could not take the place of the rulers.[16] On the one hand, the popular forces which they could use or manipulate were themselves divided; the only effective popular associations were those based on the quarters, there were no effective professional or 'political' organisations on a city-wide basis, except for certain 'marginal' and 'anti-social' associations whom the higher orders of the city could only control and use up to a point. On the other, the active leadership tended to be in the hands of the *'ulama,* the religious element in the upper bourgeoisie, and they, because of their very conception of society and of their place in it, were not able to integrate the various elements of the city into a political whole. This could only be done by the military rulers; hence the long predominance of 'Turkish' or Mamluk ruling groups, acting both as rulers and as patrons or local leaders, until, much later, the decline of Ottoman authority led to the re-emergence of local leaders in the provincial cities.

At times indeed the 'popular' forces, the instruments of political action, could escape from the control both of the government and of the urban leaders and throw up their own leaders. Hence those long-lived bodies which both Lapidus and Cahen have studied— *'ayyarun, harafish,* and so on. They might continue to exist for centuries, but, as Lapidus has shown, their basis was not the city as a whole but a small unit, the quarter or group of quarters, and their aims were essentially non-political. They could trouble ruler and urban leaders alike, but could not take their place.[17]

V

It would be a mistake to try to see the physical shape of the Islamic city simply as an expression of its social structure—of such factors as these: the predominance of a commercial bourgeoisie linked with the upper *'ulama;* the distinctive religious institutions of Islam; the ethnic difference between ruler and people; and the moral distance between the ruler's household and the society around it. A city cannot be just an external sign, in stone or wood or mud-brick, of a system of social ethics or social institutions. Aubin reminds us that there are many factors which affect the shape of a city, and first of all there are physical factors. A city must have an adequate supply of water, it must have an adequate hinterland of cultivable land, its streets and buildings will follow the contours of the land on which it is built. Apart from these physical factors, its shape will be affected by an uncounted multiplicity of individual choices not always known as such.

With such reservations in mind, it may however be possible to construct a picture of what a 'typical' Islamic city would look like. To do so is of course a dangerous task, as innumerable variations will be found in so large an area and over so long a period of time. But, speaking very roughly, we may say that we should expect to find such features as the following. First, there would be a citadel, very often placed on some natural defence work, and serving indeed to explain why there is a city at all in that place; Sauvaget for example has shown that Aleppo is where it is because of a natural *tall* dominating the countryside around, and Elisséeff suggests where the *tall* of Damascus must have been. Secondly, there might be a royal 'city' or 'quarter' which would have grown up in either of two ways, as shown in the difference of emphasis between the papers of Lassner and El-Ali about the origins of the Round City of Baghdad:[18] it might be a royal enclave implanted in an already existing urban conglomeration, or it might be a new foundation on virgin soil and around which a conglomeration later grew, attracted by the power, wealth and prestige of a court. However it began, it tended to be more than a palace: it would be rather a 'compound', grouping royal residence, administrative offices, places for the bodyguard or personal troops. Its situation, shape and size depended largely on the relations of government and society. In disturbed times, the compound might also be the citadel, the strong point of defence; in times of ease and confidence, of prosperity and a sure control of society, the court might move to more spacious surroundings, out of a desire for peace and tranquillity, for solitude, or magnificence; and when it moved it tended to draw the government after it. Rogers' study of Samarra shows how difficult it is to disentangle motives or to discern the exact nature of a royal foundation, which may have been pleasance, palace, and administrative centre at once.[19]

Thirdly, there would be a central urban complex, which would include the great mosques and religious schools, and the central markets with their *khans* and *qaysariyyas,* and with special places assigned for the main groups of craftsmen or traders. The great houses of the merchant and religious bourgeoisie would be in this district, although, as Raymond has shown, the houses of the 'military aristocracy' would be near the centre of political power, wherever that might be.[20] To explain why religious and commercial buildings should be close together, we may refer partly to that alliance of bourgeoisie and *'ulama* of which we have already spoken, but also, at least in cities of Greek or Roman origin, to a process analysed by Sauvaget. The Muslim conquerors planted themselves in the complex of *agora,* central avenue and temple or church which stood at the heart of the Greek city; the mosque replaced or stood near the church or temple, the central bazaars and what went with them took over the avenue and *agora.*

Fourthly, there would be a 'core' of residential quarters, marked by at least two special characteristics: the combination of local with ethnic or religious differentiation, and the relative separateness and autonomy of each quarter or group of quarters. The development of both these characteristics again is not hard to understand. As a new city developed or an old one expanded, the immigrants—soldiers, merchants, peasants, nomads—tended to settle in compact groups: Massignon has shown how this happened in Kufa,[21] and it can be seen today in the *bidonvilles* of the great cities of the Middle East and North Africa. Methods of administration and tax-collection strengthened and perpetuated the separateness of these groups: it was simplest and most satisfactory to hold each group collectively responsible, and recognise one member of it as local chief.

The separateness was still further strengthened when the authority of the ruler weakened, both because the quarter provided a viable unit of defence, and because of that 'ambiguity' of leadership which has already been mentioned: chiefs of quarters would have more of the character of 'subordinates' when the government was strong, more that of 'leaders' when it was weak. But it is doubtful whether the autonomy of the quarters reached the point where, to quote Sauvaget again, the moral unity of the city dissolved; as Scanlon's paper shows, there must always at the least have been some kind of general arrangements for traffic, water-supply, the removal of refuse, and so on.[22]

Fifthly and finally, there would be the 'suburbs' and outer quarters, where recent and unstable immigrants would live and certain occupations be carried on: in particular the 'caravan' quarters spread out along the main roads. Here whatever planning the city centre showed would leave little trace; even in the cities of Roman and Byzantine Syria, there must have been such 'Semitic' conglomerations around the central core. Some of these would be outside the city walls, built around the shrines of holy men, and touching the great cemeteries which surrounded the cities. Outer suburbs and cemeteries might—as Scanlon shows to be true of Fustat—lie outside the jurisdiction of the urban authorities, and be the home of outlaws.

VI

How far are such features as we have described, in the city as human community and as physical entity, peculiar to the Muslim world, and how far are they to be explained in terms of Islam? Both Cahen and Aubin warn us that it is more correct to talk of cities in *dar al-islam* than of Islamic cities. Cahen shows that many of the characteristics of what we call the 'Islamic city' are in fact those of the 'medieval' city: of the Byzantine city, of the Italian city before the eleventh century, even of the Chinese and central Asian city to some extent.[23]

Even some of the features which seem to be peculiar to the city in *dar al-islam* may not be due to Islam as a religion. Ought we, for example, to explain that special balance between military élite and bourgeoisie, between authority and rebellion, by the Islamic theory of politics? It is tempting to do so but it may be dangerous.

We must at least ask whether there are not other explanations, economic or political: the conditions in which settled agriculture was carried on in the Middle East, the need for irrigation and urban capital; the pressure of Arab and Turkish nomads on the countryside and the trade-routes; and so on.

But when all this has been said, there still remains something which may be explained in terms of Islam. To say that 'Islamic civilisation was urban' may be commonplace but is still valid to some extent. The Islamic institutions were concentrated in the cities: mosques, schools, *zawiyas*. They possessed a kind of prestige and strength which neither rulers nor bourgeoisie could ignore, and it was for this reason that they provided a framework for urban life. Through them the ruler's acts could be legitimised, the city-dwellers could take corporate action, and the two could be morally linked. The close connection of the *'ulama* with the bourgeoisie gave a distinctive shape to the urban society of the Islamic world.

Islamic law too helped to shape the city. As we have said, it did not recognise the corporation, only the individual and the community of believers. In the interests of the community, the ruler had a duty to intervene in order to regulate the relations of individuals, to prevent one individual infringing the freedom of others. It was in this way, as Brunschvig has shown,[24] and as Scanlon reminds us, that the existence of the city was given a kind of indirect recognition by the *shari'a*: regulations had to be made for roads, drainage, the burial of the dead, and so on. But otherwise, all the emphasis was on the freedom of the individual to seek the goods of this world and the next in his own way, and to dispose freely of them. Both Brunschvig and Sauvaget have pointed out that this tension between the freedom of the individual and the rights of his neighbour, with the balance weighted in favour of the first, is relevant to the problem of how the classical was transformed into the medieval 'Islamic' city.

The individual, in Islamic law, belongs to the *umma,* but he is also enclosed within another unit, the family, the basic and irreducible unit of social life, the possessor of property. What is in essence a much older conception of the family was carried by the spread of Islam to regions where it may not have existed, and was strengthened and sanctified by the *shari'a*. The right of the family to live enclosed in its house led, as Torrès Balbas has remarked,[25] to a clear separation between public and private life; private life turned inwards, towards the courtyard and not towards the street; in the thoroughfares, the bazaars, and the mosques, a certain public life went on, policed and regulated by the ruler, active and at times rebellious, but a life where the basic units, the families, touched externally without mingling to form a *civitas*.

3 Ottoman Reform and the Politics of Notables

This paper was presented to a conference on the beginnings of modernisation in the Middle East, held at the University of Chicago in 1966. It was intended as a brief first statement of certain ideas which I hoped to formulate more fully and to justify in a longer work. I did not therefore think it necessary at the time to provide full references for what I wrote, and now it is too late. I have given references only to a few works which are explicitly or implicitly mentioned, and to one or two more recent ones in the light of which some of my statements might need to be revised. I acknowledge with thanks a number of useful criticisms and suggestions made by Professors J. Berque, P.M. Holt and Stanford J. Shaw and Dr. E.R.J. Owen.

It is a commonplace that we cut up history into periods at our peril: the artificial frontiers made for convenience may seem to be real, and a new generation of historians will have to spend time removing them. Nevertheless, to think we must distinguish, and the best we can do is to try to make divisions which reveal something important about the process we are studying. The old division of history in terms of states and dynasties was not without its value; the imposition for example of Ottoman rule on the western part of the Muslim world was an event of great importance, however we look at it. But it is too simple and therefore misleading to go beyond that and make a further distinction simply in terms of the strength or weakness of Ottoman rule; the traditional division of a period of Ottoman greatness followed by one of Ottoman decline does not help us much to find out what really happened. Perhaps it would be more satisfactory to begin by making a distinction in terms of the kind of sources which we as historians must use; this might have a significance beyond itself, both because the sources we use help to determine the emphasis we place within the complex whole of the historical process, and because the appearance of a new and important type of source, or the disappearance of an old one, may reveal a change in the social order or intellectual life.

From this point of view we may make a very rough division of Ottoman history into four phases. In the first, we must rely mainly on Islamic literary sources (using the term 'literary' in its widest sense) and archaeological evidence. In the second, we must add to these the Ottoman archives; they form a unique source for the study of how a great Islamic government worked, but one which must be used in combination with the literary sources if we wish to study also how Ottoman society changed. In the third—stretching roughly, we may say, from 1760 to 1860—the relative value of types of source changes once more. The control of the central government over Ottoman society weakens or is exercised in a more indirect way; the archives in Istanbul keep their value as showing what the Ottoman government thought or intended, but that may have been very different from what actually happened. In some provincial centres important archives exist—Cairo and Tunis are obvious examples; but in others those kinds of document which Professor Shaw has used to good effect[1] may not have survived. In most great cities we can probably find documents kept in the *qadi's* court, but once the reforms began the *qadi* lost his central position in the provincial administration, and the documents we most want to see may not have been registered in his court. Once new courts were established to administer new legal codes, however, their records were systematically kept and can be used to throw light on the effects of the reforms upon Ottoman society.

In this third period the European sources come to have the importance which an earlier generation of historians thought they had for the second. We refer not so much to the travellers; their books are usually to be treated with suspicion unless like Russell they spent a long period in the place they are describing, and in the nineteenth century they are perhaps even less reliable than for earlier times, because the coming of the steamship made it possible to travel rapidly and superficially, the power and wealth of Europe cut the traveller off from the people among whom he moved semi-regally, and romanticism cast the shadow of the observer's own temperament across what he was supposed to be observing. We refer rather to the reports of European diplomats and consuls, and also of Europeans in the Ottoman or Egyptian service. In this period they contain evidence of more direct importance than before for both political and economic history (although rarely for the history of thought). Even a serious and well-informed ambassador, in the seventeenth century, found it difficult to know what was really going on in the *saray*. But by the early nineteenth the ambassadors and consuls of the major powers were not just repeating information picked up haphazardly and from a distance. The growing weight of European interests in the Middle East made it necessary for the governments of Europe to be fully and precisely informed, while the desire of the Ottoman government (and the dependent governments in Egypt and Tunisia) to maintain their independence and reform their methods obliged them and their local governors to take the representatives of the European states at least partly into their confidence.

The process of change which took place in this period was one which, by and large, the population of the empire and its dependent states—even the educated part of it—did not understand. It was change imposed from above, not yet accepted by most elements in the population, affecting the system of law and administration but not as yet the organisation of society. For this reason the indigenous 'literary' sources change in nature and value. The Muslim tradition of chronicles, biographies and descriptions continues for a time: apart from al-Jabarti, we may point in a later generation to Ibn Abi Diya'f in Tunis, al-Bitar in Damascus, Sulayman Fa'iq in Baghdad, 'Ali Mubarak in Cairo, and the official historiographers in Istanbul. But those who write within the religious tradition now have a different relationship with authority. The faith in the continued existence of a strong, autonomous and God-preserved Islamic *umma* has been shaken, and the impulse to record the names and virtues of those who have preserved and transmitted the heritage of Islam through history grows weaker; the men of the old culture, looking on their rulers as alien in ways of thought, no longer find it possible or desirable to record their acts. On the other hand, a new school of Christian writers arises in Syria and Lebanon, the product of a new education which has taught them both better Arabic and the languages and ways of thought of Europe. But they too are far from the sources of power, and (except in regard to the princely government in Lebanon itself) possess neither the knowledge nor the self-identification with power which is necessary for the political historian.

In the fourth period, which begins roughly in 1860, the importance of this last factor changes and the historian can use a new combination of sources. The importance of the diplomatic and consular records continues; that of the Ottoman and Egyptian documents increases, as the governments impose a more direct and pervasive control over society, and thus require and are able to obtain fuller and more accurate information. But what distinguishes this fourth from the third period is that the changes which had been imposed from above are now increasingly understood and accepted. There is a new self-awareness and, linked to it, a new and more active interest in the political process, a new concern to take part in the movement of change and determine its direction. We are entering the modern age of the continuously and consciously self-changing society, and once more the indigenous literary sources become important: not so much works of history (although modern history-writing begins with Muhammad Bayram and Cevdet Pasha) as the play, the novel and most of all the press-article aiming to inform, advise, criticize or arouse feeling, written not by the *'alim* responsible to an existing order regarded as of eternal value, but by the politician concerned with power or the intellectual acknowledging no sovereign except his own vision of what should or what must be.

II

We are here concerned with 'the beginnings of modernisation'; that is to say, with the third of our four periods. What kinds of source are important for this period we have already said, and in regard to each of them we can ask a further question: what can we expect it to tell us? Each of them can of course be used for one purpose at least, to throw light on the opinions or assumptions of those who wrote it; but can it be used beyond that, and for what?

There is no need to answer this question in detail here. Some of the main lines of an answer are clear. The archives of governments, in a region and age where outside the large cities custom was still king, tell us what rulers or officials wanted to happen but not always what really happened. To take an obvious example, that of land-tenure: as Professor Lambton has shown,[2] the relationship which existed between landlord and peasant was never in exact conformity with the theory of ownership laid down by law, whether *shari'a* or modern statute. Again, diplomatic and consular reports must be treated with caution because those who wrote them were themselves actors in the political process, and wrote their reports not simply as a historical record of events but, often, to justify themselves to their government or persuade it to adopt a certain line of action; moreover, ambassadors and consuls tended to be drawn into the struggles of parties in central or local government, and so reflect (sometimes more than they knew) the views of the party which looked to them for help and to which therefore they had access.

One limitation is common to most of our sources, and it is this which concerns us here. The voice of an important part of the population is scarcely heard in them, or heard only in a muted, indirect and even distorted form: that of the Muslim town-dwellers and their traditional and 'natural' leaders, the urban notables. For example, from all our vast documentation about the events of 1860 in Syria and Lebanon, we can discover with some precision and from within the attitudes and reaction of Maronites, Druzes, Turks, and European governments, but we have scarcely an authentic record of the attitude of the Muslim population and its leaders, except for a short work by al-Hasibi and some passages in al-Bitar's collection of biographies. Again, from our still vaster material about Muhammad 'Ali, we can trace in detail the development of each aspect of his policy, and the growth of a new ruling caste, but we cannot easily discover how the Muslim urban population and its leaders reacted to it. Some reaction there must have been, and we come on traces of it in the later pages of al-Jabarti or when 'Umar Makram is sent into exile. But it is not easy to build anything from these hints, and our usual picture of Egypt in the nineteenth century is an odd one: at one end, a gradual increase in the political activity of the urban population, going on throughout the eighteenth century and reaching its height in the period between the first revolt against French rule and the movement which carried Muhammad 'Ali to power; much later, in the 1870s, a sudden upsurge; and in between virtually nothing, a political vacuum.

This is an important gap in our knowledge, for the urban politics of the Ottoman provinces (at least of the Muslim provinces) cannot be understood unless we see them in terms of a 'politics of notables' or, to use Max Weber's phrase, a 'patriciate'. There are many examples in history of 'patrician' politics. They differ from one place and time to another, but perhaps have certain things in common. This type of politics seems to arise when certain conditions exist: first, when society is ordered according to relations of personal dependence—the artisan in the city producing mainly for patrician patrons, and the peasant in the countryside, whether nominally free or not, also producing mainly for a landowner, either because he cannot otherwise finance himself or because the landowner holds the key to the urban market; secondly, when society is dominated by *urban* notables, by great families which (like those of medieval Italy but unlike medieval England and France) reside mainly in the city, draw their main strength from there, and *because* of their position in the city are able to dominate also a rural hinterland; and, thirdly, when these notables have some freedom of political action. This freedom may be of either of two kinds. The city may be self-governing, and the notables its rulers, a 'patriciate' in Max Weber's full sense; or else the city may be subject to a monarchical power, but one on which the urban population wishes and is able to impose limits or exercise influence.

It is this second kind of situation which we find in Muslim history. Very rare exceptions apart, what exists is not the republic ruled by patricians, but monarchy, rooted in one or more cities and ruling their hinterland in cooperation with, and in the interests of, their dominant classes. In such circumstances we find certain typical modes of political action. The political influence of the notables rests on two factors: on the one hand, they must possess 'access' to authority, and so be able to advise, to warn, and in general to speak for society or some part of it at the ruler's court; on the other, they must have some social power of their own, whatever its form and origin, which is not dependent on the ruler and gives them a position of accepted and 'natural' leadership. Around the central core of this independent power they can, if they are skilful, create a coalition of forces both urban and rural. But this process does not necessarily end in one notable or one party of notables drawing all the forces of society into its coalition. In such political systems there is a tendency towards the formation of two or more coalitions roughly balancing one another, and for this several reasons may be given: leadership of this kind is not an institution, and there will always be those who challenge it; since the leader has to combine so many interests, and to balance them against the interests of the ruler, he is bound to disappoint some groups, who therefore tend to leave his coalition for another; and it is in the interest of the ruler to create and maintain rivalries among his powerful subjects, as otherwise he may find the whole of society drawn up against him.

The two aspects of the notable's power are of course closely connected with each other. It is because he has access to authority that he can act as leader, and it is because he has a separate power of his own in society that authority needs him and must give him access. But for this reason, his modes of action must in normal circumstances be cautious and even ambiguous. At moments of crisis direct action may be possible and even be needed. The notables lead a revolution against the ruler, or themselves become rulers during an interregnum; when one dynasty is displaced by another, it is the notables who act as caretakers and surrender the city to its new master. But at other times they must act with care so as not to lose touch with either pole of their power. They must not appear to the city to be simply the instruments of authority; but also they must not appear to be the enemies of authority, and so risk being deprived of their access, or, through the full exercise of the ruler's power, of the very basis of their position in society. Thus in general their actions must be circumspect: the use of influence in private; the cautious expression of discontent, by absenting themselves from the ruler's presence; the discreet encouragement of opposition—but not up to the point where it may call down the fatal blow of the ruler's anger.

III

Ottoman Istanbul was above all a centre of government, comparable, as a Muslim city, not so much to those great organic growths which held the deposit of many ages of Islamic history, but rather to the imperial foundations by which new dynasties marked their greatness. The greatest strength of the government was naturally concentrated in its capital, and there was almost no local countervailing power independent of it. Istanbul had not existed as a Muslim city before the conquest, and the conquerors found there no ancient Islamic society with its inner structure already full grown and having its 'natural' leaders in ancient families with an inherited social prestige. Trade was largely in the hands of foreigners or members of religious minorities, who as such were not able to exercise leadership or obtain power (except for such derived influence as the Phanariot Greeks had for a time); and the obvious need to keep the capital supplied with food made it necessary for the government to prevent that growth of urban domination over the rural hinterland which in other places made it possible for city notables to control the economic exchanges between countryside and town.

Moreover, the class which, in other cities, provided the spokesmen for popular grievances and demands—the 'ulama—was here very much of an official class, owing its influence to the holding of high religious office in the government, and therefore nearer to the ruler than to the subject; in course of time too it tended to be dominated by privileged families passing on wealth and the tradition of state service from one generation to another. It is true that, at least in the later Ottoman period, the Janissary organisation gave the members of the regiments a means of expressing their discontent. But while they could disturb the government they could not themselves control it, and they were themselves indeed the instruments of political forces inside the government. The politics of Istanbul were not the 'politics of notables' as we have defined them but something different, court or bureaucratic politics. The political 'leaders', those who formed and led combinations and struggled for power, were themselves servants of the ruler and derived the core of their power from that, not from their independent position in society. But, as Professor Itzkowitz has shown,[3] the path to power and leadership within the government changed from one Ottoman age to another: in the sixteenth century, it had led through the schools and service of the palace, but by the eighteenth it was more common for civil servants to rise to the top.

In the provincial centres, however, Ottoman power took a different form. Here the distinction of 'askar and ra'aya could have many undertones, ethnic, religious and other. Ottoman governors and officials came from far off, spoke often a different language, did not usually stay long enough to strike roots; the standing forces they could rely on were normally not sufficient to allow them to impose their authority unaided. To rule at all they had to rely on local intermediaries, and these they found already existing. At least in Asia and Africa, the lands the Ottomans conquered were lands of ancient Islamic culture, with a long tradition of urban life and separate political existence; both by necessity and because of a certain view of government, the Ottomans when they came tried not to crush and absorb but to preserve or even revive good local customs. In such conditions, when authority can only maintain itself with local help, a 'politics of notables' can grow up.

But who were the 'notables'? The concept of a 'notable', as we shall use it, is a political and not a sociological one. We mean by it those who can play a certain political role as intermediaries between government and people, and—within certain limits—as leaders of the urban population. But in different circumstances it is different groups which can play this role, groups with different kinds of social power. In the Arab provinces there were three such groups. First there were the traditional spokesmen of the Islamic city, the *'ulama,* whose power was derived from their religious position. They were necessary to the Ottoman government because they alone could confer legitimacy on its acts. But while in Istanbul they were an official group, in the provinces they were local groups: apart from the *qadi,* the others—*muftis, naibs, na'ibs*—were drawn from local families. Their positions alone would have given them influence, but they derived it also from other sources: from the inherited reputation of certain religious families, going back many centuries perhaps to some saint whose tomb lay at the heart of the city; from the fact that, in spite of this, the corps of *'ulama* lay open to all Muslims; from the connection of the local *'ulama* with the whole religious order and thus with the palace and the imperial *divan;* and from their wealth, built up through the custody of *waqfs* or the traditional connection with the commercial bourgeoisie, and relatively safe from the danger of confiscation because of their religious position.

Secondly, there were the leaders of the local garrisons. They too were necessary to the government because they had immediate control of armed force, but they also had a certain independence of action. They could rely to some extent on the *esprit de corps* which an armed and disciplined body of men develops; and the leaders of the Janissaries in particular controlled the local citadels under direct orders from Istanbul and were not responsible to the local governor. In some places also the Janissaries in course of time took roots in the city: they enlisted local auxiliary troops; membership of a regiment became hereditary; particular regiments indeed became closely identified with particular quarters of the city. Thus they served not only as military bodies but as organisations for defence or political action.

Thirdly, there were those whom we might call 'secular notables' *(a'yan, aĝas, amirs)*: that is to say, individuals or families whose power might be rooted in some political or military tradition, the memory of some ancestor or predecessor; or in the *'asabiyya* of a family or of some other group which could serve as its equivalent; or in the control of agricultural production through possession of *malikanes* or supervision of *waqfs*. (This last factor was of particular importance, not so much because it gave them wealth as because it enabled them to control the grain-supply of the city, and thus indirectly to affect public order and put pressure on the government.)

From whichever of these three groups the local leadership arises, we find it acting politically in much the same way. On the one hand, its leaders or their representatives are members of the governor's *divan*, and thus have formal access to him. On the other, around the core of their own independent power they build up a coalition, combining other notable families, *'ulama*, leaders of armed forces, and also the organisations which embody the active force of the population at large: some of the groups of craftsmen (in particular that of the butchers), the Janissaries in places where they have become a popular group, *shaykhs* of the more turbulent quarters, and those unofficial mobilisers of opinion and organisers of popular action who, under one name or another, go back into the distant past of the Islamic city. The combination may even spread beyond the city and its immediate hinterland and include Beduin chieftains or lords of the mountains. But it is a precarious combination: forces attracted into the orbit of one notable can be drawn away into that of another, or can themselves become independent agents, or can be won back to direct dependence on the government.

This much was true of all the provincial centres, but there were great differences between the provinces in regard to which group of the three took the lead, and how far it could go vis à vis the Ottoman government along a spectrum stretching as far as complete and permanent seizure of power. At one extreme, in the North African provinces, distance from Istanbul and the loss by the Ottoman navy of control of the central Mediterranean made it possible for certain local forces to take over the government, to rule in the name of the sultan and with his investiture, and to hand on their rule to their chosen successors.

In Cairo however the balance was more even. True, the local

Ottoman power was comparatively weak once the first phase was over, and was unable to maintain a large enough standing army to impose its authority. Nevertheless, Egypt was too important from many points of view for the Ottomans to let it go. Ottoman sea power still counted for something in the eastern Mediterranean, and so did the prestige of the sultan as defender of Sunni Islam and protector of the Holy Places; it was still possible for the Ottoman government to assert its authority, either by a direct act of force or by balancing local groups against each other. But the Ottoman administration in Egypt never rested, as it did in Anatolia and the Balkans, on a social basis of Turkish military landholders. It was thus possible for local leaders to rise, and hope to strengthen and consolidate their position by seizing hold of the land and the land tax. The nature and development of this local leadership has been made clearer by the recent writings of Professors Ayalon, Holt and Shaw.[4] It did not come either from the religious class or from the leaders of the military corps. It is true, the religious leaders (not so much the teachers of the Azhar as the heads of families which possessed a hereditary leadership of important *turuq*) had certain weapons in their hands: a connection with the Muslim merchants who engaged in the Nile and Red Sea trade, control of *waqfs,* a close link with the population of the small towns and the countryside, and of course the prestige of religious ancestry and learning. But the long experience of military rule, and the whole tradition of the Sunni *'ulama,* had taught them to play a discreet and secondary role, and taught the people to look elsewhere for political leadership. The leaders of the 'seven regiments' also had certain obvious advantages; but it may be that, once the military corps began to be drawn into Egyptian society and military discipline to relax, the solidarity of the regiments was not enough to provide that *'asabiyya* which was necessary for one who wished to seize and hold power. In the absence of local families with a tradition of leadership, the only groups which could provide the needed *'asabiyya* were the 'Mamluk' households: these were not military corps but élites created by men possessing political or military power, composed of freedmen trained in the service of the current heads of the household, and held together by a solidarity which would last a lifetime. The training and tradition of the household produced individuals who knew how to gather around them religious leaders, the commanders of the regiments, popular guilds, and behind them one or other of the loose rural alliances *Nisf Haram* and *Nisf Saʻd*, and then, with this combination, to secure real power—to obtain for themselves and their followers from the governor the rank of *bey* and therefore access to the great offices to which *beys* were appointed, and to seize control of the tax farms. But the combination was fragile: one household might be destroyed by others, as the Qasimiyya were destroyed by an alliance of the Faqariyya and Qazdughliyya; but in its turn the new dominant party might split, as did the Faqariyya and Qazdughliyya, or might have to face new rivals; and the Ottoman governors, as well perhaps as other local forces, could use their rivalries to weaken them all.

In the Arab provinces to the east of Egypt also here existed 'notables', but in different forms. In two provincial centres, Sayda (later Acre) and Baghdad, we find the same phenomenon of the Mamluk household as in Egypt. In both of them, however, we find a single Mamluk household, which has a tendency to split but still keeps its solidarity. In each of them, the household has been formed by a strong governor, and after his death secures the governorship for itself and keeps it until the 1830s. Why was it that the Ottoman government accepted this formal monopoly of power by a household? Various reasons may be suggested. First, both Baghdad and Acre were 'frontier' posts. Baghdad lay on the disturbed frontier with Persia, and with a potentially disloyal Shiʻi population all around, and Acre lay near the frontier of almost independent Egypt and open to the Mediterranean, and also at the foot of the hill country of northern Palestine and southern Lebanon, whose inhabitants had in the past shown more than velleities of independence and a willingness to ally themselves with outside forces; in the 1770s a combination of semi-autonomous mountain rulers, Egyptian forces coming up the coastal road through Palestine, and Greco-Russian sea forces in the eastern Mediterranean had gravely threatened the Ottoman hold over southern Syria. In both places (as in some other provinces of the empire) it was therefore in the interest of the Porte to acquiesce in the rule of a group which could maintain efficient armed forces, collect taxes, and keep its province loyal to the sultan in the last resort.

In both of them, again, the rural hinterland had been gradually eaten away: in Acre-Sayda by the lords of the Palestinian and Lebanese hills, in Baghdad by such tribal leaders as the *shaykhs* of the Muntafik, who controlled the greater part of the land and therefore the collection of the land tax, as well as many customs posts. There did not therefore exist the same spur to the ambitions and rivalries of urban forces as was provided by the *iltizams* of Egypt. Moreover, those urban forces were weaker than in Cairo, and therefore there was less scope for the creation of powerful combinations. Sayda and Acre were small towns, without great religious families; their hinterland was largely in the possession of Christians, Druzes and Shi'is, and did not contain large *waqfs*. In Baghdad there were great families of Sunni *'ulama,* but their social power must have been limited by the hold of Shi'i divines and tribal chiefs over the countryside. In both of them, commerce was controlled largely by foreigners or members of minorities. Jews and Armenians in Baghdad, Orthodox or Uniate Christians in Sayda and Acre.

Mosul again showed a different picture. It was like Acre and Baghdad in that a local group was able to impose itself on the Ottoman government and insist on a governor drawn from the city itself, but unlike them in that the governor came not from a Mamluk household but from a family, that of Jalili, and one which as so often in Islamic history came from outside (it was probably of Christian origin) and so was able to serve as the focal point for many different groups. Perhaps here too we can find an explanation for these facts in certain characteristics of the city. Mosul had a small hinterland. The range of influence of the urban economy scarcely stretched beyond the plains and river valley immediately around it; beyond that lay Beduin territory and the principalities of the Kurdish mountains. Within this small enclave, almost a city-state, urban politics could work themselves out without much interference. The city itself was a centre of orthodox Muslim education, and around its mosques and schools had grown up some families with a religious tradition and prestige, like the 'Umaris, the guardians of the religious orthodoxy of northern Iraq. It was also an important centre of trade, lying on the main route from Istanbul and Asia Minor to Baghdad and the Gulf, and being a collecting and distributing centre for parts of Anatolia and Persia; and its trade was largely in Muslim hands. Here once more we find the combination of a religious group with a commercial bourgeoisie. Moreover, it was not a military centre of the same importance as Baghdad. The main armed forces were local ones raised by the Jalili governors, and the Janissaries had become mainly a political organisation of the city quarters and under the control of local leaders. There was therefore no military body which could counterbalance the ascendancy of the local notables.

There remain to be considered the cities of Syria and the Hijaz: Damascus, Aleppo, the Holy Cities and their dependencies. Here we find the 'politics of notables' in their purest form. On the one hand, Ottoman authority remained real; it *had* to be a reality, because its legitimacy, in the eyes of the Muslim world, was bound up with its control of the Holy Cities and the pilgrim routes, and also because it was control of the Fertile Crescent which determined that Istanbul, not Cairo or Isfahan, should dominate the heart of the Muslim world. Although this authority might appear to be ceded to a local group, as with the 'Azms in Damascus throughout most of the eighteenth century, it could be taken back either by the time-honoured method of setting one governor against another, or by direct military methods: the imperial road to Syria and the Hijaz lay open.

On the other hand, the power of the notables was particularly great in these cities; and here the 'notables' were not a Mamluk group but an ancient bourgeoisie with its leaders, the *sharifs* in the Hijaz, the great families in Damascus, Aleppo and the smaller Syrian towns, some of them with a religious and learned tradition (and in Aleppo and its province claiming the title and privileges of *sharifs*). This class was strong enough to absorb into itself families of military origin around whom rival loyalties and Mamluk households might have grown up, to restrain the power of the local governor or at least ensure that it was exercised in its own interest, and at times even to revolt successfully against the governor and itself rule the city for short periods (in Aleppo several times, in Damascus in 1830).

In both Aleppo and Damascus, this class was represented in the governor's *divan* and so had access to the governor. In Aleppo the members of the *divan* included the *muhassil*, a local notable who had the farm of the most important taxes; the *serdar* of the Janissaries who, as we shall see, was open to influence by the notables; the *mufti*, the *naqib*, and the principal *'ulama*; and the *a'yan* in the restricted technical sense of those notables who were hereditary members of the *divan*. In Damascus the composition of the *divan* was similar. But the notables not only had access to the governor, they also were in a position to make it impossible for him to rule without them. They controlled the sources of power in the city, not only the wealthy and established classes but the populace. This control was exercised through the religious institutions, the popular quarters, and above all the Janissaries. In both cities there was a formal distinction between *kapikul*, imperial Janissaries, and *yerliye*, local auxiliaries or their descendents. In Aleppo however this distinction had lost its meaning and both alike were local groups open therefore to local influences, while in Damascus the *kapikul* were imperial troops sent from Istanbul, but the fact that they were not under the control of the local governor, only under the distant control of their *ağa* in Istanbul, meant that they too were exposed to local pressures. In both cities they had close connections with certain trades (once more here we come upon the ubiquitous butcher) and with certain popular quarters where immigrants from the countryside and men engaged in the caravan trade gathered: in Aleppo the Banqusa and Bab Nayrab quarters, in Damascus the Maydan, which a French consul called 'le faubourg revolutionnaire' of the city. They and through them the notables could make and unmake public order; they could also control the urban tax system, since taxes were collected through the *shaykhs* of quarters and crafts.

The notables derived their wealth from two sources, trade and the land. Historians have relied so much on consular reports that they have tended to exaggerate the importance of the trade with Europe, with which of course the consuls were mainly concerned. But the wealth of Damascus and Aleppo came very largely by other routes, the pilgrimage route and those across the desert to Baghdad, Persia and the Gulf, and at this time the first of these was wholly and the second partly in Muslim hands. The wealthy Muslim trader appears less in the consular records than the Armenian or Uniate or Jew, but was perhaps more important in this period. As for the land, the orchards of Damascus and the rich plains around the cities were to a large extent virtually owned by the notables, either as *malikanes* or as *waqfs;* when they were not so owned, the notables could hope to obtain the tax farms. Whatever form their control of the villages took, it gave them control of the urban wheat supply, and in both cities we can see them using this in order to create artificial scarcities, and so not only to raise prices and gain wealth but to dominate the governor by causing disorders which only they could quell.

In Syria as in Egypt indeed it may be that the struggles of factions were mainly about control of the food supply and the land tax, both for their own sake and as political instruments. It was for this that political combinations were formed, and because of this that they could be formed. But simply because the prize was so great the combinations were fragile. By the beginning of the nineteenth century, at least in Aleppo, the notables as such seem to have been losing their hold over the combinations they had formed, and power to be passing to their former instruments the Janissary chiefs. It was these who were now obtaining control of the villages and making alliances not only with the forces of the city but with the Beduin and Kurdish chieftains of the countryside. But their power too was more fragile perhaps than that of the Mamluks in Egypt, because urban and settled life in Syria was so much more precarious: the independent power of Kurd and Beduin chiefs was eating up the countryside.

IV

It is clear that the reforms of the *tanzimat* period in the Ottoman Empire and the similar reforms in Egypt (as also in Tunisia) would, if carried to their logical conclusion, have destroyed the independent power of the notables and the mode of political action it made possible. The aim of the reforms was to establish a uniform and centralised administration, linked directly with each citizen, and working in accordance with its own rational principles of justice, applied equally to all. But these aims, although they could be fulfilled to some extent, could not be carried out completely, and in Istanbul and Cairo alike the effect of the reforms was deflected and made more complicated by such factors as the existence of an absolute ruler who was only willing to apply the new ideas so far as they did not threaten but instead strengthened his own position; the gradual development of a public consciousness among certain groups, who were no longer willing to be ruled for their own good from above but wished to take part in the process; and the very size and variety of the Ottoman system of government, which worked differently in different places.

In Cairo (and also, it would seem, in Tunis)[5] the reforms worked primarily in favour of the ruler. In fact, the first and main aim of Muhammad 'Ali was to destroy all rivals to his power. The destruction of the Mamluk notables has been much written about, although perhaps too much attention has been paid to the famous lunch party, and too little to an event of more permanent importance, the abolition of the *iltizams*. The control of the Mamluks over the *iltizams* had been weakened by the French occupation, and this made it easier for Muhammad 'Ali to end the system. This act destroyed both the means by which the military households had secured power and the goal of their ambitions. By collecting the taxes directly, Muhammad 'Ali ensured that no new class of *multazims* should arise; when, towards the end of his reign, a new class of landowners began to come into existence, they did not at first possess the same means as the Mamluks of putting pressure on the government. It is true that they were soon able to achieve a position of much power in the rural economy, but landownership by itself did not create political power once more until Isma'il began to need their help and support in the 1870s.

The ascendancy of the Mamluk households in the eighteenth century had prevented in Cairo the process which had taken place in Istanbul, the growth of the political power of the civil servants. They were therefore not an independent force for Muhammad 'Ali to reckon with, and they lost their importance as a new kind of administration grew up for which new types of skill were needed. The new administrators were often Copts or other Christians, who as such had no power of their own, or else men of humble origin trained in the educational missions or the special schools and owing their advancement to the ruler's favour. The old religious families too, although clearly their social prestige remained in great part, lost their political power and freedom of action, which had been at their greatest in the years after the French occupation. The abolition of the *iltizams* (from which they had profited in the confusion caused by the French defeat of the Mamluks), the weakening of the *waqf* system, the development of new legal codes and Muhammad 'Ali's neglect of the old system of religious education, all these helped to weaken them. At the same time the old merchant class lost much of its power and prosperity, with the opening of the Red Sea to steam navigation in the middle of the nineteenth century (even before the Suez Canal was made), and the growth of the large-scale trade in cotton with Europe, which was almost entirely in the hands of Europeans or local Christians or Jews.

The former possessors of power were replaced by Muhammad 'Ali. Like them he built up his own army and his own group of high officers and officials to control it. But he succeeded in doing what his predecessors had failed to do and created around himself a single unchallenged 'Mamluk' household: soldiers of fortune or young boys, Turks, Kurds, Circassians and Albanians (with a few Europeans and Armenians for special purposes); strangers to Egypt, trained in his service, owing their advancement to him, with something of the *'asabiyya* of a Mamluk household but with something else as well, a European education, a knowledge of modern military or administrative sciences, and of the French language through which it came. (Here too we may refer in passing to a similar development in Tunisia: Khayr al-Din can be taken as typical of these last groups of Europeanised Mamluks.)

No doubt there was discontent with the predominance of the ruler and his household, and this was to find expression much later (first of all in the events of 1879-82), and later still to become a recurrent theme of Egyptian nationalism. But in the time of Muhammad 'Ali it could not express itself because the instruments of political action had also been destroyed. The tax farms had gone; the associations of craftsmen remained, as Professor Baer has shown,[6] later than had been thought, and so did the *turuq,* but the stricter policing of the streets and bazaars made popular action more difficult. In the countryside, the sedentarisation of the Beduin, and the growth in the power of the *'umda,* the government's agent in the villages, destroyed other possible means of action.[7] It seems too that Muhammad 'Ali set himself deliberately to dispose of those popular leaders who, in the period of confusion before he came to power, had served as mobilisers of popular support in favour of the contenders for power, and, in particular, 'Umar Makram; for, although modern Egyptian historians tend to look on 'Umar Makram as a national leader, it would be better to think of him as an intermediary, someone who as *naqib* had access to the military chiefs but also had a popular following. He had indeed used his talents on behalf of Muhammad 'Ali himself: but in regard to him as to the Albanian soldiers, Muhammad 'Ali knew that the first act of a prudent despot is to destroy those with whose help he has seized power.

It is these two factors, the preponderant power of the government and the absence of instruments of political action, which explain why politics (except for 'court politics') virtually disappeared in Egypt, during the period from the 1820s to the 1870s. In the late 1870s, however, the situation changed. The power of the ruler weakened as foreign pressure on Isma'il grew, and new channels of opinion and action sprang up, as an unofficial press was established, the urban population increased, rural security broke down, the Azhar revived under the khedive's patronage, and Egyptians of peasant origin became officers in the army. Once more then we find political activity, and once more it is the 'politics of notables'. The leaders who arise come, as might be expected from the 'Mamluk' household formed by Muhammad 'Ali. It was beginning to split up, and its leading members had greater independence of action because by now they had become landowners, through land grants by the ruler and in other ways. Riaz, Nubar, Sharif, Barudi are the new politicans, and behind them one can see in the shadows different groups inside the ruling family. As politicians they still work in the traditional way, by building up their own 'households' and systems of clients. 'Urabi and the army officers were not in the first instance leaders so much as instruments used by the politicians: we have perhaps paid too much attention to 'Urabi, too little to Mahmud Sami al-Barudi and others like him. It was the shock of the Anglo-French intervention which destroyed the politicans' delicate game of manoeuvre and the balancing of forces; the sword, struck from the hand which wielded it, for a moment seemed to have a power of its own as it flew through the air, before falling to the ground.[8]

After the first shock of the British occupation, however, the 'politics of notables' began once more. British rule was indirect; its official purpose was to make possible the end of the occupation, and for many years it was unsure of itself; it needed intermediaries, even after Cromer had found a policy and secured the essential positions of power in the government. Moreover, there was a certain polarisation of authority, between the agency and the palace. In such circumstances the notables could play a part, and as usual an ambiguous one, supporting the British occupation but also discreetly serving as the focal points of discontent. It was not until the middle 1890s that their role became less important, as Cromer began to rule more directly through British advisers and puppet ministers, while on the other hand the new khedive began to experiment with a new type of politics, that of the nationalist students and the urban mass.

In Cairo then the effect of the reforms of Muhammad 'Ali was to destroy the old political leadership and replace it by an absolute ruler supported by a new military household; but in Istanbul the process was not so simple, for many reasons but mainly perhaps because of the existence of old and deeply rooted institutions. The reforms brought about the destruction of one such institution, the Janissary regiments. Another was weakened, but only up to a point. The palace was no longer the only source of fear and favour: its wealth was more limited, its men fewer and it could only rule through a skilled and specialised bureaucracy, although, on the other hand, the house of Osman was still the focal point of loyalty, and a whole complex of political habits still gave the sultan a final ascendancy over his officials and subjects. But a third institution increased in power: the higher bureaucracy. Their military rivals had been eliminated. Apart from that, they were needed more than ever because they were the only people who could work the new administrative system; and, as Sharif Mardin's classic book has made clear,[9] that system largely embodied their ideas, or at least the ideas of those who had been trained as diplomats or translators, about how society should be ruled. They were a solid enough group to remain in control; they were held together by certain common values—belief in the empire, belief in modern European civilisation, a certain interpretation of the strength of Europe in terms of justice, rationality, efficiency; to a great extent they were a hereditary group, belonging to families with a long tradition of public service, and when the ancient system by which the property of dead or disgraced officials was seized by the state came to an end, their wealth and therefore their stake in the existing order grew.

The division of power between palace and civil service, the differing interests and intervention of the European powers, and the very size and complexity of the civil service, all led to a certain political activity. But it was still court or bureaucratic politics rather than that of notables: the politics of men whose power was based ultimately on their position in the public service, struggling to ensure their dominance and that of their ideas. Here, even more than in Egypt, the conditions of a more open type of political activity had been destroyed. The Janissaries had gone, and, apart from a few isolated incidents, the mob of Istanbul played no great political part until towards the end of the century. The new army officers were not drawn into politics by contending groups, perhaps because the memory of the Janissaries was still there to teach the danger of it. The 'ulama lost much of their importance, as in Egypt, as their official functions in the systems of law and education dwindled. The upper 'ulama, as Professor Heyd has explained,[10] were to a great extent supporters of reform, for many different reasons: they too in their way wished the empire to be strong again, some of them understood the conditions of its becoming strong, out of conviction and interest they were on the side of established order, and the bureaucratic ideal of rule from above in the light of a principle of justice was not without its appeal to men brought up in the Sunni tradition of politics.

To make up for the loss of internal instruments of action there were, it is true, certain outside forces which could be brought in. Different groups of officials were linked with different European embassies. There were also links with powerful forces in the provinces or dependencies of the empire. The relations between Muhammad 'Ali and the reforming groups in Istanbul need to be studied further, but it is clear from the diplomatic sources that between 1838 and 1840 one aim of Muhammad 'Ali's forward policy in Syria and Asia Minor was to bring to power in Istanbul his own friends among the Turkish court politicians. Again, the possibility that there were links between groups in Istanbul which were opposed to the reforms and such movements as that of Damascus in 1860 needs to be explored.

But such external forces could not make up for the lack of instruments of political action inside Istanbul. Here as in Cairo the period of the *tanzimat* was one of political quiescence, but here too a change begins in the 1860s and 1870s, and for similar reasons: on the one hand the weakening of the power of the government and the growth of European pressure; on the other, the appearance of new instruments of action—the press, the intelligentsia (officials and officers of humble origin and rank, students and graduates of the higher schools), and the new ideas of the Young Ottomans, forming as they did a powerful critique of the principles underlying the reforms.

Thus once more there was scope for the politicians, but who were the politicians? Here as in Cairo they came from inside the system of government. For all his panoply of a traditional Muslim despot, Sultan Abdülhamid II was in a sense the foremost politician of the empire: the first sultan who descended into the political fray, using various means to generate popular feeling and mobilise support vis à vis his own government as well as the European powers. But once the monarchy became political, it could no longer serve as a rallying point for all the forces of society. Other members of the Ottoman family, and of the related Egyptian khedivial family, begain to come forward as points around which loyalty or discontent could crystallise. What was more important still, Abdülhamid broke the connection between palace and higher bureaucracy which had continued in spite of strains throughout the period of the *tanzimat:* some of the high officials, with an inherited position and wealth, supported by the official class and one or other European embassy, became rallying points for discreet opposition. The situation was radically changed by the process which began with the Young Turk Revolution and brought Turkey into the modern age of mass-politics. But it is significant that the leaders of the Young Turk Revolution, and of the Kemalist Revolution which followed it, were also drawn from the ranks of the Ottoman officials and officers. Modern Turkey like the later Ottoman Empire was built around the framework of strong and well-rooted institutions of government.

Both in Cairo and Istanbul therefore the reforms worked in favour of the power of the government as against that of the subject, although in each city a different element in the government drew the main profit from the change. In the provinces of Arab Asia however this development was not to come until towards the end of the century, and even then not completely. Before this, the reforms, in so far as they were applied, did not weaken the power of the urban notables and in some ways strengthened it.

There were many reasons for this. It would not be enough to explain it by the distance of Damascus, Aleppo, Baghdad and Jidda from Istanbul. Distance may it is true have counted for something in regard to Baghdad, but Syria and western Arabia felt the impact of modern means of communication even before the Suez Canal was opened and the first railways were built. Steamship lines were opened from the 1830s onwards (at the time of the events of 1860 in Syria, it was possible to reinforce the Ottoman army there rapidly by sea), and telegraph lines were laid in the 1860s. For the main reasons why the Arab provincial cities reacted in a different way to the *tanzimat* we must look elsewhere, and first of all to the very fact that they *were* provincial cities. The hand of the government was less heavy there than in the capital, and there is plenty of evidence that, as the century went on, it came to be regarded as in some sense alien, as it had not been earlier when political thought and sentiment naturally took a religious form. Both the Egyptian government which ruled Syria and the Hijaz in the 1830s, and the Ottoman government which replaced it, were regarded by the Muslim city-dwellers as westernising governments going against religious tradition and against the ancient principle of Muslim supremacy; and it seems that this view of the new Turkish officials as innovators, almost infidels, sharpened the perception that they were Turks.

Moreover, the long tradition of leadership by the local *a'yan* and *'ulama* was too strong to be broken. It is true, in each of the provinces Ottoman control was sharply imposed or reimposed: in Baghdad and Mosul by military expeditions in the 1830s, in Syria and the Hijaz after the Egyptian withdrawal in 1840. This experience certainly left its mark. It meant that old ruling groups or families lost the power they had had in the eighteenth century, but it did not necessarily mean that they were destroyed, and during the nineteenth century there was perhaps a tendency for families of 'Turkish' or Mamluk military origins to blend with those of 'Arab' and religious origin to form a single class with social prestige. This class still had at its disposal the instruments of political action which had been weakened in Cairo and Istanbul. The *'ulama* remained more important than in the capitals, both because they were largely drawn from a locally rooted aristocracy and not an élite of service, and because the religious schools, although in decline, still had a monopoly of religious education. There were no modern professional high schools in the provincial centres, and it was not until towards the end of the century that Muslim families of standing began to send their children to the French and American mission schools or the professional schools of Istanbul.

The 'popular' organisations still remained. Ottoman policing of the cities was less effective than Egyptian, and the quarter remained very much of a unit with its local leadership. The associations of craftsmen still existed, and there is some evidence that they had more autonomy in Syria at least than in Cairo or Istanbul: for what it is worth, Iliya Qudsi speaks of the *shaykhs* of the Damascene crafts as being elected by the members,[11] and it seems that in Jerusalem the *shaykhs* were drawn from the poorer *sharifs* and under the control of the *naqib*. The Janissaries also, although formally dissolved in the 1820s, continued to be an important political force for at least another generation. They were largely responsible for the rising of 1854 in Mosul, and they were reported to be still meeting secretly in Aleppo in 1860. There was perhaps greater popular discontent to build on than before. The coming in of European textiles led to a rapid decline of local crafts: raw materials which had previously been manufactured for a wide market in Aleppo or Damascus were now exported to the factories of western Europe. The number of looms fell sharply: in Aleppo, from 10,000 to 4,000 at most during the 1850s. This meant a decline in the prosperity of the artisans and of the merchants whose work was bound up with theirs: a decline the more sharply felt because at the same time a new merchant class was rising to deal with the trade with Europe, and this class tended not be drawn from the local Muslim population. In Damascus, it is true, some Muslim merchants held their own even in the European trade. But in Baghdad it was Jewish and Armenian merchants who prospered; in Aleppo, local Jews and Christians and Europeans; in Beirut, local Christians; in Jidda, Europeans as against the Hadrami merchants.

Again, in spite of efforts the Ottoman control of the Syrian and Iraqi countryside was to remain limited and precarious until much later. It gradually spread over the more accessible plains, but in the hills some degree of autonomy continued, and the power of the Beduin chiefs remained as it was. As late as the 1850s indeed, when in Egypt the process of sedentarisation was well under way, the opposite process was still taking place in some parts of Syria, and peasants were abandoning their lands to the pastoral nomads. The traditional connection of the urban *a'yan* with the mountain or Beduin chiefs could still therefore play a role in the politics of the cities.

In some ways indeed the influence of the notables was even strengthened in the first phase of the *tanzimat*. The Ottoman governors needed them more than before. A governor was sent, usually for a short period, to a city he did not know, with a small number of officials to help him, no organised police force or gendarmerie, and inadequate armed forces. He was sent not simply to carry on as before, but to apply a new reforming policy which was bound to arouse opposition. In these circumstances, he could only rule with the help of the local notables: without their local knowledge and their credit with the population he could scarcely hope, for example, to raise conscripts or new taxes. Some at least of the new governors moreover were men out of sympathy with the reforms and for that reason exiled by the central government to posts in different provinces. It was no doubt for these reasons that, with the acquiescence of the government, the local *majlis* in most provincial centres came to be controlled by the notables. The *majlis* included several Muslim notables either appointed by the governor or in some sense elected, as well as the *qadi* and the *mufti* and perhaps the *naqib* ex officio. All the consular reports agree that, at least until the 1860s, this local Muslim element dominated the *majlis*. The Jewish and Christian members, who had played an active part during the Egyptian occupation, were reduced to silence, and in one way or another the *a'yan* were able to do as they wanted with the Turkish officials.

Not only were the notables needed more by the government, their intervention was also more sought after by the population in its dealings with the government. Conscription, new legal codes, new methods of assessing and collecting taxes, the establishment of garrisons or government offices in smaller towns, the attempt to weaken or destroy the local autonomies, all meant that more than ever before the population was brought into connection with the government and the notables could play their traditional role of intermediaries. This strengthened their control over the city, and extended it over the countryside. Notables became 'patrons' of villages, and this was one of the ways in which they came to establish their claims to ownership over them. They also created useful alliances with country notables. In Lebanon, for example, the abolition of the princedom meant that the government in Beirut and Damascus could intervene more than before. Different families or factions in the mountain began to find powerful friends and supporters in the provincial capitals: it was in this period for example that the connection between Druze chiefs of the Shuf and Muslim notables of Beirut grew up. The destruction of the Kurdish principalities had similar effects. Disaffected Kurdish chiefs like Badr Khan formed alliances with discontented urban notables in Mosul; some of the Kurdish ruling families, like that of Baban, themselves settled in Baghdad, became urban notables, but from the city still had a certain influence over their former territories. In those territories, their place as local leaders was taken by the hereditary *shaykhs* of religious orders, like the Barzanji *shaykhs* of the Qadiri order and the Naqshbandi *shaykhs* of Barzan; these too had connections through their orders with the religious aristocracy of the cities.

The notables used their possibilities of action fully in this period. On the whole they threw their influence against the reforms, not only from prejudice or conviction, but because the general direction of the reforms ran contrary to their interests: the political conception underlying the *tanzimat* was that of a direct and identical relationship between the government and each of its citizens, and this was not compatible either with the privileges of Muslim notables or with their role as intermediaries. As was to be expected, they also used their power to increase their wealth. They no less than other classes were deeply affected by the change which was taking place in the trading system. The trade from which their wealth had come was in decline. Long before the Suez Canal was opened, steam communications between Istanbul and Egypt, as well as the disturbed state of Persia and of the desert routes, had cut down the number of pilgrims going to the Holy Cities by the difficult overland route from Damascus: as early as 1843 it was reported that no pilgrims had come to Damascus from Persia, and only 200 from Asia Minor, compared to several thousand in previous years. The merchants of Damascus suffered most from this; those of other cities in Syria, Iraq and the Hijaz suffered also from the decline of the old textile crafts, the insecurity of the transdesert routes, and the opening of steamship communications between Iraq and India. On the other hand there were new possibilities of becoming wealthy from the land, and notables and merchants made the most of them. After the restoration of control by the central Ottoman government, many of the *malikanes* seem to have been abolished, but the land tax as well as other taxes was farmed annually. When the farms were auctioned, the large merchants and notables, in collusion with Ottoman officials, were in a good position to obtain them. The land tax was now paid in kind, while previously it had been paid in money. The tax-farmer would delay levying the tax, under some pretext or other; but the cultivator could not send the rest of his produce to the city market until the tax had been paid. This caused an artificial scarcity in the city, prices went up, and the merchants could then release the stocks of grain they had stored up for this purpose and sell them at a high price. Such manoeuvres, which we find described again and again in the consular sources, were the more profitable because the control of the government was being extended from the city over the more accessible countryside; regions like the Biqa', which had for a long time been under the control of the mountain lords, now came under that of Damascus, and their tax-farms went to Damascene families or Ottoman officials. Later, when the new Land Law was issued, it was used from the beginning by members of the *majlis* and their partners in the Ottoman administration to obtain the title to villages.

In the Syrian and Iraqi provinces, the balance of power between notables and government did not swing decisively in favour of the latter until towards the end of the nineteenth century, when the control of Istanbul grew much more effective for various reasons. But even then this did not mean the end of the local predominance of the notables. Under Abdülhamid they began to send their sons to Ottoman professional schools and from there into the civil or military service; they could preserve their position by becoming part of the Ottoman aristocracy of service. Later, under the Young Turks and then the Mandatory governments, the idea of Arab nationalism provided them with a new instrument of resistance. Here indeed we find one of the ways in which the history of Syria and Iraq in modern times has differed from that of Turkey and Egypt. The nationalist movement was led by the urban aristocracy and moulded in their image; the change did not begin to come until after 1945.

V

Thus far we have talked in terms of two factors: the government, and the urban notables acting as a focus for local forces and able either to oppose the government or else oblige it to act through them. But there was a third factor involved: the European embassies and consulates, particularly those of England, France and Russia. Their influence was changing in scope and nature. Since the early seventeenth century the European states had had interests of their own to preserve, and had done so by allying themselves with one or other party in the palace, the imperial *divan* or the provincial *divans*. But in the nineteenth century a new situation came into existence. Their power and interests were now so great that they were no longer willing simply to act through whatever government existed, or in other words to allow the Ottoman central or local governments to provide the framework within which the activities of Europe should be conducted. They were now in a position to put pressure on the government to become the kind of government they needed. In particular, they were not willing to deal with the various populations of the empire through the government. European trade with the empire (in particular the textile trade) was growing quickly, and this meant, not only that European merchants should be protected, but that those involved in the trade with Europe, whether foreigners or Ottomans, should be able to deal directly with the population: to travel freely, not to bear vexatious burdens and impositions, to widen the market for imports, to collect materials for export, to tell producers what to produce and lend them the money to do it. At the same time, for various reasons different groups in the population wanted the protection of the European powers, who were willing to give it them. Rich and prominent individuals could be protected by attaching them in some way to the consulates and embassies, and during the 1830s something new happened: for the first time Ottoman subjects were themselves made consular agents. But beyond that, whole communities were taken under protection. A policy of protection, which had been pursued by the French since the seventeenth and the Russians since the late eighteenth century, was pursued by them and others more consciously and deliberately in the 1840s and 1850s; it was then that the British government, which had no obvious protégés of its own, established a connection with the Jews in Palestine, some of the Druzes in Lebanon, and the new Protestant churches. Behind the protection of trade and religious minorities there lay something else, the major political and strategic interests of the powers, and these also might make necessary a direct connection with the peoples of the empire: British communications with India must be kept open, and for this purpose British consuls must have direct and friendly relations with the chiefs of Beduin tribes which lay across the routes.

In their own interests therefore the European powers needed a certain kind of Ottoman government and a certain position for themselves inside the empire; to obtain this they were prepared to put pressure on the government, and they were able to do so both because of their military strength and because of their connection with different groups in the empire. The Ottoman government for its part needed *them:* only the armies of one European power could protect it from the threats of another. In addition, political groups inside the government looked more than before to the support of European embassies and consulates in their struggles with other groups; this in its turn strengthened the position of the ambassadors and consuls even further.

In general, their influence was used in favour of the reforms of the *tanzimat*. They wanted a better position for their Christian and Jewish protégés' and they wanted an efficient and rational government with which to deal. (This is probably true of the Russian not less than other governments, although we shall not know definitely until the Russian sources are fully used. We should beware of what is written about Russian policy on the basis of British and French sources; there seems no reason to doubt that in this period of change Russia like other states wanted reform, so long as that did not mean the domination of some other power.)

But European help to the reformers was given on one condition: that the reforms did not harm the interests of the European states, and in particular their free and direct access to the peoples of the empire. The decisive struggle in this connection was that between the British government and Muhammad 'Ali in the 1830s. The aim of Muhammad 'Ali's policy, so far as his relations with Europe were concerned, was to create a new framework within which European activities could be pursued, but to make sure that Europe would deal with his territories through *him,* not only as ruler but as merchant-in-chief, principal broker between the rural cultivator and the European market. This claim was not acceptable to the British government, and battle was joined over a number of matters: the rights and privileges of consular agents, the British expedition to open up the Euphrates to navigation, and above all the question of monopolies. After the defeat of Muhammad 'Ali, the claims of Europe were generally accepted. Ottoman and Egyptian reformers needed European help too much to risk a major quarrel, even had they had the strength to pursue it.

The consequence of this was not only that foreigners and protégés secured a better position, and that merchants, consuls and missionaries could travel and work more freely than before, but also that ambassadors and consuls came to have a larger role in the politics of the empire. Once more the role was different in Istanbul, Cairo and the cities of the Fertile Crescent. In Istanbul, no power could allow any of the others to establish a permanent ascendancy; the embassies remained in a permanent tension, each on its guard against the others but all (until the last years before World War I) conscious of the overriding need to prevent the outbreak of war and to preserve the common interests of Europe in the Middle East. Since Istanbul was the capital and its politics, as we have seen, were primarily those of a court and a bureaucracy, the embassies served as centres not so much for the independent forces of society as for groups at court or in the government. In Cairo, at the other extreme, the British military occupation of 1882 meant that one of the foreign representatives became in effect ruler of Egypt, in uneasy collaboration with the palace; this conferred on the other representatives, in particular that of France, and on the Ottoman high commissioner, a new importance as the only possible foci of opposition but also limited their efficacy, since the presence of a British army gave the British consul-general a power which they could not challenge.

In the cities of the Fertile Crescent the influence of the consuls was exercised within a different framework again. Because they were known to have power with the government, and because they had free access to the population, their intervention was sought, and they began to play the part of intermediaries which had belonged for so long to the notables. Innumerable examples of this could be given. To take a few at random: in 1822, after the great earthquake in Aleppo, the *a'yan* asked the French consul to intervene with the government so that the city could be exempted from taxation for five years; in 1830, the *shaykhs* of the Mawali and Anaza tribes asked him to make peace for them with the governor of Aleppo, who himself was willing to accept this intervention; in the 1850s the revolt of Jabal Druze against conscription was ended by the intervention of both the British and the French consuls. Such intervention tended to place the consuls in direct opposition to the interests of the notables. It gave the consuls, whether or not they wanted it, a role in local politics. Both in the town and countryside they could mobilise political forces for local political ends: in fact, they could scarcely avoid doing so. The famous intervention of 'Abd al-Qadir in the Damascus massacres of 1860 is a good example of this. His action to save and protect Christians has usually been regarded as an act of Muslim *noblesse,* and so no doubt in a sense it was. But it is clear from the French records that it was the French acting consul who, in anticipation of what happened, distributed arms to the Algerians and agreed that they should act as they did. Seen in this light, it is the French consulate which now plays the traditional part of the notable, and 'Abd al-Qadir and his Algerians that of his clients. The *noblesse* of 'Abd al-Qadir's action remains, but mixed with it is something else: the desire to win the favour of the government of Napoleon III, through whom his own political plans might be accomplished.

The rise of the consulates also threatened the economic power of the notables. While the old trading system declined, the growth of the European trade gave wealth and economic power to Christian or Jewish merchants who were for the most part either formal protégés of one or other consulate or morally attached to it. Even the hold of the notables over the land was challenged. As Chevallier has shown,[12] in parts of Syria the merchant from the seaport was replacing the local landowner as provider of capital for the peasant and organiser of his production. Even more widely, Christian and Jewish merchants were becoming moneylenders and thus acquiring some of the claims of landowners, and were looking to the foreign consulates to support their claims against the peasant: in the early 1860s a large proportion of the village debts in the province of Damascus were owed to Jewish protégés of the British consulate.

The opposition of the notables to the centralising tendency of reform was in this way coloured with anti-European and anti-Christian feeling, and the growing influence of the European governments and their local protégés provided a common grievance through which the notables could hope to mobilise popular support. The great disturbances of the 1850s (Aleppo in 1850, Mosul in 1854, Nablus in 1856, Jidda in 1858, Damascus in 1860) follow a common pattern. In Mosul for example the events were organised by the relics of the Janissaries, in agreement with the 'ulama, aiming to restore their own former position, linked with the Kurdish ağas who were fighting for their own position in the mountains, strengthened by control of the tax-farms of the villages, which the governor had given back to them, and using anti-Christian feeling to win popular support. Again, in Jidda in 1858, those who set on foot the revolt were some of the large merchants and 'ulama, with the help or acquiescence of some Ottoman officials, and they used the grievances of the Hadrami traders against the foreign merchants who were replacing them.

After 1860 the fire dies down for a generation, but the rivalry of notable families and consulates as intermediaries, political organisers and potential claimants to rule continued. As one Arab province after another fell under European rule it came to the surface in a new form, the opposition of alien ruler and nationalist movement.

4 A Note on Revolutions in the Arab World

The title of this essay raises several questions, the first of them being: what do we mean by 'revolution', and which of the innumerable violent movements which have taken place in the Arab countries in modern times should we call by that name? There is no need to go deeply into the matter of definitions. Let us simply, to begin with, take the definition given in the *Shorter Oxford English Dictionary:* a revolution is a 'complete overthrow of the established government in any country or state by those who were previously subject to it; a forcible substitution of a new ruler or form of government'. If we extend this definition, and include movements which aim at such an overthrow and substitution as well as those which result in it, then there appear *prima facie* to have been a large number of revolutions in the Arab Middle East since the beginning of the nineteenth century (although, as we shall see later, on further inquiry some of them may turn out not to have been revolutions in this sense). The following come to mind without much effort—with more thought it would no doubt be possible to think of many others: the revolution against French rule in Cairo in 1798; the 'Urabi movement in 1882; the Egyptian revolutions of 1919 and 1952; the risings of Aleppo in 1819, of Damascus in 1830, of Palestine, Hawran, and Lebanon against Muhammad 'Ali in the 1830s; the movements in the Syrian towns which culminated in the Damascus massacre of 1860; the revolt of the Druzes and Syrians against the French in 1925; the various *coups d'état* in Syria since 1949; the Lebanese civil war of 1958; the Arab disturbances and risings in Palestine from 1920 to 1939; the Iraqi rising of 1920; the military movements in Iraq from that of Bakr Sidqi in 1936 to that of Rashid 'Ali in 1941; the Iraqi revolution of 1958; the revolt of Sharif Husayn and his associates against the Ottoman Government in 1916; and the Yemeni revolution of 1962.

As soon as we look at this list another question arises. Have such movements anything in common, and is there any reason to think that they should have? It is possible to talk of successive Turkish or Persian revolutions and reasonable to suppose that they should have a common character, because they were all phases in a single process of political change, all aimed at overthrowing or controlling a machine of government and administration which, in spite of changes, had a clear continuity. But the revolutions we have mentioned took place in many different centres of political life and aimed at the overthrow of many different governments—Ottoman provincial governments, British or French administrations, governments of several Ottoman successor-states. Why should we expect them to have a character in common? Is the fact that those who led or took part in them for the most part spoke Arabic significant in this context? Can we speak of such a thing as an Arab style of revolution, shared by those who speak Arabic and not by those who do not?

The attempt to answer such questions might lead us to formulate ingenious theories about national character or the influence of language on ways of thought and action. It is better perhaps to resist the temptation and begin with a simple fact: all the movements we are concerned with took place in regions which were once part of the Ottoman Empire, and in cities which for the most part had been Ottoman provincial centres. It is worth while to ask whether this fact has given them a common character, and one which has persisted long after Ottoman rule vanished; and if we ask this question we may indeed find that many of these movements (at least the earlier ones) are expressions of a common form of political life. I have written at greater length about this form of life in another essay.[1] To put briefly what is said there, in the Ottoman provincial centres there were two kinds of political role, and political life sprang from a complicated relationship between them. There was the role of governing and administering, which was in the hands of members of the Ottoman ruling group; and there was the role of mobilising and directing public energy, which was in the hands of local 'notables'. These 'notables' did not form a single sociological type, and the form and origin of their social power and prestige might vary: in Egypt, throughout most of the Ottoman period, it had been Mamluk *beys* who played this role, with a power based on the *'asabiyya* of a Mamluk household and strengthened by possession of the *iltizams;* in the Syrian cities, the role belonged to members of local families whose power was based (beyond the solidarity of the family) on the inherited prestige of an ancient socio-religious position and on wealth derived from commerce or from *iltizams*. But these notables of differing kinds tended to be alike in their methods of obtaining political power and in their aims. Their political actions had three main aims: to acquire leadership over the active forces of society—the craftsmen, the urban mobs, the popular religious leaders, the lords of the hill-valleys and the chiefs of Kurd, Turcoman or Arab tribes; to eliminate or neutralise rival claimants to leadership; and to obtain influence with the Ottoman governor. These three were inseparably connected with one another: when formal institutions do not exist, all political roles are ambiguous, and the notables could act at times as agents of authority, at times as spokesmen of the people in the halls of power—to do either, in fact, they had to be able to do both. In general their aim was not to replace the Ottoman authority (although in some circumstances this might happen) but to become its sole and indispensable channel of communication with those it ruled, and thus to impose a certain policy on it, either in their own interest or in a broader local interest.

Seen in this light, the earlier movements we have mentioned were perhaps not true revolutions at all: their aim was not so much to overturn an existing order as to change it and then to restore it; not to replace the system of government by another but to change its policy or its personnel and to preserve or indeed to make more stable the balance between local governor and local leaders on which Ottoman provincial society depended. Social anthropologists have taught us that feuds do not break up societies: they are themselves the expression of an underlying unity of customs or values, and they serve indeed to restore and strengthen the equilibrium of a society by bringing about a necessary change in the relations within it. Most of the earlier movements we have mentioned may have been feuds rather than revolutions. Thus the popular movement in Cairo in 1805, which modern Egyptian historians tend to regard as a kind of plebiscite, bringing Muhammad 'Ali to power by national choice, may rather have been an attempt to restore an older political system which had been shaken by the events of the last half-century—such events as the overshadowing of Ottoman authority by 'Ali Bey and his household, its destruction by the French invasion, and the weakening of the Mamluks by French policy in regard to *iltizams*. Muhammad 'Ali later succeeded in almost throwing off Ottoman authority, but in the first phase he was in fact restoring it in the only form in which it could be restored; and 'Umar Makram, in so far as he played an independent role, was acting as the 'notable', the mobiliser of political energy, and may have aimed at becoming the link between the new Ottoman Pasha and the people of Cairo. Again, the events of 1860 in Damascus should perhaps be seen not just as an explosion of popular fanaticism but as an attempt by one group among the notables of Damascus to use a popular feeling which certainly existed in order to establish their position as local leaders, against other notables and the new local power of the European consuls, and once having established it to use it to prevent the application of the *tanzimat;* it may even be (although there is no clear evidence of this) that these notables were encouraged by political groups in Constantinople opposed to the *tanzimat* and the domination of Fuad and 'Ali Pashas. To take a third example, we may ask whether the 'Urabi movement was really what it appears to be, a precursor of later nationalist and military revolutions, or whether it too should not be seen in the context of Ottoman provincial politics. It may be that, in the first phase at least, the real protagonists were not 'Urabi and the officers, still less 'Abduh, Nadim, Blunt and all the familiar figures, but such politicians as Sharif, Riaz, Mahmud Sami al-Barudi, each trying to secure a position of influence over the khedive, doing so by the familiar method of mobilising opinion and generating pressure, and using for this purpose not only the old instruments but a new one, the army, just as their predecessors had used the seven regiments of Ottoman Egypt. It was the unfamiliar factor of strong foreign pressure which shifted power from the politicians to the officers; but even in the later stages 'Urabi may not have been trying to abolish the khedivate, make himself military ruler and destroy foreign interests, but rather to act as intermediary between the people of Egypt and the khedivial, Ottoman and foreign authorities. If he failed, it was because of a factor which, being what he was, he could scarcely have predicted: the British government was not willing to play the game in the same way, and thought of its relationship with Egypt in quite other terms

After 1882 there is a generation of political quiescence, not only in Egypt but in the other Arab regions of the Middle East. This can be explained partly by the greater and more direct control over society assumed by modern or modernising governments, and partly by the weakening or destruction of the instruments through which political leaders had formerly obtained influence. A new wave of revolutionary events begins in the early years of this century, with the formation of the Watan party in Egypt, the Young Turk revolution, the Arab revolt in 1916, and the disturbances in Syria, Palestine, Iraq, and Egypt in the years after the end of World War I; this series may be thought of as ending with the Iraqi revolt of 1941 and the Syrian and Lebanese crises of 1943-5. The movements in this phase may appear to have been real revolutions in the sense of our definition, but here again a doubt may be expressed. Did the nationalist leaders of the first generation, in Iraq, Syria, Palestine and Egypt, really want independence and really want to excercise power? Of course, they did not believe full independence was possible and so were willing to settle for something less, but perhaps their inherited attitude towards politics made them more comfortable than they would otherwise have been in that 'something less'. The Syrian, Iraqi and Palestinian movements were led by members of the old families of urban notables or by army officers who had been drawn into the Ottoman system of control; the Arab revolt was started by members of the family which had for long played the part of notables in the Holy Cities; and the first leader of the Wafd, Sa'd Zaghlul, came from a stratum of Egyptian society without a tradition of ruling, and belonged to a generation still accustomed to thinking of government as being in alien hands. The effective aim of the movements which they started and led was not to drive the Ottoman or the European ruler out, but to create a new balance between him and them; they would act as the notables had acted in the traditional system, as intermediaries between rulers and ruled, and would use their power to shift the balance in favour of local interests but would not try actively to destroy it completely.

To take some obvious examples: it may be doubted whether most of those who supported the Sharif Husayn's revolt in 1916 really contemplated a complete break with the Ottoman Empire, or whether their aim was not rather to rally support, in the Arab provinces and from the British Government, in order to bring about a change of policy in Constantinople. 'Aziz 'Ali al-Misri said as much in later years, and the Sharif Husayn himself kept some links with the Ottoman Government for as long as possible. It was the British invasion of Palestine, and then the collapse of the Ottoman Empire, which brought about a change in the aims of the nationalists. Again, the willingness of the Wafd to make a treaty with the British, and of the National Bloc in Syria to make a treaty with the French, cannot be explained only by their bowing to superior force and accepting the best terms they could obtain; other nationalists, both in Egypt and in Syria, did not accept the treaties and stood out for complete independence, and in a sense it would have been easier for Zaghlul and Nahhas, Quwwatli and Mardam, to do likewise. If they did not, it was because there was something short of complete independence which was for them an acceptable aim: to bring about, of course, some relaxation of foreign control and some shift in the balance between government and nation; and to make sure that they became the sole intermediaries between the imperial ruler and the people, that England or France did not negotiate with their rivals. This explains, for example, why Zaghlul in 1921 put forward his theory of a division of functions between government and Wafd: it was the government's task to carry on the local administration, but only the Wafd, in office or out, could negotiate with the British on behalf of the Egyptian people. It explains also why the Wafd (at least until its last period of office after the War) was never much interested in the processes of government or the problems of social and economic progress. Similarly, when the Syrian nationalists came out firmly against the French in 1943-5 and refused to make a treaty with them, it was because they thought it was possible, and in the interests of their party and their country, to establish with England the type of relationship they had tried to establish with France in 1936—but to do so on far more favourable terms, conceding to England only the final hegemony over the Middle East.

It was possible for the nationalist leaders to act in the tradition of Ottoman local politics, after the old Ottoman Empire had disappeared, because the new rulers needed them. Most of the Young Turk leaders understood that, now that the Empire had become virtually a Turco-Arab state, it could only survive if a working agreement could be reached between the government in Constantinople and some at least of the political forces in the Arab provinces. After 1918, the British and French could not rule without a partner, a leader or party which could control local forces but at the same time would accept the final authority of England or France. This was necessary because of the provisions of the Mandates, the new climate of political thought in England

and France, the expense of ruling directly and by means of an army of occupation, and the fact that the British and French governments, being alien in religion and language, could not act in the double way in which indigenous governments can act, both as rulers and as political leaders.

The balance which both sides wanted for different reasons was achieved sometimes and for short periods, but it was never as stable as that balance between imperial government and Arab notables which the Ottomans had created, which the second phase of the *tanzimat* had overturned, and which might have been restored had not Turkey entered World War I, and entered it at a moment when Turco-Arab relations were strained. That it was never stable can be explained in many different ways, but perhaps there were two factors more important than the others. First, the aims of British and French rule were themselves unstable: caught between political parties which wanted to withdraw from the imperial responsibility as soon as possible and political parties which wanted to remain for ever in spite of mandates and declarations, between armies thinking in terms of military rule and diplomats striving for delicate relationships between political forces, the British and French Governments were never able to pursue in an unwavering way the aim of reaching an agreement with their Arab subjects; and Arab politicians in their turn could only make it worth while for the rulers to negotiate with them by mobilising forces which might make agreement impossible. Their appeal had to be to the sentiment of nationalism, and behind it that of religious solidarity: sentiments which no doubt they themselves shared, but which in them could be controlled by ideas of political prudence. Thus the ambiguity which, as we have said, attaches to the role of political leadership in such situations, became even greater and could lead to more violent alternations of policy: a Nahhas would at times be willing to make an agreement with the British and come to power with their help, but at others would withdraw into an attitude of defiant opposition—partly no doubt compelled by pressure from his followers, but partly from the exhilaration of riding on a wave of feeling which was barely controllable.

After 1945 the situation changed, and the conditions for the use of the old kind of political expertise no longer existed. The withdrawal of England and France meant that the office of ruler was vacant, and those who wished for political power had to put themselves forward, not as popular leaders in the face of an alien or unshakable authority, but as possible rulers; it meant also that the division between the two political roles no longer existed. The ruler, being no longer alien, could also be leader; his possession of new means of coercion made it possible for him to rule directly and without an intermediary; and self-interest made it necessary for him to weaken or destroy other claimants to leadership, since those other claimants had now to attempt not only to persuade the ruler to accept them as partners, but to become rulers themselves. In a few countries (Lebanon, Israel, Turkey) where there existed a strong sense of common interest and an accepted system of conventions about how political power should be exercised and transferred, political life could be carried on in other ways. But for the rest, the age of the politics of notables had passed, and had been replaced by a different age—that of the politics of courts and bureaucracies. In this new age, the political struggle takes place on two levels. Those inside the system of government compete for favoured access to the ruler and control of important positions of power in the administration. Those outside must aim at a total overthrow of the government, using the only method which seems likely to be effective: the armed forces. In such circumstances, real revolutions take place, aiming at the total overthrow of the old régime and the overturning of the social system in which it is rooted, and they justify themselves in terms of revolutionary ideology: the total worthlessness, even the unreality, of what has been overturned, the appeal to a more distant past or to an imagined future. The revolutions are not always violent; some old régimes can be swept away with ease. But once they have occurred, the path from political change to radical social change (whether successful or not) is one which it is difficult not to take. The history of the Egyptian revolution, 1952-61, makes this clear; so does the train of events in Syria since 1963, the Ba'hist revolution leading to the gradual destruction of the Syrian bourgeoisie.

5 Sufism and Modern Islam: Mawlana Khalid and the Naqshbandi Order

Much has been written in recent years about modern movements in Islam, and the origins and direction of some of them are by now well known: a new emphasis on virtuous activity, justified in terms of certain traditional sayings, but derived in fact from the European 'scientific' thought of the nineteenth century, and tending sometimes towards a revolutionary nihilism; a sharper distinction between what was essential in religion and those laws, customs and practices which were subject to the principle of progress and therefore liable to change; and a 'protestant' rejection of Islam as it had in fact developed, and in particular of the mystical tendencies which marked its later history, in the name of the real or imagined purity of the faith in its first period.

The relations between such movements are not so clear as they may at first sight seem. In a book published some years ago, I tried to show that the attempt to return to the primitive simplicity and fervour of the faith might have an effect opposite to what was intended, and lead to a more or less complete secularism.[1] Moreover, the position of those who put forward 'modernist' views was not always so free from ambiguity as might appear. There are of course exceptions to this: all that Muhammad Rashid Rida wrote is marked by the same harsh and uncompromising logic. But the more one studies the thought of Muhammad 'Abduh the less clear its outlines become. In particular, we should beware of attributing to him that rejection of the Sufi interpretation of Islam which marked the thought of Rashid Rida and others of his Syrian disciples. His early religious training had been within the mystical tradition; his early relationship with Jamal al-Din had in it something of the relationship of *murid* and *murshid*; and until the end of his life he held that it was necessary to go beyond external obedience to that 'interiorisation' of the faith which is the starting point of Sufism, and ascribed value to the kind of spiritual discipline taught by the more orthodox masters of the Sufi way. 'Were I to despair of reforming the Azhar,' he once said to Rashid Rida, 'I should choose ten students, make a place for them in my house at 'Ayn Shams, and there give them a Sufi upbringing while completing their education.'[2]

The rejection of Sufism by Muslims of modern education is indeed a recent development, and by no means a universal one. Throughout the nineteenth century most educated Muslims who took their religion seriously interpreted it within the framework created by the great masters of the spiritual life, and many still adhered to one or other of the brotherhoods founded by them or in their names. Far from a decline, there was in many ways a revival and development of these brotherhoods. Some of them were active in organising and leading resistance to European conquest: the Naqshbandiyya in the Caucasus, the Sanusiyya in Libya. New brotherhoods were founded and old ones given a new direction; in some of them we can see an emphasis on strict observance of the law, and a claim to exclusive possession of the truth, preparing the way for those 'modernist' movements which in the end were to turn against the brotherhoods themselves.

What follows is an attempt to deal with a small but not unimportant part of this subject, the spread of one *tariqa* or order, the Naqshbandiyya, in one region of the Muslim world.

II

The man after whom the *tariqa* is named, Baha al-Din Muhammad Naqshband, was born in a village near Bukhara in 717/1317, spent most of his life in that region, and died there in 791/1389. His tomb has always been an important centre for pilgrimage, not only for villagers and city dwellers from the district, but for devout Muslims from as far away as China.[3]

But the order was not founded by Naqshband himself. In modern times its members have traced its spiritual genealogy from the Prophet along three lines of descent: the first by way of 'Ali ibn abi Talib, the Imam Husayn, the Shi'i Imams, Ma'ruf al-Karkhi, and Junayd; the second from 'Ali through Hasan al-Basri and again to Junayd; and the third through Abu Bakr al-Siddiq,

Salman al-Farisi and Abu Yazid al-Bistami.⁴ Writers of the order also distinguish different phases in its history marked by different names. From Abu Bakr al-Siddiq to Abu Yazid Tayfur al-Bistami they call it the 'Siddiqiyya'; from Abu Yazid to 'Abd al-Khaliq al-Ghujdawani the 'Tayfuriyya'; from al-Ghujdawani to Baha al-Din Naqshband, the 'Khojaganiyya'; from Naqshband to Shaykh Ahmad al-Sirhindi, the 'Naqshbandiyya'; from Ahmad al-Sirhindi to Shaykh Khalid the 'Mujaddidiyya'; and after Shaykh Khalid, the 'Khalidiyya'.⁵ These changes of name mark certain shifts of emphasis under the impact of powerful personalities.

The origins and development of the order have been studied by M. Molé in a number of important writings.⁶ According to his interpretation, its roots lie in the mystical tradition of Khurasan, itself a reaction against certain Sufi tendencies in Baghdad in the fourth Islamic century. The Sufism of Khurasan was strictly Sunni, but touched by the *malamati* teaching, that one should abase oneself in other men's eyes by acts appearing to be contrary to the law, since earthly reputation was of no account; it preserved the tradition of the *futuwwa* and the memory of al-Hallaj. In this complex of ideas there were implicit contradictions, and the Sufis of Khurasan gradually split into two main groups. Both traced their descent from Yusuf al-Hamadhani. One line from him passed through Ahmad al-Yasawi and ended in the Baktashi order; the other through 'Abd al-Khaliq al-Ghujdawani to Baha al-Din Naqshband.

The connections and divergences between these two lines are not easy to trace. They were not mutually exclusive: Hajji Baktash was himself a Naqshbandi. But Molé has been able to make certain distinctions. First of all there may have been a certain ethnic difference. The Yasawiyya and its off-shoot the Baktashiyya were mainly Turkish; Naqshband himself was a Tajik, and in its early days his order spread mainly among the Persian-speaking population of central Asia. But the importance and validity of this distinction should not be stressed too much: Naqshband himself had some relationship with the Turkish shaykhs of his time, and, as we shall see, the order named after him spread later in countries of Turkish speech. The essential distinguishing mark of the Naqshbandiyya was one of doctrinal emphasis and attitude towards the *shari'a*.

The primary emphasis of the Naqshbandi teaching has always been on the need for a life wholly turned towards God: lived in

His presence, filled with love towards Him, directed to worshipping Him without distraction or mediation, and without earthly reward, even that of human praise. Even when speaking to other men one's inner self should remain turned towards God. Baha al-Din is said to have been given the name 'Naqshband' ('painter') because he traced the form of perfection always on his heart.[7] Following a certain Sufi tradition, he kept his distance from the courts of rulers, because power enmeshes the heart in the affairs of the world and turns it away from God. In his early life he had had a certain experience of public affairs, when one of his teachers, Shaykh Khalil, had been for a time ruler of Transoxiana, but after Khalil fell from power Baha al-Din turned away from things of the world: one of the stories recorded of him is that he refused to eat food prepared for him by the king of Herat.[8]

Secondly, 'fidèle à la grandeur austère de l'islam sunnite',[9] the order adhered strictly to the tradition of *ahl al-sunna,* and to the *shari'a* as Sunnism understood it. As a Sufi order, it did not make external observance of the law an end in itself; on the other hand it avoided the danger of antinomianism inherent in the *malamati* teaching. (But not all those associated with it were immune from this danger: some of the *qalandaris* attached to it were less strict in their observance of the *shari'a,* [10] and in recent times C.J. Edmonds has noted that the Naqshbandis in the Kurdish villages, but not in the towns, are prone to eccentric practices.[11]) The role of the order was the traditional one of the more orthodox orders: that of defending Sunnism from attacks, not by rejecting the doctrine of those who attacked it, but by accepting it and incorporating it into a more complex system.

The aim of Naqshbandi Sufis is to arrive at direct contemplation of God, through direct contact with the Prophet and the *awliy'a,* friends of God: if God can and should be known directly, then it must be possible to rise above the need for visible teachers and make contact with invisible masters, the mighty dead. (Here lies the significance of the claim that Baha al-Din himself was an Uwaysi. The reference is to Uways al-Qarani, a contemporary of the Prophet who became Muslim without ever having seen him; an Uwaysi is thus one who attains spiritual knowledge without a visible guide or *murshid.*[12])

This aim determined both the public and private ritual of the order. In the public liturgy, there was no music or other external aid, simply a repetition of the name of God, *Allah,* or *la ilah illa* 'llah, accompanied by certain 'tricks' of breathing or balancing the body. The public ritual was perhaps less important than the private *dhikr* (a practice shared with the Baktashis): the name of God was spoken in private, silently, perpetually, even when engaged in other activities, with concentration (*tawajjuh*), with the eyes closed and all the senses turned towards the heart, and with the image of the *murshid* or the *awliy'a* evoked in the heart. For the same purpose, the moral discipline of the order was based on respect and obedience to the *murshid* or *shaykh*, but conceived as a first step in a spiritual ascent: from self-annihilation in the *murshid*, through the *awliy'a* and the Prophet, to self-annihilation in God.[13]

III

In Iran and Transoxiana, the great age of the Naqshbandiyya was that of the Timurids. Under them it was indeed the dominant order, but its influence waned with the rise of the Safavis in Iran and of the Uzbeks in the region beyond the Oxus. In Bukhara it still continued to be important, and it found a new sphere of expansion in India, where it was spread by Khwaja Baqi Billah (d. 1012/1603). The Indian Naqshbandis seem to have abandoned or interpreted anew the principle that they should avoid the temptations of power, and to have set themselves to win influence with rulers: 'the well-being of the king is the well-being of the world; his corruption is the corruption of the world'. They found a welcome at the court of the Moguls, themselves of Timurid descent, during the period of orthodox reaction against the syncretic teaching of the Mogul emperor Akbar.

The spread of the order in India in this period is closely connected with Shaykh Ahmad al-Sirhindi (d. 1034/1624), known to his followers as the *mujaddid* or renovator of Islam, appearing at the beginning of the second Islamic millennium. (Hence the name *mujaddidi* given to the order in the next phase of its history.) A man of influence at the Mogul court and an enemy of illicit innovation, *bid'a*, Shaykh Ahmad was also a writer in whose work can be seen that process whereby doctrines which might by themselves be dangerous to orthodox belief are incorporated into it. He accepted the need for *ijtihad*, but strictly within the bounds of Qur'an and *sunna;* taught the Sufi way of spiritual progress towards experiential knowledge of God, but distrusted mystical intoxication and stood, as did the Naqshbandiyya throughout its history, for an austere sobriety of thought and action; and was strongly opposed to Shi'ism.

At roughly the same period the order spread westwards into Asia Minor. It came to Istanbul as early as the second half of the fifteenth century, and soon became an order favoured by the *'ulama*, to whom it offered the assurance of unchallenged orthodoxy. Its spread at this time was perhaps associated with that movement by which the Ottoman sultanate turned its back on the heterodoxy of its earlier history and assumed its responsibilities as protector and ruler of the western part of the Muslim world. The hold of the order over the population of the capital continued and even grew stronger with the passing of time. In the seventeenth century, Evliya Çelebi says that the great men of the learned hierarchy tend to belong either to the Khalwatiyya or to the Naqshbandiyya; at the end of the eighteenth century, d'Ohsson finds that it is popular with men of every class; in the nineteenth century, J.P. Brown gives a list of 52 *takiyyas* of the order in Istanbul alone.[15] It spread far beyond the capital: Hasluck has recorded a number of ancient Naqshbandi shrines in the Balkans and Asia Minor,[16] and the biographical dictionaries are witness to its presence in the Arab cities as well. For example, the famous mystic and theologian, 'Abd al-Ghani al-Nabulsi (1050/1640—1143/1730) learnt the Naqshbandi way in his youth from Shaykh Sa'd al-Balkhi in Damascus.[17]

A new wave of expansion began as the influence of Ahmad al-Sirhindi and his successors of the Mujaddidi branch of the order spread beyond India. This spread is associated with the family of al-Muradi, whose lives are to be found in the biographical dictionary written by one of them. The first we read of is the eponymous founder of the family, Murad (d. 1132/1720). By origin from Bukhara, he studied in India and accepted the Naqshbandi way from Shaykh Muhammad Ma'sum, the son of Ahmad al-Sirhindi. After long wanderings he settled in Damascus and founded a family whose later history shows clearly how sanctity or religious learning served in Islamic society as a point around which social power crystallised. His grandsons 'Ali and Husayn each in turn became Hanafi *mufti* of the city; his great-grandson, Khalil, the historian, was *mufti* too, and also *naqib al-ashraf;* later members of the family also held office. Murad had received grants of land in the province of Damascus from sultan Mustafa II, and his family grew rich on them. They founded schools: the *madrasa al-muradiyya,* and the *madrasa al-naqshbandiyya al-barraniyya* in Suq Saruja. The *mufti* Husayn is said to have had great influence with the government and to have held the leadership (*riyasa*) of the city.[18]

IV

In the early nineteenth century one more phase begins in the history of the order, at least in the western part of the Muslim world. Once more it is associated with an individual, Abu'l-Baha Diya al-Din Khalid al-Shahrizuri, known to his followers as Mawlana Khalid.[19] He was born at Qaradagh in the district of Shahrizur in Kurdistan, then ruled by the Baban family, probably at some time between 1190/1776 and 1194/1780; he belonged to a family of the Jaf tribe claiming descent from the caliph Uthman. He had his early education in his own town and then in the Baban capital of Sulaymaniyya (a new town, founded by Mahmud Pasha Baban and named after his nominal overlord Sulayman Pasha of Baghdad). Some years earlier a shaykh of the Qadiri order, Ma'ruf al-Barzinji, had established himself in Sulaymaniyya and it was with members of this family, 'Abd al-Karim and his brother 'Abd al-Rahim, that Khalid mainly studied. He taught for a time in Sulaymaniyya and then went in 1220/1805 to Damascus and from there to Mecca on pilgrimage. He seems to have been well received in Damascus, both on his way to Mecca and on his way back; he spent some time there studying with well-known shaykhs, Muhammad al-Kuzbari and Mustafa al-Kurdi, by whom he was initiated into the Qadiri order.

Two incidents are recorded of this journey which, if we can accept them, seem to foreshadow Khalid's later life. In Mecca a holy man told him that spiritual grace and enlightenment would not come to him there but in India. The other incident, which occurred in Damascus, is more difficult to attribute to him. The governor of Damascus at that time, Yusuf Genç Pasha, was also a Kurd. In 1222/1807 his character was seen to undergo a sudden change. He began to issue strange decrees: Muslims were forbidden to shave their beards, and to listen to music in the coffee houses, the sumptuary laws were applied strictly against Christians and

Jews, and some pressure was put on Christians to become Muslims. Two explanations are given by the local chroniclers. Yusuf Pasha's acts may have had some connection with the situation in the Hijaz, where the Wahhabis held the holy cities and were placing difficulties in the way of pilgrims whom they suspected of not being strict Muslims; only a year later indeed the Wahhabis were to launch an attack from the Hijaz against Hawran in the province of Damascus. The Ottoman governor of the city may well have wished to show that he and his government were no less concerned than the Wahhabis to maintain the rule of Islamic virtue and justice. The second explanation given by some of the chroniclers is that Yusuf issued the decrees under the influence of a Kurdish shaykh. Finally the *'ulama* told him that what he was doing was contrary to Islam and without precedent and he should dismiss his shaykh; he did so and returned to his normal frame of mind.[20]

One of those who narrate the story, Ibrahim 'Awra, says that the shaykh concerned in it was Khalid. Here is his version:

> At that time there came to [Yusuf Pasha] a certain Kurdish shaykh with an outward show of piety and claiming to be a shaykh of the Naqshbandi order. His name was Shaykh Khalid; he was much in the company of Yusuf Pasha, initiated him into the Naqshbandi order, and changed his habitual nature.[21]

Other writers do not mention Khalid's name, and we should hesitate about ascribing the story to him. He was young, and a transient visitor in Damascus; 'Awra wrote his book long after the event, and after Khalid (as we shall see) had settled in Damascus and become famous there. But if true, it does illustrate characteristics of his teaching and activity which showed themselves in other periods of his life as well: a certain harshness in his insistence on the importance of strictly obeying the *shari'a*, and in his view of non-Muslims, which betrays the rustic preacher coming from a region of uncertain orthodoxy, and might well have offended the heirs of the Muslim culture of the great Arab cities.

On Khalid's return to Sulaymaniyya, an Indian Sufi, Mirza Rahim Allah, known as Darwish Muhammad, repeated the advice given by the holy man in Mecca, that he should go to India to seek knowledge. In 1224/1809 he went overland to India. He spent some months in Delhi studying among others with the son of Shah

Wali Allah, 'Abd al-'Aziz al-Dihlawi. This stay although short was decisive, for it was here that he was initiated into the great orders which flourished in Islamic India: the Suhrawardiyya, Kubrawiyya and Chishtiyya, and the Naqshbandiyya of the Mujaddidi branch.

He returned to Kurdistan by way of the Gulf and Iran, and once more an incident is recorded by his followers. As so often in biographies of this kind, it is impossible to say whether it actually occurred, or is part of a perhaps unconscious process of fitting him into an intellectual and spiritual form regarded as praiseworthy. But it shows his intransigent attitude towards those who stood outside the bounds of Sunnism:

> Then he went from Bandar Masqat to the regions of Shiraz, Yazd and Isfahan, proclaiming the truth wherever he was; and many times some of the Shi'is met together to beat or kill him, because they were unable to answer his arguments whether based on reasoning or authority. But he attacked them with his sharp sword and they retreated and turned their backs in flight.[22]

In 1226/1811 he resumed his life as a teacher in Sulaymaniyya. In this new phase he incurred the hostility of the Barzinji family and their followers in the Qadiri order. Here as in Damascus, his rigidity may have offended Muslim divines who had struck deeper roots in the social order and were more inclined therefore to support the Sunni idea of broad tolerance for the sake of peace, unity and order. There may also have been other reasons for the hostility. His growing reputation as a teacher was reinforced by his claims to have the power of foreseeing the future, preserving the living from harm, and establishing contact with the spirits of the dead. Such claims struck at the root of the spiritual power of the Barzinjis, by offering the villagers and townspeople of Kurdistan a *baraka* more potent than theirs. It might also threaten their influence with the Baban family and their social position.

Several incidents are recorded in which this hostility showed itself. The Barzinjis are said to have plotted against Khalid in Sulaymaniyya and forced him to go to Baghdad. There too, according to Naqshbandi sources, they tried to slander him to the Pasha, but without success; the Pasha ordered an investigation which showed him to be innocent of that of which he was accused.

Soon the ruling Baban, Mahmud Pasha, invited him back to Sulaymaniyya, but his career there ended in 1236/1820 with an incident more dramatic than the earlier ones, and known to us not only from the writings of members of the Naqshbandi order but from a description by a detached observer, the British Resident in Baghdad, C.J. Rich, then on a journey in the Kurdish districts:

> There is a great Mahometan saint living in Sulimania. His name is Sheikh Khaled; but the Koords think it profanation to call him by any other name than *Hazret i Mevlana,* or the holy beloved one; and talk of his sayings as being *Hadeez,* or inspired. He is of the Jaf tribe, and is a dervish of the Nakshibendi order, which he embraced at Delhi, under the guidance of the celebrated Soofee Sultan Abdulla. He has 12,000 disciples in various parts of Turkey and Arabia. All the Koords call him an *evlia* or saint; and a great many of them almost put him on a footing with their Prophet. Osman Bey, who with the Pasha and almost all the principal Koords are his mureeds or disciples, told me that he was at least equal to the famous Mussulman saint, Sheikh Abdul Kader.
>
> ... October 20.—This morning the great Sheikh Khaled ran away. Notwithstanding his escape was sudden and secret, he managed to carry his four wives along with him. It is not yet known what direction he has taken. The other day the Koords placed him even above Abdul Kader, and the Pasha used to stand before him and fill his pipe for him; to-day they say he was a Kafir or Infidel, and tell numbers of stories of his arrogance and blasphemy. He lost his consideration on the death of the Pasha's son. He said he would save his life, and that he had inspected God's registers concerning him, etc. The cause of his flight is variously reported. Some say he had been making mischief between the Pasha and his brothers, who had desired that he should be confronted with them. Others say that he had formed a design of establishing a new sect, and making himself temporal as well as spiritual lord of the country. Of course a great deal more is laid to his charge than he was really guilty of. All the regular Ulema and Seyds, with Sheikh Maaroof at their head, hated Sheikh Khaled, who, as long as his power lasted, threw them into the background.[23]

Naqshbandi sources explain what happened in a way less

discreditable to Khalid. A century later Edmonds heard an oral version from which it appeared that the cause of Khalid's downfall was his engaging in a miracle-working contest with Shaykh Ma'ruf al-Barzinji, the setting of one *baraka* against another.[24] Whatever really happened, the historian of Kurdistan assures us that the tension between Qadiris and Naqshbandis arose from a 'simple difference' and left no lasting enmity behind it.[25]

For the rest of his life Khalid lived in Damascus. He was invited there by the *mufti* Hasan al-Muradi (himself, as we have seen, of a Naqshbandi family) and others; and one of his wives belonged to a famous Damascene family with a tradition of learning and piety, that of Ghazzi. From writers belonging to his order we have some stories of his life in these last years. Some of them show the same rigidity of exclusion: while in Jerusalem on his way to Mecca for the last time, he refused to enter the Church of the Holy Sepulchre:

> They said to him, 'But Shaykh 'Abd al-Rahman al-Kuzbari entered it.' He said, 'Strange that he should have done so! For he was an exponent of *hadith*, and must have heard of the saying of the Prophet, the favoured one: "he who enters a church is like him who enters a house of fire." '[26]

But others show another side of the Naqshbandi way: the withdrawal of the heart from the things of this world. When his son died, he spoke words of resignation:

> Once a man asked for his intercession, so that he should not be struck by the plague. He raised his hand and interceded for the man, who then said to him: 'My Lord, do it for yourself as well.' But he replied—may his soul be sanctified—: 'Surely I should be ashamed before my God if I did not wish to meet Him.' Now on Wednesday the 26th day of Shawwal his son Shaykh Baha al-Din fell sick with the plague. He was a boy of great excellence, about five years old at that time, and sadness and fear for him appeared on all sides. Then God took him to His mercy on the Friday morning. 'I praise God in the highest', said the Shaykh—may his soul be sanctified—'for the patience and joy He has granted me. I have sent this boy before me, and if God wills he will be a treasure laid up for me with my Lord. He will be our lodestone, and we shall all follow him.' Then a

smile appeared on his noble face, and he began to discourse of the grace of the death of sons and of patience under it, and how they would put their feet in the door of Paradise and intercede for their parents as soon as they entered.[27]

When he himself fell ill of the plague, in 1242/1826, and knew his death was near, he called his three wives together and entreated them to keep together and observe the *tariqa,* and then himself abandoned all earthly cares:

Then he said—may his soul be sanctified—: 'I beseech you, ask me no more from this time on. I have left you and my successors nothing they need ask me about; my only wish is to occupy myself wholly with my Lord. Let no one come in to me more than once, and tell those who come that I wish no one to speak to me.'[28]

Among the writings he left, there is a poetic *diwan* in Persian and Kurdish; a commentary on the *Maqamat* of al-Hariri; a collection of letters on spiritual matters; a treatise on the Naqshbandi *tariqa,* and another on the difference between the doctrines of al-Ash'ari and al-Maturidi in regard to freedom of the will.[29]

V

As we have said, the latest phase of the Naqshbandiyya is called after him, the Khalidiyya, and we can trace the influence of his teaching, and the line of spiritual descent from him, in the regions where he lived.

In his native Kurdistan, several members of the Barzinji family itself became his disciples, and other families claiming spiritual descent from him established themselves as leaders: the Tawila family in the Sulaymaniyya district and the Barzani family in the Zibar and Barzan districts in what is now the north of Iraq.[30] By a familiar process, spiritual influence bred wealth, social power and political leadership. In the Kurdish districts there were special reasons why this should be so. The imposition of control by the central government in Istanbul, during the period of the *tanzimat,* involved destroying the power of the hereditary rulers of the mountain valleys. Some of the Kurdish chieftains were removed in the 1830s; the greatest of them, the family of Baban, continued to rule Sulaymaniyya until 1850 and were then deposed (but played a part in the politics of Istanbul and Baghdad for another century). After that, the great families of Sufi shaykhs provided the only focus of political activity, and any movement of discontent with the government looked to them for leadership. The revolt against Ottoman rule in 1880 was led by the Naqshbandi shaykh 'Ubayd Allah of the Shamdinan family; in the 1920s, various movements against British mandatory policy, and the incorporation of the Kurdish districts in the new kingdom of Iraq, were led by Shaykh Mahmud of the Barzinji family; and in the present generation the Kurdish movement has been led by members of the Naqshbandi family of Barzan, first Shaykh Ahmad and then his brother Mulla Mustafa.

In Baghdad, the Khalidi branch of the Naqshbandiyya had its centre in the *madrasa al-ahsa' iyya*, which Khalid himself had acquired for the purpose; among his disciples we find mention of Shaykh Musa al-Juburi, several of the Suwaydi family, and Shaykh 'Ubayd Allah al-Haydari, a *mufti* of Baghdad, himself of Kurdish origin.[31] In Damascus, disciples and members of his family continued his line, and Sultan Abdülmecid gave the order the famous *takiyya al-sulaymaniyya* and had a tomb built for Khalid himself.[32] Traces of his influence can be found even beyond the countries where he lived. His treatise on free-will was translated into Turkish by Sulayman Pasha (one of the conspirators who deposed Sultan Abdülaziz in 1875);[33] and the Algerian hero, 'Abd al-Qadir, making the pilgrimage with his father in 1241/1825, met Khalid who also was going on pilgrimage and was by him initiated into the order.[34]

The spread of the Naqshbandiyya in the nineteenth century went far beyond the sphere of radiation of Mawlana Khalid's personality. Snouck Hurgronje notes its great importance in Mecca in the 1880s, its wealth swollen by contributions from the faithful, its influence spreading as far as Sumatra, Java and Borneo.[35] In Istanbul and Asia Minor, when the Baktashi order was suppressed in 1826, the Naqshbandi order was for a time given control of its houses (perhaps because it stood in the more orthodox line of descent from their common ancestors): Hasluck found a Naqshbandi shaykh residing in the central *takiyya* of the order, near Kirşehir, to supervise the liturgy at the tomb of Hajji Baktash.[36]

In the Caucasus, the most determined resistance of Chechens

and Daghestanis to the Russian conquest took place within the framework of the Naqshbandiyya: the aim of Shamil, leader of the resistance, was to create an imamate in which Muslims should live in accordance with the *shari'a*.[37] Across the Caspian too, in the regions in which the order had grown up, it played an important part, and in some places resistance to Russian rule found Naqshbandi leaders: for example, the revolt of Farghana in 1898.[38]

VI

If we ask why the Naqshbandiyya, and other similar orders, played this part in the modern history of Islam, we can perhaps find two types of reason, very different from each other but both rooted in the same reality, of a society threatened in its beliefs, autonomy and self-confidence.

On the one hand, it seems clear that popular Naqshbandism was not always faithful to the 'grandeur austère' of Sunnism, and did not always heed the warnings of Shaykh Ahmad al-Sirhindi against mystical intoxication. We have noted what Edmonds said about the eccentric practices of village Naqshbandis in Kurdistan; Snouck Hurgronje too found in Mecca that some Naqshbandi shaykhs (but not the most respected) encouraged dancing, violent movements of the body, and other such ways of inducing ecstasy. Shaykh Khalid himself seems to have made serious claims to be able to enter into contact with the spirits of the dead: claims which, as we have seen, are closely linked with the Naqshbandi teaching on the progression of the soul towards God. Half a century after his death, Rashid Rida joined the Naqshbandi order in Tripoli and, in a memoir written long after his total rejection of Sufism, gives special mention of the Naqshbandi doctrine of the communion of hearts, not only between teacher and disciple but between living and dead, back through all the links in the spiritual chain to the Prophet himself. He mentions also the strange phenomena, like perfumes, which could be observed at the mystical sessions.[39] To men and women living in an age of doubt, such assurances of the existence of an invisible order are doubly precious.

On the other hand, Naqshbandism offered the perplexed Muslim a faith which emphasised the importance of virtuous activity, and the claims of the *shari'a* to be a guiding rule for it; a faith which included all that was valuable in those of its opponents justified Sunni Muslims in rejecting other creeds and strengthened them in resisting attacks from outside. This rejection of all that is not Sunni, in the name of a Sunnism which comprehends the elements of truth in what it rejects, links the Naqshbandiyya both with the Islamic past and with certain modern methods of interpretation.

6 Sufism and Modern Islam: Rashid Rida

The Salafi trend of thought in the modern Muslim world has been much studied since C.C. Adams wrote *Islam and Modernism in Egypt* and Henri Laoust published his essay.[1] On the one hand, it was a reaffirmation of a comparatively simple body of doctrine, regarded as that of the 'founding fathers' of the faith, the *salaf al-salih;* on the other, a reformulation of laws and social morality in the light of new needs, carried out cautiously and responsibly, and by an extension of the accepted principle of *istislah*. In both its aspects, this process involved the rejection of much in later Islamic belief and practice, and in particular of many ideas and activities to which the epithet of 'Sufi' was attached.

A symbolic moment of rejection has been described by Muhammad Rashid Rida, the main spokesman of the Salafi movement in his generation, in a passage which has already been published in partial translation:

> They said to me, 'Won't you come and attend the meeting of the Mawlawis in their monastery—it is like the heavenly paradise, lying on the bank of the river Abu 'Ali'. I agreed, and went with those who were going after the Friday prayers. It was the opening of the season for these meetings in the spring. I sat in the spectators' space . . . until the time of the session came, when Mawlawi dervishes appeared in their meeting-place in front of us, with their shaykh in the seat of honour. There were handsome beardless youths among them, dressed in snow-white gowns like brides' dresses, dancing to the moving sound of the reed-pipe, turning swiftly and skilfully so that their robes flew out and formed circles, at harmonious distances and not encroaching on one another. They stretched out their arms and inclined their necks, and passed in turn before their shaykh and bowed to him. I asked, 'What's this?' and they told me, 'This is

the ritual prayer of the order founded by our Lord Jalal al-Din al-Rumi, author of the *Mathnawi*.'

I could not control myself, and stood up in the centre of the hall and shouted something like this: 'O people, or can I call you Muslims! These are forbidden acts, which one has no right either to look at or to pass over in silence, for to do so is to accept them. To those who commit them God's word applies, "They have made their religion a joke and a plaything." I have done what I was obliged to do; now take your leave, and may God pardon you.' Then I left the place and retraced my footsteps quickly to the city; as I was going I looked back, and found behind me a small number who had returned, while the greater number stayed on.

The purpose of the present essay is to ask what exactly it was that Rashid Rida thought he was rejecting. It is clear that he, like his master Muhammad 'Abduh, did not think he was condemning Sufism as a whole. They would both have made a distinction between what they regarded as the 'true' and the 'false' Sufism. Some of the 'true' Sufis, like al-Junayd, al-Ansari and Ibn Qayim al-Jawziyya, they would have regarded as being in the line of succession of the *salaf al-salih*, and 'Abduh at least thought the revival of the 'true' Sufism to be a legitimate and important task for a reformer of Islam.[3]

In making such a distinction, they were pointing to an obvious fact, that the term 'Sufism' covers a variety of ideas and activities. Every writer of 'Sufi' works has tended to use words in his own sense, and, as A.M. Schimmel has reminded us recently, when we are dealing with Sufi poetry it is not always easy to be sure that a poet is using a word with the full intention that its Sufi meaning be taken literally. Apart from difficulties of interpretation, what we call 'Sufi' writings can be concerned with very different kinds of thought and activity.[4]

Since Massignon, scholarly work has tended to show that Sufism developed out of some combination between an ascetic tendency, rooted perhaps in the eastern Christian spiritual tradition, and an attempt to 'interiorise' the Qur'an and *hadith:* through meditation on them to understand their true meaning, to obey the divine commands expressed or implied in them, and to do so with the correct intention, that of sincerity. Understanding, obedience and sincerity could only be attained by effort, and Sufi writers set themselves to mark out the path by which the spiritual wayfarer, the *salik*, could move towards knowledge of God under the impulse of love: the way of purgation, by which the soul turned away first from sin, then from the distractions of the world, and the way of illumination by which it grew in knowledge of its true self and of God. The various stages *(maqamat)* on the way could be described: repentance, poverty, trust in God, fear, longing, love. So too could the various practices which helped the wayfarer to overcome the distractions of life: special prayers *(awrad)*, recollection of the name of God *(dhikr)*, accompanied by concentration *(tawajjuh)*, special methods of sitting, standing and breathing, and music or poetry.

It was a matter of observable fact that, as the *salik* travelled along this path, certain affective states *(ahwal)*—sorrow for sin, love of God—might come, and these too could be described and the succession of them distinguished. It was observable too that, at a certain point on the path, those who had persevered might have an experience which all who had it explained in terms of some kind of direct knowledge of God *(ma'rifa)*: the presence of God in the soul, the immediate awareness of the oneness of God, the absence of the human self, a kind of dialogue between God and man. Another kind of writing could attempt to describe this experience, or at least hint at what was literally indescribable, and to discuss its significance in human life: once it had tasted *ma'rifa*, should the soul remain in a state of permanent 'drunkenness', in which God was all and man nothing, or should it return to the 'second sobriety', in which man was 'present in himself and God', and lived in human society under the rule of God's law, the *shari'a*, but haunted by the memory of the 'lost Beloved'?

It was generally agreed that it was dangerous, and beyond a certain point impossible, for the *salik* to tread the path alone, without a guide and teacher who would administer the medicine of the soul, teach the practice of virtue, and pass on certain secrets of prayer, recollection and meditation: 'when someone has no *shaykh*, Satan becomes his *shaykh*'.[5] The activity of striving towards virtue and knowledge was placed within the framework of two of the essential institutions of Muslim society: that of apprenticeship, the relationship between master and novice, *murshid* and *murid;* and that of the *silsila*, the chain of transmission of a special body of knowledge, coming from the Prophet, through a succession of masters of the spiritual life, to the *murshid* and his *murid*. A Sufi 'order', a *tariqa*, was, almost by definition, a body of men practising and handing on a special way of drawing near to knowledge of God, authenticated by a continuous chain of masters. Thus further subjects of Sufi writing were the *adab* or moral relationship of master and pupil, the lines of transmission, and the graces *(karamat)*, given by God to the great masters or saints, those who had come near to Him *(awliya)*.[6]

There was another kind of Sufi writing, the metaphysical or theosophic: what kind of God and what kind of universe were implied by the possibility of *ma'rifa?* The beginning of an answer was given in the image of two arcs, one of the descent of the created world from God, the other of ascent or return to Him: 'I was a hidden treasure and I wished to be known, so I made creation in order to be known.' The processes of descent and ascent were depicted by means of various systems of images, those of light, of love and of wine. They could, however, be interpreted in more than one way. What proceeds from God could be regarded as something other than Him, or as an emanation, a succession of forms of God's own being. The experience of *ma'rifa* might be explained in terms of a temporary substitution of God's attributes for man's; afterwards man should return to the 'second sobriety' of life in society under law. It might also be interpreted as a revelation of the 'unity of being' *(wahdat al-wujud)*: God was the sole reality, man had no separate being, and once the soul had attained to understanding of this, it would remain in a permanent state of 'drunkenness', knowledge of the one reality.

Once this body of ideas and practices had developed, there was virtually no total rejection of it until modern times. The differences were not of total acceptance or rejection, but of beliefs and practices within the system. Different orders varied in their prayers and rituals, and in their view of the relations between *shari'a*, the way of obedience to law, and *tariqa*, the way towards *ma'rifa*. Individual members of orders also no doubt accepted the *tariqa* with differing motives and at various levels of conviction: some wished for union with God, for others the meetings of the *tariqa* offered some of the attractions of a club, or dead or living *awliya* could work miracles and intercede with God, or their descendants or the guardians of their tombs could act as arbitrators of disputes, guarantors of the neutrality of the market-place, or leaders of movements against rulers held guilty of injustice or infidelity. There was general agreement, however, on certain matters: the validity of the *tariqa*, the journey to knowledge of God under the direction of a *murshid;* the existence of friends of God, *awliya;* and the possibility of *karamat*, signs of God's favour.

This is true even of the tendency of thought and practice which might seem furthest from Sufism, that of the Hanbalis with their emphasis on the Qur'an and the practice of the first generation. The work of Laoust himself, and then of G. Makdisi, has shown that Hanbalism and Sufism may even be said to have had a common origin, in meditation on, and imitation of, the example of the Prophet and his companions. Many famous Hanbalis were also Sufis, and the most famous Hanbali attack upon Sufism, that of Ibn al-Jawzi, was in fact an attack on certain illicit practices only, and was coupled with attacks on other forms of innovation *(bid'a)* as well. In the thought of Ibn Taymiyya, as Laoust has shown,[7] there is an acceptance of the existence of *ahwal*, and of the experience of *ma'rifa* as having some kind of validity. But it is only a fleeting experience in a life to be lived, both before and after, in strict conformity with the Qur'an and *hadith*, and it does not in any sense justify metaphysical speculations which destroy the distinction between God and man and in so doing weaken the hold of law. Makdisi has shown that Ibn Taymiyya himself was invested with the Sufi cloak *(khirqa)* by Ibn Qudama, in whose own *silsila* most of the links, back to 'Abd al-Qadir al-Gaylani, were themselves Hanbalis.[8]

Even the most famous exception may not be very significant. The Wahhabi movement in the eighteenth century (and here again we are in debt to Laoust[9]) was a neo-Hanbali movement which appears to have gone further than Ibn Taymiyya in its rejections: in particular, of the veneration shown to dead saints and the idea of human intercession to modify divine justice. A more detailed study of Wahhabism than has yet been made might possibly change our views of it, and at all events it can be regarded as a phenomenon of an abnormal situation, a violent reaction characteristic of a marginal community with a weak urban tradition, where the fragile orthodoxy of the small market-towns lying along the Wadi Sirhan was always challenged by the *jahiliyya* of the Beduin. It had no great influence in the Muslim world as a whole until the present century, and even then the influence was as much political as religious.

Throughout the eighteenth and nineteenth centuries, indeed, and until the rise of the Salafiyya movement, the most influential currents of thought and action still flowed within the channels of the Sufi orders. In some of them, both old and new, there was a great emphasis on the importance of the link between *shari'a* and *tariqa*, and therefore of activity in obeying the law, exhorting others to obey it, and attempting to create a society living under the rule of Islamic justice. Typical of such movements was the Naqshbandi order.[10] Beginning in central Asia, it spread to India in the Mogul epoch, had a certain influence at the Mogul court, and produced a considerable thinker, Ahmad al-Sirhindi, although one of less originality, perhaps, than was once believed.[11] It came into the Ottoman lands in three waves: to Istanbul and Asia Minor in the fifteenth and sixteenth centuries, to Damascus in the seventeenth with the founder of the Muradi family, and to Iraq and Syria again in the early nineteenth with Mawlana Khalid. Its marks were the silent and solitary *dhikr*, and strict emphasis on obedience to the *shari'a* and action in order to bring the world under its rule: 'to serve the world it is necessary to exercise political power'.[12]

The Naqshbandiyya was by no means the only *tariqa* to show such characteristic in the last two centuries, and it would be correct indeed to regard such movements as leading by a natural development to others which may seem more typical of the modern world. The emphasis on observance of the *shari'a* was not incompatible with a certain reinterpretation of it, and in fact the extended use of the principle of *istislah* can be traced back at least as far as another Indian thinker connected with the Naqshbandiyya, Shah Waliullah of Delhi in the eighteenth century. The emphasis on restoring the reign of Islamic justice could provide a moral basis for 'proto-nationalist' movements of opposition to governments which seemed to threaten it, whether indigenous secularising governments or European imperial ones. Resistance to the policy of the *tanzimat* and then of Atatürk in the Anatolian countryside took place within the framework of *tariqa's*, and so too did resistance to the expansion of Russia in the Caucasus, France in north and west Africa, and Italy in Cyrenaica.

How far can the thought of Rashid Rida be seen as falling within this cumulative tradition, and how far did his work and that of his successors mark a break with it? More precisely, did he intend to do more than criticise certain illicit aspects of Sufism, or did he come near a total rejection of it?

In the passage already quoted, it is clear that he is criticising certain practices of one order, the Mawlawiyya: practices through which the beauty of the visible world might distract the believer, the line between sacred and profane love be blurred, and purely human inventions replace the forms of worship which the Qur'an and *hadith* stated to be pleasing to God.[13] At this time Rashid Rida was, or had recently been, a *murid* of the Naqshbandi order, and the attack upon the Mawlawis was such as other Naqshbandis might have made from within their own tradition.

The dangers of the 'false' Sufism form a theme which recurs again and again in his work: in a long section of the *Tafsir al-Manar,* the Qur'anic commentary which he wrote with 'Abduh, in his life of 'Abduh, and in articles scattered throughout his periodical, *al-Manar,* in particular a series on the *karamat* of the saints in the earlier volumes, and another, much later, in which he defends himself against attacks made by certain shaykhs of the Azhar.[14] (This later series is more personal in tone than earlier ones, and it is from here that our quotation comes.)

The false Sufism is attacked as a cause of immorality, and still more as corrupting the purity of the faith, by introducing prayers and rituals having no basis in the Qur'an or *hadith;* one order in particular, the Tijaniyya, is criticised for using a prayer, the *salat al-fatih,* which is uncanonical, and which Ahmad al-Tijani claimed to have been imparted to him by the Prophet in a vision and to be more efficacious for salvation than the canonical prayers.[15]

The dangers of ascribing *karamat* to saints are pointed out.[16] Rida did not regard them all as false, since it was quite possible that God would give special favours to individuals, and they did not in any sense contradict the orthodox view of the way in which God works in the created world; apart from the Muʻtazilites, virtually all Muslim thinkers had accepted the possibility that God should, in His freedom, diverge from His own customary modes of action *('adat).* By no means all, however, of the strange experiences and signs attributed to saints, or which came upon the *salik* on his way, need be accepted as *karamat.* Some were simply lies, invented by the claimant to sainthood or his family or successors, in order to obtain wealth, power or glory. Others had a natural explanation in terms of God's customary modes of action. Predictions of the future or answers to prayer might be no more than coincidences. Strange visions might be dreams, or the kind of illusion which comes to us in a state between sleeping and waking, or hallucinations induced by drugs, excessive fasting, or uncontrolled practice of a certain kind of *dhikr*. The silent *dhikr* of the Naqshbandis, for example, involved five thousand repetitions of the divine name, with concentration of the heart upon that of the shaykh, and through him upon the whole chain of masters back to the Prophet; in this exercise, illusory visions of the dead might come. Even experiences which could not be explained in such natural ways need not necessarily be a sign of God's favour; they might come not from God but from demons.

Such events and experiences as did come from God might not be so significant as they were thought to be. In themselves they had no value; they could be given to sinners, unbelievers or sorcerers. Their value derived from something other than themselves; at best they strengthened the hold of the *shari'a* over him who had the experience or those who observed it. (A quotation recurs more than once in Rida's writing on this subject: if you see a man flying, do not place any confidence in him until you know whether or not he obeys the *shari'a*.[17]) Therefore it is best not to speak openly of them, in case they should lead others astray by causing them to believe that some men have been given private revelations and can ignore the commands of the public revelations through the prophets. One of the differences between the miracles of prophets *(mu'jizat)* and those of saints *(karamat)* is that the former should be proclaimed openly, since they help to prove the status of the prophets, while nothing should be said in public of the latter.[18]

Above all, Rida was critical of all kinds of speculative interpretation which went beyond what he took to be the clear meaning of the text of the Qur'an or *hadith*. One of the points he singled out for criticism in the work of al-Ghazali, a writer who had much influence on him in youth, was the practice of *ta'wil*, the mystical interpretation of the injunctions of the *shari'a*.[19] He directed a much sharper criticism, however, against such metaphysical systems as that of Ibn al-'Arabi.

In his criticisms there is a note of personal sharpness and bitterness. His attitude seems, to judge by such passages as that already quoted, to have been formed already in his early years in or near Tripoli. The Lebanese countryside was full of natural objects held sacred by Muslims and Christians alike, in accordance with traditions inherited from earlier days, and which provided ways by which ancient beliefs and rites could penetrate Islam: stones, trees, springs like that of 'Afqa linked with the story of Adonis.[20] Rida tells us that he himself in his early youth had persuaded the people of his own village, Qalamun, to stop lighting candles before certain shrines, and root up a myrtle tree associated with a woman saint.[21]

There may have been experiences more personal still, and even a certain temptation in his early life. Once more we must rely on his own version. He tells us of strange powers he was believed to possess: while reading the *Ihya* of al-Ghazali, he felt as if his mind had been released from his body; he had a sense of being outside time; he had premonitions of the future; sometimes he seemed able to heal the sick, and his prayers appeared to be immediately effective. If these experiences had been written about in the traditional language of Sufism, he suggests, they would have been regarded as signs of God's favour; members of his own family did regard him as a saint in the making, and he might have come to think of himself in the same way.[22]

Even before he left Tripoli in his early thirties, his rejection of Sufi ways of thought had gone further than was common in the slightly 'modernising' milieu in which he was educated, and he had been warned against it by his teacher Husayn al-Jisr.[23] At that time, he tells us, he knew little about Ibn Taymiyya, except for a book by Khayr al-Din al-Alusi, and next to nothing about Wahhabism.[24] Once he settled in Egypt, the lines of thought already started were carried further. On the one hand, he found in Egypt a manifestation of popular Sufism almost unknown in his own district, the saints' days or *mawlid's,* great country festivals where superstition was openly expressed and the moral precepts of Islam were ignored.[25] On the other, his rejection was given a firmer theoretical basis. He read Ibn Taymiyya and Ibn al-Jawzi, and came under the most decisive personal influence of his life. Muhammad 'Abduh had been through similar experiences in his earlier life, and had perhaps gone further than his disciple on the path of striving towards *ma'rifa*. He had certainly immersed himself more deeply in speculation and wandered in the 'world of images' *('alam al-mithal)*. From the attraction of such ideas and visions, he once told Rida, a man could not escape by himself, but only by some personal influence strong enough to draw him away. This had been the role played in his own life first by his uncle Shaykh Darwish, who had warned him of the dangers of isolation, and then of Jamal al-Din.[26]

Under such influences a new note came into Rida's criticisms. The false interpretations, he believed, had come from outside

Islam, from an ancient tradition of speculation which had arisen in Asia and spread from there into Greece. They had been brought into Islam by those who professed to accept the religion but really wished to ruin it, the adherents of the esoteric tendency, the Batiniyya, who were responsible alike for the excesses of Shi'ism and those of Sufism.[27] The Batiniyya he regarded as a kind of conspiracy to destroy 'Islam and the Arab *dawla*' and restore the Zoroastrian faith and rule.[28] There is indeed a strong anti-Shi'i tone in his later writing, the product perhaps of his Naqshbandi apprenticeship, perhaps of the threatened Sunnism of the Syrian coastal towns, with a Shi'i, 'Alawi and Isma'ili hill country lying between them and the great Sunni cities of the inner plains.

Apart from the bitterness of tone, however, the criticisms we have so far encountered are scarcely more than what can be found in Ibn Taymiyya and Ibn al-Jawzi, authors whom Rashid Rida quotes extensively. He certainly did not think of himself as attacking Sufism as such, but only 'excess', which threatened the central core of essential belief and the unity of its adherents. He pointed out that he had made similar attacks on other kinds of excess: the literalism and pedantry of the lawyers, and the speculations of the theologians.[29]

Nevertheless, there are certain ways in which he seems to go further than the older critics of Sufism. First, his writings contain an implicit questioning of the validity of the later stages on the path of the spiritual wayfarer. In some passages, indeed, he accepts the possibility that some Muslims may have reached a point where they knew and understood more than the majority.[30] On the whole, however, the *via purgativa* is more real to him than the *via illuminativa*. The rare exception apart, the furthest a Muslim need go or can go is to the station of trust in God: a station attained by meditation on the Qur'an and *hadith*, examination of conscience, and a turning away from the goods of the world which stops short of the excesses of asceticism, and expresses itself in sincere obedience to the commands embodied in the *shari'a* and exhortation to others to obey.[31] Even Sufis whom he would have regarded as belonging to the *salaf al-salih*, like Junayd, would have gone further than this, and 'Abduh sometimes spoke as if he had gone further, but there is no sign that Rida himself would have striven to do so.[32]

A more striking departure from the cumulative tradition is to be found in Rida's virtual rejection of the necessity of a relationship between *murshid* and *murid* and of a continuous chain of initiation. There were dangers in them: the Naqshbandi practice of concentration on the spirits of dead saints could open the way to trickery or to demonic possession. More than that, the idea of intercession, of the *awliya* as possessing a kind of protective role, seemed to deny the possibility of a direct relationship between God and the individual Muslim; and the idea of an invisible hierarchy of saints who sustained the order of the world seemed to imply a disbelief in God's sustaining hand.[33]

There was a more fundamental reason for the rejection: a dislike of the kind of personality produced by the close relationship of *murshid* and *murid,* as expressed in the famous saying that the novice should be like a dead body between the hands of his master. Such a personality had no place for that independence of mind and soul which was, in Rida's view, what Islam demanded and created. It was the equivalent in Sufism of the blind imitation, *taqlid,* which was for him the great danger in the Islam of legal observance.[34] While he sometimes spoke of himself as the *murid* of Muhammad 'Abduh, he was careful to add that he had never surrendered his independent judgment to him any more than to his earlier teacher Husayn al-Jisr.[35]

Such a relationship, moreover, tended to be exclusive, in a way incompatible with the openness and universality of the community of believers. It might divide the community into groups each claiming to have sole possession of the truth. There was indeed such a tendency in some of the Sufi orders of his time. The Tijaniyya, for example, appear to have claimed that theirs was the only path to the truth, and he who entered on it should avoid all other paths and never give it up.[36]

Behind such criticisms there lies a certain ideal of the virtuous Muslim life, expressed in what Rida wrote about 'Abduh, and elsewhere about his own great-uncle Sayyid al-Shaykh Ahmad: a man who gave his life to prayer, neither visiting nor receiving visits except at stated hours, grave and dignified in conversation, allowing no foolish talk or noisy laughter in his presence, avoiding the rulers of the world, but living in and for the community.[37] This ideal of the believer given to prayer, learning and moral exhortation is an ancient Muslim one, but excludes some elements of the Sufi ideal: however far the believer has gone on the road towards sincerity and trust, there still lies a limitless distance between himself and God; the mark of his virtue is sincere obedience rather than love; in this life there is no nearness to God, in the most literal sense, no *wilaya*.

In the writings of Rashid Rida and those who can be regarded as his associates and followers, another strand of criticism of the Sufi life is intertwined with these. They reject some manifestations of Sufism for social and political reasons also. The excesses of popular Sufism are thought to have brought the Muslim world into disrepute, and the quietism of Sufi teaching has weakened the will of the community and made it unfit to survive in the modern world.[38] These were themes taken up by those associated with the Salafiyya movement in North Africa even more than Syria. In Algeria, the Tijaniyya were accused of having submitted too easily to French rule, either because of opposition to the previous Ottoman rule or rivalry with the Qadiriyya, with which the movement of 'Abd al-Qadir was linked. In Morocco, other orders as well as the Tijaniyya were accused of collaborating with the French occupying power.[39]

When nationalism became explicit therefore, in Syria and North Africa alike, it had Salafi overtones, and the rejection of the *tariqa's* and their view of Islam was carried further as a secular organisation of society took root. Even beyond the educated class and the cities, the social and political role of the *tariqa's* began to change. In the modern state, the city-based government dominates the countryside more directly than before; in town and country alike, political parties and labour unions offer other forms of association. The *tariqa's* can still play an active social role to the extent to which they are able to acquire modern forms of organisation, and insert themselves into the interstices of modern society. A recent study by M. Gilsenan of the Hamidiyya Shadhiliyya order in Egypt has shown how it has been able to organise itself in a modern bureaucratic way, and makes a special appeal to certain marginal strata in a modern urban society, those who have neither the high status conferred by education nor that conferred by occupation.[40] It is clear, however, that for most adherents the *tariqa* is rather a club with a certain atmosphere of religious and moral uplift, coming into its own at certain public festivals—the end of Ramadan, the *mawlid* of the Prophet—than an association of wayfarers engaged in a common journey towards unity with God.

There is more to be said than this, however. Sufism fulfils an individual need, even among the educated, and there are signs that, at least for some concerned Muslims, the Sufi way is an acceptable alternative both to secularism and to the austere fundamentalism of the Wahhabi type which has now become worldwide. Its persistence is due as much to the survival of an old tradition as to that interest in mystical experience which can now be observed all over the world.[41]

7 The Middleman in a Changing Society: Syrians in Egypt in the Eighteenth and Nineteenth Centuries

The subject of this essay is the role played in modern Egypt by a comparatively small group of immigrants who came into the country from what used to be called Syria in the broad geographical sense: that is to say, the land lying along the eastern Mediterranean coast and stretching inland from the coast to the Syrian desert—*barr al-Sham* in the Arabic of Egypt, hence the name *shami* (plural *shawam*) for its inhabitants.[1] This role was of some but not of major weight in the political and economic life of Egypt; in the intellectual life of the country it was, for a generation or two, of great importance. Thus the subject has an interest of its own but it is also significant of two general tendencies: first, the tendency for ethnic difference and economic specialisation to go closely together in the traditional society of the Muslim Middle East (and in other societies also to varying degrees); secondly, the tendency for a society in process of change to generate a need for more special skills than it can itself provide, and so to give an opportunity for groups of an alien origin to find a place for themselves in it, at least for a time.

Egypt and Syria (to use the name once again in its broader sense) are neighbouring countries, and there must always have been a movement of peoples between them. Long before the eighteenth century a considerable trade moved between the two, by the sea routes linking their Mediterranean ports or by the coastal road through Sinai. Some of those who travelled with the caravans or profited from them were Syrian Muslim merchants, and a brief mention in al-Jabarti shows this trade still continuing in the early nineteenth century: he records that in 1801 a large caravan came from Damascus by the land-route, bringing with it soap, tobacco and other goods, and gives the names of two merchants who came with it, both of them Syrian Muslims (al-Sayyid Badr al-Din al-Maqdisi and Hajj Sa'udi al-Hinnawi).[2] Some of these merchants settled in Cairo, in particular Palestinians from Nablus and Hebron trading in soap and glass. There was also a Syrian community of a different kind long settled in Cairo, the teachers and students of the Syrian *riwaq* in the Azhar. The biographical dictionaries show us how many Syrian *shaykhs* studied at the Azhar, and that quite a number of them remained there and took an active part in its life of study and its turbulent politics. This too continued into the nineteenth century: the Syrian *riwaq* played an important role in the crisis over the choice of a new *shaykh* for the Azhar in 1812.[3]

The Syrian community took its modern form in the seventeenth and eighteenth centuries with the emergence of two new factors, probably connected with each other.[4] One was the growing importance of a certain commodity, the silk produced in Lebanon and imported into Egypt both in its raw state, as material for the workshops of Damietta, Mahalla and Cairo, and in the form of silk textiles of Damascus and Aleppo. By the early eighteenth century a certain pattern of exchanges had been fixed, and this was to remain until the middle of the nineteenth century, when the growth of the trade in Egyptian cotton once more introduced a new element. Egypt imported from Syria Indian produce coming by way of Damascus, silk and cotton fabrics, the raw silk of Lebanon, the tobacco of Latakia, soap, olive oil, sesame seed and cotton of Palestine. She exported to Syria rice grown in the region of Damietta, grain, lentils, spices and coffee, some linen and silk textiles, and some black slaves. The value of the imports usually exceeded that of exports, and the difference was made up by the export of precious metals. Some of this trade still went, as we have seen, by the land-route, but most of it passed through the Mediterranean ports—Alexandria, Rosetta, and above all Damietta.[5]

The second change was the establishment of Syrian merchants specialising in this trade in Cairo and the ports. Some of them were Muslims. For example, 'Abdallah Barbir, a member of a well-known Muslim family of Beirut and himself a poet famous in his time, was born in Damietta in 1748;[6] and al-Jabarti tells us of a famous merchant of the same city, Hajj 'Umar al-Tarabulsi, who quarrelled with the Syrian Christian merchants.[7] Most of those who engaged in the coastal trade seem indeed to have been Christians, and of these few appear to have belonged to the 'Greek' Orthodox community, and most seem to have been Maronites or Melkites, that is to say, 'Greek' Catholics or Uniates. This may however to some extent be a false impression, since we do not possess Orthodox Church registers of births, marriages and deaths before the middle of the nineteenth century, while we do possess the registers of the Franciscans of Terra Santa from the seventeenth. The first names of Syrians in these registers are of Maronites, mainly from Damascus: we find them recorded in 1643 and a few later years in the century, but they are not many, and it would appear that the community was small at that time and mainly concerned with the import of textiles from Damascus. In the early eighteenth century most of the names are still of Maronites, but more of them come from Aleppo. Then in the years 1730—50 numbers increase rapidly, and the majority of those mentioned are Melkites, not Maronites. The reasons are not difficult to discover. First, some Uniate merchant families had by now a long connection with French and other European commercial houses, as *employés* or brokers, and in this way had acquired a knowledge of trade and finance and entered into contact with the sources of supply of manufactured goods in western Europe. Secondly, in the first half of the eighteenth century there was a long struggle for power between Catholic and non-Catholic elements in the Orthodox and other eastern churches. In this struggle the Ottoman government on the whole supported those groups led by the patriarchs in Istanbul, who wished to keep their churches independent of the papacy, and the various European Ambassadors exercised what pressure they could on one side or the other. There was a period during which the Catholic groups were persecuted, in the great cities of Syria as elsewhere in the Empire. This was followed by a period of *de facto* separation, mutual toleration and calm, but it was not until 1848 that the Melkites were finally recognised as a separate *millet*. Of the eastern churches, the Maronite was the only one which was not torn by this conflict, since it had accepted the Roman obedience as a whole during the Crusades, and re-affirmed it at the Synod of Mount Lebanon in 1736. The Orthodox Church was deeply divided, and there is some evidence that this conflict led to the emigration of a large number of Melkites from ,Aleppo and

Damascus to Egypt. They may have been helped in this by the Franciscans, who were by this time well established in Egypt; they may have hoped also for a greater toleration from the Mamluks than from Ottoman provincial governors, for there was a certain tendency for local ruling groups desirous of greater autonomy within the Ottoman Empire to support the Uniates. (The Shihabs and Jumblats in Lebanon are other examples of this).

From the 1740s onwards we find mention in the registers of many of the Melkite and Maronite families who were to remain leaders of the Syrian community until the present century. In Cairo, a Zananiri is mentioned in 1749, a Sabbagh in 1750, an 'Anhuri and a Sakakihi in 1752, a Farazli in 1753, an Ayrout in 1760, a Kahil in 1761, and a Debbané in 1768; in Alexandria, an Eid in 1770, a Taghir in 1788; in Damietta a Far'awn, a Surur, a Tawil and a Turk before the end of the century. In the registers of the Franciscan monastery of Cairo about 400 Syrian families are mentioned by the end of the eighteenth century, and this more or less accords with other figures we have.[8] The *Description de l'Egypte* says that there were about 5000 Syrians in Cairo out of a total population of 260,000 at the time of the French occupation;[9] this makes them about 2 per cent of the whole population, but a considerably larger proportion of the merchant class. (Writing a little later, in 1823, Mengin gives a rather lower figure: 3000 in Cairo, 500 in Damietta, 250 in Alexandria and Rosetta.)[10]

They were for the most part merchants, brokers, or retailers of cloth, of hardware and haberdashery, of precious metals and precious stones. The main centres of the Syrian Muslim merchants had long been in the Khan al-Hamzawi and the Jamaliyya quarter, where some of the *wikalas* were largely occupied by them and given over to the Syrian trade: for example, *Wikalat al-Sabun* and *Wikalat al-Tuffah*. When the Christians began to come in, they too traded in and around the same places and gradually replaced the Syrian Muslims in some of them: by 1760 the Khan al-Hamzawi was almost entirely occupied by them. They lived in various quarters: there were some in Old Cairo, but most lived in the Frankish quarter *(Harat al-Afranj)*, near the French and other European merchants and not far from their places of work.[11] Here as elsewhere they lived clustered around their churches. In Damietta there was a Syrian church throughout most of the eighteenth century. It belonged to the Maronites, but the Melkites also had the use of it; it was served by the Maronite order of the

Lebanese Fathers from 1745, and by the Melkite order of the Basilians of St Saviour. There was a Melkite church in Old Cairo, but none in Cairo itself until a later date: Maronite and Melkite priests officiated in the two Catholic churches of Harat al-Afranj, that of Terra Santa and that of the Propaganda.[12]

The *Description de l'Egypte* says that the Syrian churches were the poorest, smallest and least frequented of any, but they were by no means a poor community.[13] By the end of the eighteenth century, indeed, they were in control of a large part of the trade of Egypt. One sign of their wealth is the amount which the head of the community paid the government for his annual investiture: the head of the Copts paid 25,000 *paras* a year, that of the Greeks 10,000, that of the Jews 6750, and that of the Syrian Christians 12,000.[14] Their prosperity was connected with the close links some of them established with the European merchants and the Mamluks. The church registers record many marriages between European merchants and the daughters of Syrians. Some of them acted as middlemen, buying the luxury goods which the Europeans imported and selling them to the Mamluk *beys* and other notables of the city. (We hear of one of them, a Maronite of the Kusa family, as official purveyor of broadcloth to the Mamluk chief Murad Bey.)[15]

It was no doubt through this commercial link with the Mamluks that, in the middle of the century, a number of Syrian merchants became administrators of the customs houses. The *iltizams* of the customs of Cairo and Bulaq, of the three Mediterranean ports, and of Suez and Qusayr were held by the Mamluk *beys,* who administered them through officials or *mu'allims*. For long the *mu'allims* had come from various Jewish families, but during 'Ali Bey's tenure of power a Syrian merchant of Damietta, Hanna Fakhr, set on foot an intrigue which resulted in 'Ali Bey's confiscating the wealth of the Jews and putting Syrian *mu'allims* in their place in 1767. From then until the coming of the French one Syrian or other held this office in most of the customs houses; the families of Farhat, Fakhr, Jamal, Bitar, Kassab, Fara'un and Kahil are mentioned in this connection.[16] Naturally the *mu'allims* used their position to their own advantage: they influenced the *beys* in their favour, increased taxes on the European merchants, and enriched themselves. But, as was equally to be expected, the Mamluks were always on the watch to seize their wealth. They had a powerful weapon which they could use to this end: the fact that the Maronites and Melkites were not formally recognised as separate communities. The Ottoman government recognised the Orthodox and Armenian *millets*, and the European or 'Latin' Catholics, but in its eyes the Melkites were still members of the Orthodox church. On occasion the Greek Patriarch of Alexandria tried to interfere with them, and in this he received some support from the government in Istanbul: a *berat* of appointment of one of the Patriarchs promises him help in fighting Roman Catholic activities in his province,[17] and at least once the Sultan issued a *firman* forbidding members of the Orthodox *millet* in Egypt to enter Catholic European churches.[18] But they were able, in one way or another, to obtain *fatwas* in their favour, and they appeased the patriarch by an annual payment. When they wanted, however, the Mamluks could use the ambiguous position of the Syrians for their own profit. In 1796 Murad Bey imprisoned the Syrian Catholic priests of Damietta, and only released them in return for money.[19]

The history of one family, that of Far'awn, illustrates clearly the fortunes of the Syrians in this period. They came from Damascus, and when the split took place in the Orthodox community in that city they took the Uniate side. A certain member of the family, Ibrahim, found it best to leave Damascus for Damietta with his three sons. There they prospered, and one of the sons, Antun, became chief *mu'allim* of the customs; under him, one of his brothers was *mu'allim* of the customs house at Bulaq, another at Damietta, and a cousin at Alexandria. They became leaders of the community, built churches at Damietta and Old Cairo, had close links with the Franciscans, established a family connection with the famous merchant Carlo Rossetti, and obtained titles of nobility from the Holy Roman Emperor and the Pope. When with the death of 'Ali Bey and then of Abu Dhahab their position grew weaker, they were able to leave Egypt in 1784, to settle in Trieste and Livorno, great centres of the Levant trade, and from there to found a family whose branches are still found in several cities of the Mediterranean.[20]

The French occupation of Egypt ended the special relationship of Syrian merchants and Mamluk *beys*, but opened a new path to influence for some Syrians. When Bonaparte was planning the expedition, he sent instructions to Monge, who was then in Rome, to enlist interpreters and other officials from the Syrian priests and students there, and other interpreters were found when he landed in Egypt, among Syrians who added to their native Arabic a knowledge of Italian learned from the Franciscans.[21] The most famous of them was 'Don Raphael', Father Ruf'il Antun Zakhur (1759-1831): a Melkite of a family from Aleppo, but born in Cairo, who entered the order of St Saviour early, studied for several years in Italy, then returned to Egypt some years before the coming of the French. As well as being chief interpreter he was a scholar of some distinction, who became a member of the 'Institut d'Egypte' and the 'Commission des Sciences et Arts'.[22] But there were others also and they played many parts, as translators, printers, interpreters of courts and councils, and on semi-political missions. When Bonaparte sent an emissary to Ahmad Pasha al-Jazzar, governor of Acre, there went with him two Syrian merchants, one of them of the family of Zughayb—once more we come on a name which was to remain well-known throughout the history of the community.[23]

What is more surprising is to find a company of 'Syrian Janissaries' among the local troops recruited by the French when they lost control of the sea and could no longer bring reinforcements from France. They appear to have been drawn not from the Syrian families of the Egyptian cities but from Nazareth, Shafa 'Amr, and other Christian centres in northern Palestine. Some of them went with the French army back to France, were absorbed into the 'Mamelukes de la garde' and took part in the later wars of the Empire.[24]

One or two of the leaders of the Syrian Community played a more important role. When the general *divan* was restored in December 1798 after the insurrection of Cairo, it was to have a smaller standing *divan* of fourteen members. Two of them were Syrians from among the great merchants of Cairo, Yusuf Farhat and Mikha'il Kahil;[25] the latter indeed might be called a victim of his public position, for shortly afterwards al-Jazzar confiscated the property of his partner in Syria, and when Mikha'il Kahil heard the news he had a heart attack and died.[26]

In general, the Syrian Christians appear to have been on the side of the French, and were accused of using the French presence to improve their position. Al-Jabarti records with clear disapproval that during the popular festival of the Nile flood the Syrians went in illuminated boats, accompanied by their women-folk, wearing clothes more suitable to Mamluk *beys,* joking and talking in a disrespectful way; they rode horses, imitated French manners, used insulting words, and ate and drank openly in the *suq* during Ramadan.²⁷ Sometimes however they overplayed their hand. Three Syrians at one point tried to convince the French that the Muslims were plotting against them; they were proved wrong, and the French then tried to restrain their behaviour and restore the sumptuary laws.²⁸ It is easy to see why a minority already within the range of European ideas and manners should respond in this way to the French presence; but the Syrian Muslims at the Azhar reacted in quite a different way—the four men accused of killing Kléber were all Syrians, and the act was planned in the Syrian *riwaq*.²⁹

The withdrawal of the French does not seem to have led to any strong reaction against the Syrians, and when Muhammad 'Ali became governor of Egypt he too looked to them for the same kind of services they had given Bonaparte. He also needed translators, but for a new purpose, to render into Arabic the textbooks needed for the new professional schools. Don Raphael returned to Cairo after some years in Paris, and spent his last years as a translator. There were others, particularly in the School of Medicine ('Anhuri, Far'awn, Sakakini);³⁰ and a Maronite from a famous Damascene family, Niqula Masabki, was sent to Italy to study printing, and was the virtual founder of the Bulaq press.³¹

As Muhammad 'Ali's interest in Syria grew, he established contact with Syrians other than those already settled in Egypt: with members of those families who provided clerks and financial officials for the Ottoman governors and the princes of Lebanon. Some of them came to Egypt to work for him. Faris Shidyaq spent some years of his youth there; of greater importance was another family, that of Bahri. Such Christian and Jewish families of clerks and financiers attached themselves to the fortunes of a local leader, and this is what happened to the Bahris. Greek Catholics settled in Damascus; here they were closely attached to Yusuf Genç Pasha, governor of Damascus from 1807. In spite of outbursts of religious feeling, he gave them his favour, and they shared in his fall. He was deprived of the province in 1810, and succeeded by Sulayman Pasha of Acre. Sulayman brought with him his own clients, the famous Jewish family of Farhi, and two of the Bahri family, the brothers Germanos and 'Abbud, went with Yusuf Pasha to Cairo and entered the financial service of Muhammad 'Ali.³² Of 'Abbud it is recorded that Muhammad 'Ali liked him, that he was good at his work, and that he built a splendid house where he lived in a princely fashion.³³ A third brother, Hanna, remained in Damascus, but his time was to come when Ibrahim Pasha conquered Syria in 1831: Hanna Bahri became his financial controller for the whole of Syria, and one of his closest advisers.³⁴

The Syrian families of Cairo and Alexandria shared in the prosperity brought by the increase in the foreign trade of Egypt. It is true, they still lived under some disabilities. At one point the *muhtasib* tried to apply the sumptuary laws strictly and they had to secure the intervention of the Pasha himself,³⁵ and as late as 1840 they were still paying their annual tribute to the Orthodox Patriarch of Alexandria.³⁶ But some of them were drawn into the group of large merchants engaged in the import and export trade. In the Bowring report of 1837, 10 out of the 55 large merchants of Cairo are said to be Greek Catholics, and there are 6 or 7 Syrian names among those of the 72 commercial houses of Alexandria. Significantly, it appears from the list that almost all of them by this time have foreign protection or nationality—British, French, Austrian or Tuscan.³⁷

Most of the names are of families already there in the eighteenth century, and there does not seem to have been much immigration from Syria in this period. Muhammad 'Ali, it is true, brought in several hundreds of Syrian peasants to begin cultivation of the silk-worm in Wadi Tumaylat in 1812, but the experiment did not succeed.³⁸ Lane in 1836 and Clot Bey in 1840 give the total number of Syrians as 5000,³⁹ and this is the same as the number recorded by the authors of the *Description de l'Egypte* forty years earlier.

In the second half of the nineteenth century, however, there was a sharp increase in the size of the community and some change in its nature. The old families for the most part remained, and 'Ali Mubarak in his survey of Cairo found many of them living and working in the same quarters as before. Many of them still lived in the old Frankish quarter, where by the end of the century Maronite, Melkite and Syrian Catholic churches stood near the older churches of the Roman Catholic mission. In the *Wikalat al-Tuffah* and elsewhere in the Jamaliyya quarter there were still Syrian Muslims, largely Palestinians, working in glass or selling soap. There were still many Christian merchants in and around the Khan al-Hamzawi: some of them were among the first to open antique shops in the Khan al-Khalili, taking advantage of the conjunction of the increase in the number of foreign tourists and residents with the destruction of old houses and palaces, as new roads were built and rich families moved out into new quarters.⁴⁰

But around these families there grew up a larger community of more recent immigrants. Figures of growth are difficult to give, because different census returns estimate them in different ways. The census of 1882 gives the number of Egyptians originally from other parts of the Ottoman Empire as 16,403, and perhaps the majority of these were Syrians;⁴¹ the census of 1897 has a total of 40,126.⁴² In that of 1907, the total number of 'Ottoman Syrians' appears as 33,947; of these roughly one half live in Cairo and one third in Alexandria.⁴³ The census of 1917 gives a figure of 31,725 for 'Syrians', including local subjects, Ottoman subjects, and foreign nationals (mainly French);⁴⁴ that of 1927 states that 29,429 were born in Syria.⁴⁵ The variations in these figures can perhaps be explained by the growing number of persons of Syrian origin born in Egypt and absorbed into the general population. It is impossible to give a precise figure which would include these as well, but an estimate of 60,000 or so, for the 1920s and 1930s when the community attained its greatest size, would seem appropriate. This larger community spread out from its old centres of places of residence and work, along both main lines of the growth of Cairo: to the north, Syrians formed an important element in the new quarters of Faggala, Zahir and 'Abbasiyya, and then in a further extension beyond the railway station and along the Avenue de Choubra; some of the wealthier of them moved westwards into the new residential districts growing up between the Azbakiyya and the Nile, where Isma'il encouraged building by grants of land.⁴⁶ Through living in these new quarters, going to foreign schools and working in trades or professions of which the clientele was largely foreign, many Syrian families were drawn into the cosmopolitan society of the Levant: a society which had in common French as its *lingua franca,* Italy and France as its spiritual homes, and a commercial *ethos,* but which was nevertheless still fragmented into separate communities by ethnic and, even more, religious loyalties. The new Syrian immigrants, like the old (and like the Italians, Greeks and Armenians), still clustered around their churches.

There were two main reasons for the new immigration. The first was the attractive force exercised upon ambitious business men from all over the Levant and Mediterranean by the vast expansion of the Egyptian cotton trade in all its ramifications: the lending of money to peasants to finance their crops or pay their taxes, the ginning and other processes connected with the preparation of raw cotton, the export of cotton, the import of cotton textiles and agricultural machinery. By the reign of Isma'il there had appeared the Syrian village money-lender, whose services were much in demand but much resented during the later days of the reign, with the great increase in peasant indebtedness and the foreclosure of mortgages.[47] But there had also appeared a number of large merchants and financiers. Almost the first house to have an international fame was Sakakihi Frères, owned by one of the old-established Melkite families. In the 1860s they were Cairo agents for the Paris banking house of Dervieu and the London house of Oppenheim, and were associated with them as well as with leading Egyptians in founding the Egyptian Steam Navigation Company in 1863.[48] Their house became the focal point of a new district in the northward extension of the city. To them and other such family houses there were added new houses founded by branches of the great merchant families of Beirut: Sursuq, Bustrus, Trad.[49]

Most of the activities of these merchants took place in Cairo and Alexandria; the local trade between Damietta and the Syrian coast continued into the later years of the century—in 1872, 317 boats arrived in Damietta port from Syria, and 350 left[50]—but it gradually ceased to be important. As a community, they were not of the same weight in commercial and financial life as the great European, Greek and Jewish families; out of a list of 35 important firms engaged in the export of cotton from Alexandria in 1911-12, only one or two are Syrians.[51] But they were important in cotton ginning: in 1908, 2 out of 10 ginning establishments in Kafr al-Zayyat were owned by Syrians, 2 out of 8 in Mahalla, 2 out of 9 in Mansura, 4 out of 6 in Tanta.[52] They were important also on the stock exchange and in some branches of the retail trade. The Sidnawi family, owner of large retail stores, began like so many Syrian merchants in the Khan al-Hamzawi. They owed their success, their biographer tells us, partly to their fortune in becoming purveyors of goods to some members of the khedivial family, partly to their being the first such firm to buy directly from Europe; they had their office in England from an early date.[53]

As capital accumulated from trade, an Egyptian investment boom began in the last decade of the century, and we find the names of Syrians among the directors and large shareholders of companies for banking, finance and land-mortgage, irrigation and agriculture, insurance, the production of soap and cotton goods.[54] As the modern Egyptian laws of land-ownership took shape in the reigns of Sa'id and Isma'il, foreigners as well as Egyptians rushed to put their money in land, the safest and most profitable investment. Syrian land purchase began in the reign of Isma'il. The 1882 census gives the names of owners of *'izbas*. The numbers of those with clearly identifiable Syrian names owning land in the Delta provinces are as follows: Buhayra 12, Daqahliyya 1, Gharbiyya 3, Minufiyya 3, Qalyubiyya 4, Sharqiyya 3.[55] A mere comparison of numbers is by its nature crude, but for what they are worth here are the figures for 1897: Buhayra 20, Daqahliyya 16, Gharbiyya 10, Minufiyya 6, Qalyubiyya 9, Sharqiyya 8.[56]

By now, we find many of the most famous families, both old and new, among the landowners: Sursuq, Bulad, Sidnawi and Far'awn in Buhayra; Debbané, Sa'b, Zughayb, Karam and Chedid in Daqahliyya; Kahil in Gharbiyya; Bustrus and Qar'ali in Minufiyya; Ayrout and Eid in Qalyubiyya; Ayyub and Zananiri in Sharqiyya.[57] Later census reports do not give these details. But 1897 was near the beginning of the main phase of the investment boom, and it is clear that the numbers and holdings of Syrian landowners increased between then and the outbreak of war in 1914. By that time there were even a few who owned land in Upper Egypt. The Lutfallah family, for example, held land in the province of Minya: this was part of the *Da'ira al-saniyya* estates which had been pledged by Isma'il as security for foreign loans and were later sold off to private owners.[58]

The other reason for the immigration was the increasing need of Egyptian society for certain types of skill which Egypt could not at first provide and Syria could. A rapidly developing society like that of Egypt, with a population of ten millions by the end of the century, with an agriculture of high technical standards and an economy geared to that of Europe, with large foreign communities and a new culture grafted on to an old, needed officials, journalists, writers, and entertainers, teachers and doctors. It could not itself produce all it needed as rapidly as it needed them; possessors of high professional or technical skill it could import from Europe, but at a price, and some kinds of skill were linked with a knowledge most European immigrants did not have, that of the Arabic language. The intermediate positions in the new professional class were filled mainly by members of different 'Levantine' communities, Greeks, Cypriots, Armenians, oriental Jews and Syrians; and among these the Syrians had a unique place because they had a native knowledge of Arabic as well as various kinds of professional training. By now the love and knowledge of the Arabic language, fostered by the educated Uniate priesthood trained in the colleges of Rome and by the families of *katibs* and officials, was widespread in Syria, and in the schools boys could become accomplished Arabic scholars, and at the same time learn French or English well and acquire a knowledge of modern Europe and some training in its intellectual skills and habits. They could not find scope in Syrian society, and the heavy, oppressive atmosphere of the era of Abdülhamid II was difficult to breathe for those brought up on the ideas of the French Revolution or English liberalism. Egypt, on the other hand, offered them greater freedom, wider opportunities, and the attractive climate of a more modern urban society.[59]

The immigrants who came in this way were different from the earlier ones. Some still came from the old Christian bourgeois families of Aleppo and Damascus, but most belonged to Lebanese village families. They came for the most part by way of the schools of Beirut, the Jesuit Université Saint Joseph, the American Syrian Protestant College, the Maronite Ecole de la Sagesse. Many of them were Maronites and Melkites, but some were Orthodox, some Protestant (few in numbers but significant for a reason we shall see later), some Druzes. Towards the end of the century a new element came in: Muslims from leading families of the cities of the interior or the coast, graduates of the mission schools, to which they had begun to go rather later than the Christians, or else of Ottoman government schools, virtual political exiles as the rule of Abdülhamid became more oppressive.

This movement began in the middle years of the century, under Sa'id and Isma'il. Muhammad 'Ali, as we have seen, established relations with the Christian secretarial families of Syria, both before and during his period of rule there. These links were maintained by his successors, not only out of interest but because of a natural affinity between modernising groups in different parts of the Middle East: the new Christian intelligentsia of Beirut had contacts with the ruling élite in Cairo and Istanbul alike. In 1859 there took place a significant event: Sa'id Pasha visited Beirut, and stayed there not with the Ottoman governor or one of the Muslim notables, but with the Christian merchant family of Bustrus in their splendid new Italianate house.⁶⁰ From about this time the links grew closer. Isma'il gave subsidies to the Syrian journalists: to Khalil al-Khuri, editor of *Hadiqat al-Akhbar*,⁶¹ and Salim al-Bustani of *al-Jinan* in Beirut,⁶² and to Ahmad Faris al-Shidyaq, who had worked for his grandfather so long before and now published *al-Jawa'ib* in Istanbul.⁶³ He also helped Butrus al-Bustani and his family in publishing their encyclopaedia.⁶⁴

At this time too a number of Syrians entered the service of the Egyptian government. Those of them who had been educated in French Catholic schools had acquired certain intellectual skills, in the drafting of documents and the handling of figures, which were useful to a modern administration; they knew French as well as Arabic, and could therefore help the increasing number of European advisers and officials in the service of the khedive. One or two Syrians were among those sent by Isma'il to Europe on educational missions to fit themselves for work in the government. After European financial control was imposed, and still more after the British occupation, the number of Syrian officials increased. The first British head of the Account Department, Sir Gerald Fitzgerald, and his successors wished to reform the ancient Coptic system of keeping the state accounts. They succeeded in doing this, but only by breaking the Coptic monopoly and bringing in Syrians with an expert knowledge of office-routine and book-keeping.⁶⁵ More generally, the new administrative system, with British advisers working through Egyptian ministers and with Egyptian officials, made it necessary to have a class of intermediaries: secretaries and clerks who knew not only English and Arabic but also French, the language in which exchanges between British and Egyptian colleagues took place. 'In the early eighties' wrote a British official, Coles Pasha,

> 'I do not know what we should all have done without Syrians and Armenians to interpret for us, and consequently the number of clerks of these nationalities rapidly increased, to the detriment of the true Egyptian ... I fancy that most of the letters we Englishmen and Egyptians wrote to each other in French were drafted by Syrian clerks.'⁶⁶

Some of them became much more than clerks: for example, Joseph Saba Pasha who was head of the Post Office and 'Abdullah Sfayr Pasha who was head of Security.⁶⁷

Lord Cromer in his *Modern Egypt* expressed great respect for the persons and services of such officials, but showed also that he was aware of Egyptian suspicion and resentment of British reliance on a group which, in spite of language, was foreign to Egypt by origin and more at home in Levantine European society than in Egyptian.[68] His oriental secretary, Harry Boyle, thought there was a danger of British officials falling under the sway of their Syrian secretaries.[69] When Riaz Pasha was Prime Minister he tried to limit the number of Syrian officials. Cromer opposed this to some extent, and at the very end of the century a compromise was reached: persons whose ancestors were established in Egypt before or during the reign of Muhammad 'Ali, and Ottoman subjects established there for at least fifteen years, were to be regarded as Egyptian nationals and therefore eligible for government service.[70]

On a small scale, Syrians played a similar part in the consulates of the European states. As we have seen, even in the time of Muhammad 'Ali a large proportion of the richer Syrian merchants had obtained foreign nationality or protection, and this movement continued; some of them also acquired foreign titles—the Debbanés from the Emperor of Brazil, the Sa'bs and Chedids from the Pope, and the Zughaybs from the house of Savoy.[71] Employment in a foreign consulate was much desired by the greater families: it gave them legal protection, commercial privileges and social prestige. Early in the nineteenth century the family of Surur held consular appointments from England and France in Damietta;[72] and by 1914 in Alexandria the interpreters of the German and American consulates, the vice-consul of Belgium (Eid), the consuls general of Brazil (Debbané) and Denmark (Zughayb) were Syrians.[73]

But a larger number of Syrians went into the professions. They were not only the new immigrants, but the new generations of those born in Egypt, for by the 1870s and 1880s a large proportion of them were going to the foreign schools, as well as those of their own communities, in Cairo and Alexandria. In 1878, there were 241 Syrians out of 4329 students in the schools of Cairo, and 270 out of 4613 in those of Alexandria.[74] Many of them became doctors, lawyers and teachers. A full list would be of no great interest, but three groups in the professional class call for special notice. The first two Muslim girls' schools, the one established under the patronage of a wife of Isma'il in 1873, and the other under the *Awqaf* administration soon after, had Syrian headmistresses, Rose and Cécile Najjar;[75] and the first indigenous woman doctor, who took her degree from Edinburgh and began to practise in 1900, was also of Syrian origin.[76] The growth of girls' schools in Lebanon, founded by Catholic nuns and Protestant missionaries, and the social freedom of women in the Lebanese villages (more than in the Christian quarters of the cities of the interior) made it possible for Syrian women to play a certain part in Egyptian life in the generation before the movement for emancipation began there. May Ziyada, who was not only a writer but a friend of other writers in an age when the literary salon was just beginning to exist, can be taken as the representative figure of this group.[77]

A similar role of innovation was played by the Syrian actors. Here again there was no indigenous tradition, and the adoption of something new from Europe began earlier in Beirut than in Cairo, partly because of the work of the Jesuit and other mission schools, with their tradition of using drama as a means of moral education. A Maronite merchant of literary tastes, Marun Naqqash, brought back to Beirut from Italy the idea of starting a theatre and writing or translating plays for it.[78] Here once more we find the growing population and wealth of Egypt providing a scope for Syrian talents which Syria itself could not. In 1876 Marun's nephew Salim Naqqash brought his troupe to play in Alexandria: it included, significantly, four actresses as well as actors.[79] Others followed, and the Syrian contribution to the birth of the drama in Egypt culminated in Georges Abyad, sent by the Khedive 'Abbas Hilmi to study acting in France, and who on his return formed a company which acted the plays of Shakespeare and Molière in translation.[80]

The main contribution of educated Syrians was as journalists, writers and publishers. Once again, the origins go back to the age of Isma'il. There was already a reading public which wanted news in Arabic: not only local news but news of what was happening in Europe, for the eastern crisis of the 1870s was the first event of the kind which aroused widespread concern and anxiety in the Muslim countries of the Middle East. To meet the need a number of Syrian writers started newspapers. The two Taqla brothers established *al-Ahram* in 1876, first in Alexandria and later in Cairo; Salim Naqqash founded *al-Tijara* in 1878 together with a gifted young writer educated by the French Lazarists, Adib Ishaq, who himself started *Misr* in 1880; and Salim 'Anhuri began publishing *Mir'at al-Sharq* in 1879. These first years were difficult: the public, although growing, was still small; times were disturbed, the Khedive Isma'il kept a firm control over what was printed, and *al-Ahram* at least once was in grave difficulties with him. After the British occupation, the life of a journalist became easier. There were more readers as foreign and official schools expanded. At first, the British gave much freedom to the press, until the assassination of Butrus Ghali Pasha in 1910, the appointment of Kitchener and the outbreak of World War I led to stricter censorship. The capitulations gave protection to journalists who could claim foreign nationality, and international rivalries meant that newspapers could hope for subsidies from one source or another. At the same time, the growing difficulties of life in Syria under Sultan Abdülhamid induced ambitious young writers to seek their fortunes in Egypt. In 1885 two young former teachers at the Syrian Protestant College in Beirut, Faris Nimr and Ya'qub Sarruf, moved *al-Muqtataf*, a periodical they had started there in 1876, to Egypt. They were encouraged in this by Riaz Pasha, and four years later, in 1889, they were encouraged by Cromer to start an evening newspaper, *al-Muqattam*. For the next generation or more it was to be the leading newspaper, far above its rival *al-Ahram* in circulation and influence. Other newspapers followed. Out of 166 papers published in Cairo between 1828 and 1900, about 36 were owned by men whose names were recognisably Syrian; out of 188 between 1900 and 1914, about 21 were Syrian. In Alexandria, there were 31 Syrian newspapers out of 61 between 1873 and 1900, and 7 out of 27 between 1901 and 1914.[81]

Besides the newspaper of news and political comment, the other characteristic product of the Syrian journalist was the periodical of *vulgarisation*, containing articles on history or science, often translated or adapted from English or French, and perhaps stories as well, and putting forward, at least by implication, certain views of the universe or human society. Such periodicals were of great importance in a period when a writer could live by writing articles but not by publishing books, and when the periodical press provided all the reading-matter that most readers had. Once more, the Syrian share is well indicated by some simple figures. In Cairo, there were 28 Syrian out of 130 periodicals started between 1848 and 1900, 12 out of 161 between 1900 and 1914. In Alexandria, 9 out of 23 periodicals started between 1881 and 1900 had Syrian editors, and 6 out of 34 between 1901 and 1914. Apart from *al-Muqtataf*, a few of them should be mentioned because of the extent of their influence or the quality of their writing: *al-Huquq* (Amin Shumayyil), 1886; *al-Hilal* (Jurji Zaydan). 1892; *al-Manar* (Rashid Rida), 1898; *al-Diya* (Ibrahim al-Yaziji), 1898; *al-Jami'a* (Farah Antun), 1899. Of these *al-Hilal* and *al-Manar* are of special importance, since around them there grew up publishing houses which printed and distributed books as well as periodicals.[82]

Fully to assess the contribution made by the Syrian writers and journalists to the modern literature and thought of Egypt would be beyond the scope of this essay. At least for the period stretching from the 1880s to World War I their influence was deep and perhaps decisive, and it continued to some extent for another generation after that. Some of the reasons for it are not difficult to find. The Syrians were fluent and lucid writers, even if their style appeared too European to those brought up in the tradition of the Azhar; they had learned from Butrus al-Bustani and his colleagues a manner of precise and logical exposition well suited to discussion of the subjects which concerned them. From foreign schools and trade with Europe, from reading and travel, some at least of them had a full and accurate knowledge of the society and politics, the science and technology, of western Europe.

Among them were some who were more than brokers of other men's ideas or words. One or two were original writers of high quality: above all perhaps the poet Khalil Mutran. Some were thinkers capable of taking the great ideas of the modern world and applying them to their own society. To this task they brought a combination of qualities valuable at a moment of transition: a sense of cultural tradition together with a willingness to innovate. In Syria and Lebanon, as elsewhere, modern education brought with it not only a general intellectual curiosity but a desire for self-knowledge, and educated Christians began to identify themselves imaginatively with the past embodied in the language they used, even if that past had been moulded by a religion other than theirs and if their fathers would have regarded it as in some sense alien. The re-interpretation of the Islamic past, not as religion but as human culture, in the light of a romantic vision of history: this was one aspect of the contribution of the Syrians, and we should associate it in particular with *al-Hilal* and its editor Jurji Zaydan, and with his historical novels even more than his formal works of history.

On the other hand, the Syrians were specially receptive to the new ideas and ways of life of modern Europe. The merchants and professional men in Cairo and Alexandria, in particular the more successful of them living in the new quarters, were drawn naturally into the cosmopolitan society of the age, even if they had not been half drawn into it already by their education in mission schools. They were able to accept its values with fewer reservations than educated Muslims of their time, because it did not seem that they were sacrificing something essential of themselves in the process. Foster-children of Victorian Europe, they accepted the idea of progress: the world was moving forward, Europe was in the vanguard of the march, the secret of its success was to be found in the development and application of science and in a certain ordering of social and political life, the East had been left behind and must try to catch up on the same path. This acceptance of the modern world (even if with a touch of nostalgia for the past) we can associate with the other great periodical of the age, *al-Muqtataf*, with its editors Sarruf and Nimr, and with such writers in it as Shibli Shumayyil. Its pages are filled with articles on science and technique, on social customs and social ethics.

The two periodicals did not deal directly with political problems, but much of what they said had political implications, and these were made explicit in other writings and in the newspapers. Some of the papers owned by Syrians were pro-British, like *al-Muqattam*, others pro-French like *al-Ahram*. Some were supporters of Egyptian nationalism, like those of Salim Naqqash and Adib Ishaq at the beginning of our period and *al-Ahram* later. Most of them continued to take a lively interest in the fate of Syria and the Ottoman empire. *Al-Muqattam* provided a platform for those who opposed the tyranny of Abdülhamid in the name of Ottoman liberalism; after the Young Turk revolution, it and other papers tended more in the direction of a 'Syrian' nationalism, although overtly at least it remained within the bounds of Ottoman unity and had links with the Ottoman liberals who believed in decentralisation.[83]

This support for the idea of nationalism sprang from a questioning if not a rejection of the traditional order of society. In his memoirs, Mikha'il Mishaqa has told how, as a young boy sent from Lebanon to his uncle at Damietta in 1818, he had found that many of the inhabitants had religious doubts stirred up by works of European philosophy and science circulating in Arabic translation.[84] The great European conflict of science and religion had its echo in Beirut and Cairo. As young men, Nimr, Sarruf, Shumayyil and Zaydan had all been involved in the great controversy about Darwin and evolution which split the Syrian Protestant College in the 1880s.[85] They did not all of them go as far as Shumayyil in rejecting the claims of revelation and accepting a materialist view of the universe. But most of them believed that a society organised on the basis of a revealed law and religious loyalties could not be strong, progressive and civilised. This belief did not (except for Farah Antun and a few others) lead to criticism of the traditional theology of Islam; not only prudence but also that imaginative absorption of the Arab past of which we have spoken restrained them from this. It took rather the form of an attack on the accepted system of authority in the Christian church; hence the importance of the small group of Protestant converts among them, for, in a country still organised into religious communities, to become a Protestant was as near as a Christian could come to rejecting authority and living as an individual.

So far we have been speaking of the Christian writers. There was also a smaller but important group of Syrian Muslim writers and journalists, 'Abd al-Rahman al-Kawakibi, Rashid Rida, Rafiq al-'Azm, Muhammad Kurd 'Ali, 'Abd al-Rahman Shahbandar. The line between them and the Christians was not sharply drawn. They had much in common: language, attachment to Syria, a concern for the future of the Ottoman empire, a certain distance from the country in which they lived. Some of them wrote for *al-Muqtataf* and the great newspapers. But in some ways their view of the world was different. They too professed belief in the reorganisation of society on the basis of national loyalties, and took an active part first in the movement against Abdülhamid and then in the struggles between Young Turks and liberals. As the belief in an Ottoman nation dissolved, their national idea became articulate in an 'Arab' rather than a 'Syrian' form. But the difference should not be exaggerated; during World War I Faris Nimr as well as Rashid Rida was involved in the various negotiations with the Allied authorities about Arab independence. Some of them were social innovators, but in general they were more reluctant than the Christian writers to accept a wholly secular order of society: at the same time, they were far removed from those who wished to retain the law and doctrinal formulations of the Muslim faith unchanged. Grouped around Rashid Rida's periodical *al-Manar,* they formed a distinctive element among the disciples of Muhammad 'Abduh, moving in the direction of a neo-

Hanbalism which would combine rigid adherence to the essentials of the faith with flexibility in reinterpreting law and social morality in the light of the interests of the Muslim community.[86]

After World War I, the position of the Syrians and Lebanese (as we must now call them, once Lebanon emerges as a separate country) might well have seemed to be unchanged or even to have grown stronger. Numbers remained at more or less the same level. The great newspapers and periodicals, and the publishing houses, kept their position: *al-Ahram* under the second generation of the Taqlas and Antun Jumayyil, and *al-Muqtataf* under the nephew of Ya'qub Sarruf, still served as meeting places for those who took an active part in the political and intellectual life of Egypt. Economically, Syrians and Lebanese found less scope in government employment, but played a leading part in the development of industry, and not only in textiles; in 1951, more than ten per cent of company directors with clearly identifiable names were of Syrian or Lebanese origin.[87]

Nevertheless, the historic role of the community was coming to an end. The interstices within Egyptian society, and between Egypt and the modern world, into which the Syrian middle man had fitted, were becoming narrower. Egypt was by now beginning to produce the professional and technical skill demanded by its development. The distance between modern Europe and modern Egypt was narrowing, and at a later stage 'modernity' would be detached from its origins in western Europe and become something universal.

8 Lebanon: the Development of a Political Society

This essay was written in 1963, long before the civil war of 1975, which I did not anticipate. I have not tried to alter it in the light of what has happened.

The history of Lebanon is history on a minute scale. Every Lebanese can find his ancestors or his own village in it; its tiny conflicts are family quarrels, carried by Lebanese emigrants wherever they go, its triumphs are causes of personal rejoicing, like village weddings. But why should the outer world care about decisive battles which were scarcely more than skirmishes on a terraced hillside or among the olive trees, or members of an obscure ruling family who put out the eyes of their cousins? Several answers could be given to this question, and some of them might be valid. One only will be given here. Lebanon can be of interest to the historian or political scientist because he can see there with peculiar clarity the development of a political society: that is to say, a system of customs and agreements defining the ways in which power should be exercised and neighbours deal with one another. What is rare in the Middle East is that this is a development which has been continuous over several hundred years, and, although it cannot be fully understood without taking into account influences from outside, the most important of its causes are to be found inside itself: in a common social and political consciousness, gradually becoming explicit and spreading among all the inhabitants of the Lebanese mountain valleys and the surrounding districts, and in the freedom with which they have been able to think and act, the absence of the distant, almost unknown, overriding force of coercion from outside (the state or the urban landowner) which in other parts of the Near East has prevented the growth of rural liberty.

A continuous process of development has pitfalls for the historian:

he may be misled by similarity of names or the persistence of formal institutions, and interpret the past in terms of the present. Because Lebanon today is an association of several religious groups, living together on the basis of equality and common citizenship, and within a political framework which in some sense embodies a secular principle, we may be tempted to think that it was always so: some modern historians, for example, write of Fakhr al-Din in the seventeenth century almost as if he were an ideal President of the Lebanese Republic. But to do this is to obscure the precise nature of the continuity of Lebanese history. It is not that of sameness, it is that of real development: the elements which make up the Lebanon of today did not always exist or stand to each other in their present relationship. It was only gradually that there appeared the shape of the Lebanon we know.

Only a brave man would venture into the tangled problems of the early history of the mountain: whether the Maronites were Mardaites, whether they were Monotheletes, who the Druzes were and where they came from. For our purpose we need go back no further than the Mamluk period, when we find the main protagonists of Lebanese history already present. The last great disturbances which violently changed the nature of the population were the Mamluk expeditions into the north of the mountain in 1283 and into Kisrawan in 1292, 1300 and 1305. After that, we find the different groups either in the same positions as today or else in positions which make it easy to understand how later changes took place: Maronites in the Bsharri district in the north, Shi'is in Kisrawan, the Biqa' and Jabal 'Amil, Sunnis in the coastal ports, Druzes in the Gharb, the Shuf and Wadi al-Taym, Orthodox Christians in Kura at the northern extreme of the mountain range and living among Druzes of the south and Sunnis of the ports. Already we find in existence the basis of Lebanese society: the peasants, living by mixed farming on small patches of terraced and irrigated land, in small villages held together by a strong sense of solidarity; the lordly families, perhaps descended from military settlers planted there by rulers of Syria to guard the coasts and keep the local inhabitants in order, but gradually, like border chieftains everywhere, acquiring a virtual autonomy by playing off one ruler against another; and between peasants and lords a relationship which gave the latter a certain ascendancy— they had a hereditary right to part of the produce of the land, to labour, to service in time of war—but left the cultivator liberty to move from one lordship to another. Some of the leading families have disappeared: the Maronite *muqaddams* of Bsharri, the Turcoman family of 'Assaf whom the Mamluks placed in control of Kisrawan and the coast, the Buhturis or Tanukhis of the Gharb, the Arslans who perhaps have little more than the name in common with the present Arslan family, the Ma'nis of Shuf, the Harfush and Banu Hamra of the Biqa'. But at least one remains: the Sunni Shihabs, who were to dominate a century and a half of Lebanese history, were already established in their stronghold of Wadi al-Taym. After the Mamluk invasions these families by and large were free from interference by the Mamluk and then the Ottoman governors of the surrounding cities and countryside. Mamluks and Ottomans could, it is true, occupy the mountain when they wished: the Ottomans did it in 1584 when raiders from Lebanon threatened the imperial roads. But in general it was not worth their while to rule Lebanon directly. It was simpler to recognise local chiefs as tax-collectors of their districts and leave them in charge so long as the tax was paid. Thus the Buhturis, the family about whom we know most, were given a place in the Mamluk 'feudal' system, to guard the harbour of Beirut and the coast against raids from Cyprus.

By the early Ottoman period, then, three elements in the structure of Lebanon already existed: the population, the system of lordship, and the autonomy of the local rulers. A fourth was also coming into existence: Arabic was becoming the common language, although some Syriac continued to be spoken among Maronites, and easy mastery of the literary language was not to come for another century or so. Certain other factors, however, existed either not at all or only in a rudimentary form. There was as yet no hierarchy of lordly families; some were more powerful than others, some had close relations with others (we hear of a Ma'ni, a Tanukhi and an 'Assaf going off together to meet the Ottoman conqueror of Damascus); but there was no formal gradation of ranks, and no supreme ruler who would stand at the peak of the system. Nor were there more than the rudiments of the other great institution of later times, the Maronite patriarchate. The patriarch of course existed: he had long recognised the papal supremacy, and during the Crusading period had had close relations with Rome and been invited to the Council of 1215. But the community over which he had spiritual power was small, weak, and limited. Temporal power was neither in his own hands nor ultimately in those of other Maronites, it belonged to Muslim lords, the 'Assaf and then the Banu Sayfa; after the end of the Crusading states he had only a loose, intermittent connection with Rome, and had to struggle with the Jacobites for spiritual authority over his flock.

There did not moreover yet exist an organic unity between the different parts of what we now call Lebanon. Between the main areas of Maronite, Druze and Shi'i population lay sparsely inhabited regions. North and south had different overlords: in the Crusading period, the one had been part of the County of Tripoli, the other of the Kingdom of Jerusalem; then under the Mamluks and early Ottomans the one fell in the province of Tripoli and the other in that of Damascus. Between coastal towns and mountain valleys there also was a separation. The Buhturis, it is true, ruled Beirut for a time, but the coast and its ports were too important for the Mamluks or Ottomans to leave them to the lords of the mountains; and Tripoli was a great centre of government, of Sunni population and of Islamic learning.

The emergence of a ruling institution, the princedom or *imara*, is the dominant feature of the next period, which stretches roughly from 1590 to 1711. This was a process which took place from within, by the rise of one of the lordly families to supremacy over the others. The family was that of Ma'n and then, when the Ma'nis became extinct in 1697, their kinsmen the Shihabs assured this position. It was the Ma'ni Fakhr al-Din II (1590-1635) who first created a close and permanent union of a number of hitherto separate lordships, and gave them a leadership which most of them recognised and which had at its disposal a standing army and some kind of regular administration. He did not, it is true, establish the Lebanese state as we know it today, but he created the political institution around which Lebanon would eventually crystallise. This institution was the princedom. It embodied a secular principle: indeed, from that day to this it has been part of the political tradition of Lebanon that the holder of authority, whether the local lord or the supreme ruler, should stand in a sense above his own community, should protect the religious men and laity of faiths other than his own. The origins of the Ma'ni family are obscure, and there is some doubt what Fakhr al-Din's own religion was; he may have been Sunni Muslim or Druze, and it has even been said (with some but not conclusive evidence) that he was a Maronite. What is certain is that the Ma'ni claim to authority had no religious sanction, and potentially their princedom could serve as a rallying point for adherents of all religions. Nevertheless, the coalition of families which he built up was essentially Druze, and so was the region over which he had stable rule. His 'kingdom' indeed can be clearly divided into two parts. The nucleus consisted of the districts of Shuf, Gharb and Kisrawan; here he was the heir of the Buhturis, whose power had declined and then disappeared. Around them lay a personal 'empire' which he had conquered and dominated: Safad, Sayda, Beirut, certain northern districts conquered from the Banu Sayfa, who had replaced 'Assaf in northern Lebanon. But these slipped away when he died. The north of Lebanon was given by the governor of Tripoli as a fief to the Shi'i family of Hamada; Sayda became the seat of an Ottoman governor to watch the south—the mainly Muslim towns of the coast might fall beneath the control of the mountain lords when the Turks were weak, but no strong Ottoman government would willingly lose hold of them. Only the nucleus of Fakhr al-Din's principality passed ultimately to his successors, and here the Druzes were dominant. The Maronites played a subordinate part in his system. It is true, he used Maronite priests in his dealings with the courts of Europe, but that was because they knew Italian; in his administration he used Muslims and Jews rather than Christians. He did indeed give Kisrawan to the Maronite family of Khazin, but this was because he wanted men on whom he could rely to guard a frontier district with a mixed population. The stirring of political consciousness among the Maronites of the time was focused neither on the concept of Lebanon nor on the institution of the princedom. In 1584 the Maronite College in Rome had been founded, and a little later Catholic missions had begun to work regularly in Lebanon and the surrounding districts—the Capucins in 1626, the Jesuits in 1652; among the clergy trained in the College or by the missionaries there emerged a group of scholars and writers who, having acquired the sciences of the Arabic language from Muslim shaykhs and a knowledge of Christian history from their teachers, began to write in Arabic about the traditions and history of their own people. The focus of their interest was the Maronite community, not the Lebanese nation or the land of Lebanon, and if there was an institution which they regarded as having a legitimate claim to leadership, it was not the princedom but the patriarchate, which by now was acquiring greater control over the community, although its political power was still limited.

Even within the nucleus, the authority of the prince was not yet universally recognised. It was accepted when embodied in the strong personality of Fakhr al-Din, but not yet regarded as in itself legitimate. All through this period indeed Ma'nis and then Shihabs had to fight to secure acceptance of their rule, and they succeeded only by putting themselves at the head of one party in its struggle against another—a struggle which expressed itself in a revival of the ancient Arabian tribal conflict of Qais and Yaman. By and large, Ma'an, Shihab, and Khazin were Qays, 'Alam al-Din, Sayfa, and Arslan were Yaman.

Nor was the prince's authority unchallenged from outside. The Ottoman government was able to intervene effectively when it wished. It did so several times when Fakhr al-Din grew too strong, and finally defeated and killed him. On the other hand, it was perhaps only because of Turkish approval that the princedom came into existence at all. It was convenient to have one tax-collector for the mountains, provided he did not become too strong and free; it was through Ottoman help that the Ma'nis had established their rule in the first instance. After Fakhr al-Din's death the Turks tried for a time to support the Yamani faction, but soon went back to support of Ma'n; and when the last Ma'ni died it was with Ottoman permission that the lords of Lebanon met at Sumqaniyya in 1697 to choose a successor; and when they chose the house of Shihab it was the government which decided which member of the family to recognise as prince. Fakhr al-Din had tried but failed to call in another force to counterbalance that of the Turks; through the growing silk trade of Lebanon he had relations with the states of Italy, but none of them could help him effectively. There was indeed a certain growth of French influence, but French contacts were mainly with the Maronites, and they could do little for them except at a distance, by diplomatic intervention in Constantinople.

It was only in the eighteenth century that the princedom became more fully autonomous, ruler of north as well as south Lebanon, and with a secular authority recognised as legitimate by most of its subjects. At the Battle of 'Ayn Dara in 1711 the Qaysi forces under the Shihabs finally defeated those of Yaman. Some of the Yamani families disappeared, and some of their followers moved across the plain of Hawran to what is now called Jabal Druze; the Arslans remained, shorn of part of their lands but too powerful to be destroyed. From this time, the rule of the Shihabis was generally recognised. One of them might revolt against another, but the family's right to rule was scarcely questioned. Yet it was by no means the richest of the great families or the most powerful, and could only impose its authority with the help of others. The basis of Shihabi rule lay in the support of the lordly families: Jumblat in the Shuf, Abi Lam'in the Matn, Talhuq in the Gharb, Khazin in Kisrawan. After 1711 their mutual relations were defined more precisely than before, and what we now think of as the traditional hierarchy of families was established.

The province of Sayda had been created to keep Lebanon in order, but did not always have the strength to do so. During much of the eighteenth century a large part of it was controlled by a local ruler, Dahir al-'Umar of northern Palestine. The Shihabi princes therefore had much freedom of action, and in 1749 were able to occupy Beirut, an important point because it was the port of shipment for Lebanese silk. It was not until the 1770s that a strong ruler of the province of Sayda, Jazzar, was able to reverse the process. From his capital at Acre, he re-established control over the coastal towns, including Beirut and Tripoli; from this time there was to be a strong Muslim authority and, ultimately, a revived Muslim political consciousness on the coast. He also extended his authority into the mountains: the Shi'is of Jabal 'Amil were brought under his rule, and he gained influence in Lebanon itself by setting one member of the Shihabi family against another.

Thus curbed in two directions by the rise of Jazzar and his Mamluk group, on the coast and in the northern Palestinian hills, the princedom was able to expand in two others, and was perhaps encouraged in this by the rulers of Sayda. In 1748 a Lebanese force had defeated that of the governor of Damascus and seized control of the Biqa' valley: for a time the lords of Lebanon owned the villages and the governor of Sayda received their taxes. A little later, the Maronite north of Lebanon accepted Shihabi rule. By this time the Shihabis were making increased use of Maronite and other Christian officials, drawn from the new class of Christians with a mastery of Arabic; and from 1756 a number of the Shihabi princes were themselves converted to the Maronite faith. Whatever the reason for their conversion, it did not bring with it a shift in policy from Druzes to Maronites. The extension of Shihabi rule northwards seems in fact to have been caused partly by internal conflicts inside the family, partly by the wish of the governors of Sayda to extend their control, and above all by the development of the Maronites themselves. Their religious and intellectual life had moved to a higher level: they had an educated priesthood, and after the Synod of 1736 they had a close and agreed link with the Holy See. Their numbers were increasing: they had spread southwards into the rich farming district of Kisrawan, and Maronite merchants in Beirut were growing prosperous from the silk trade. They needed economic security and religious freedom and the Shihabs could give them both. In the 1750s and 1760s they drove out their Hamada overlords and accepted the rule of the Shihabs. Henceforth the whole range of the mountain was politically united, but the political consciousness of the north was still Maronite rather than Lebanese, focused on the Church rather than the land. The patriarch still lacked political power. He had escaped from the control of Hamada by moving south from his ancient seat in the district of Bsharri to the safety of Kisrawan, and this brought him and his hierarchy under the control of the Khazin family, lords of Kisrawan, who in this period provided what leadership the Maronites had.

In popular legend as well as the eyes of the world, the reign of Bashir II (1788-1840) marked the apex of Shihab power. He crushed his enemies inside Lebanon, extended his influence into northern Palestine and the plains of the interior, obtained the right to deal directly with the Ottoman government, and ruled Lebanon with a stern justice which is still not quite forgotten. But in his time there took place two changes which were to weaken the basis of the princedom and affect its relationship with the people. The first was the direct intervention of outside forces. 'Ali Bey in the 1770s and Bonaparte in 1799 had advanced from Egypt almost to the south tip of Lebanon: in the 1820s their successor as ruler of Egypt, Muhammad 'Ali, established contact with the local rulers of Syria, and Bashir, driven from Lebanon by a combination of enemies, spent some time in Cairo as his guest. When Muhammad 'Ali's army under his son Ibrahim conquered Syria in the 1830s, Bashir became a pillar of Egyptian rule. But the alliance with Egypt had its dangers. Ibrahim carried further Jazzar's policy of establishing strong rule in the coastal cities—a rule now exercised from Beirut near the heart of the mountain; and he brought to Syria the modern concept of direct centralised administration, which in the end was to threaten the traditional autonomy of the mountain. Moreover, the alliance with the Egyptians brought foreign intervention of another kind: the British ambassador in

Constantinople, being opposed to the Egyptian presence in Syria, made contact with the enemies of Egypt and Bashir, and encouraged local discontent which broke out into revolt in 1840.

Within Lebanon itself there were challenges to the authority of the prince. The most serious came from the Druze family of Jumblat. Their power and wealth had grown from the seventeenth century. They had become leaders of one of the two parties in the conflict of 'Jumblat' and 'Yazbak' factions; this was a struggle different from the earlier one of Qays and Yaman, since it took place within the structure of the princedom and did not query its authority. But a time came when Jumblat grew strong enough to challenge Shihab. In his early days Bashir had relied on the Jumblats; this gave them great influence, and in the 1820s they came forward as rivals to the prince. In 1825 he turned against them and their followers and destroyed their power for the moment. But having done so he found himself isolated at the summit of power. He could try to build up other Druze families or call on the Maronites for soldiers, but nothing could replace the solid basis which the Druze hierarchy had given his power. In the end he had to ask his Egyptian overlord for soldiers. This brought into the mountain not only Egyptian power but a new concept, that of a direct relationship between the government and the individual subject. Bashir found himself called on to do things which were contrary to the whole tradition of Lebanon: to disarm the mountaineers and conscript them for service in the Egyptian army. When the Druzes revolted against this he used the Maronites against them; but then the Maronites thought their own turn had come. They revolted in 1840, and when, a little later, an Anglo-Turkish force compelled the Egyptians to withdraw, it was easy to depose Bashir and send him into exile. With him there went something important: the legitimacy of Shihab rule. The link which bound the princes to their subjects had been loosened; the basis of their power, the hierarchy of landed families, had been weakened; the good relationship of religious groups had been threatened; and since Bashir had been deposed by foreign hands, those hands were henceforth the final repositories of power.

It is at this point that the communal question becomes the dominant problem in Lebanese life. Bashir's policy had set Maronites against Druzes and encouraged certain tendencies inside each community. The Maronites were increasing in numbers, spreading southwards, and developing in ways which could not be contained inside the traditional social structure. The merchants and artisans of the new Christian market-towns, Zahla and Dayr al-Qamar, were no longer willing to accept the lordship of the local Druze families. The cultivators were establishing a direct link with the silk merchants of the ports, who gave them advances or loans; they were the less willing to give their ancient lords the traditional services and share of the silk crop, because they were no longer so economically dependent on them. The various discontents of the Maronites found leaders in the patriarch and clergy. By now the Church was freeing itself from the control of the great families. Drawn largely from the people, the priests tended to support popular grievances and put forward claims to leadership. Implicit in their claim was the principle that the Maronites were a nation as well as a Church. This principle was incompatible with the ancient basis of the princedom and the hierarchy of lordly families; the Druze lords, weakened by Bashir and now challenged by the Maronites, struggled to hold on to their position.

Lords, cultivators, Maronite hierarchy, peasants, all in different ways looked for help to the European consulates. In the last years of Egyptian rule the British consulate in Beirut had established a close link with a section of the Druzes; meanwhile, the ancient French link with the Maronites grew stronger and changed its character, and the French consulate became a centre of local influence and a focus of Maronite political feeling. There was another party to the conflict: the Ottoman government, restored to Syria by the intervention of Europe. It brought with it a new concept of direct administrative control: here as elsewhere it wished to limit if not destroy the old autonomies of the mountain districts. It was backed by the Muslim population of the large cities of the coast and interior, whose political consciousness was given a new turn by the sense of Islam being in danger. It was able to make use of the processes already at work inside Lebanon: the weakening of Shihab authority and the growth of communal feeling. In 1842 the government deposed Bashir's successor and brought Shihab rule to an end. A new system was adopted, providing for the division of Lebanon into Druze and Maronite districts, each with a governor of the dominant religion, but with a council representing the various religious groups; here we find the first embodiment of the communal principle which has since then been the basis of the legislature.

Ostensibly the new system was based on the principle of

religious equality, but it went against the developments of the last century. By now there was a political consciousness which included the mountain as a whole; there were interests in common and the tradition of a secular authority extending over the whole mountain. These interests and this consciousness no longer had an institution to express them: the only links between the two districts and the various communities were the European consuls and the Ottoman administration in Beirut, which were drawn into the affairs of the mountain without having the same recognised authority as the former prince. This period without authority ended in the crisis of 1858-60: the peasant revolt in Kisrawan, the communal war of 1860, and the massacres of Christians by Muslims in Damascus. These events showed how completely the traditional authority had disappeared. At the moment of crisis, communal feeling, stimulated from outside and not held in check by a common authority, turned into religious hatred. Orthodox Christians, who had hitherto opposed the claims of the Patriarch, now sided with the Maronites; Sunnis and Shi'is joined forces with the Druzes; the only local forces which could have provided an authority standing above the conflict were themselves drawn into it, the Shihabs on the side of the Christians, the Ottoman officials on that of the Druzes.

Once legitimate authority had disappeared it could not be restored from within. In Damascus it was still intact and could reassert itself to end the massacres: the Ottoman government intervened to restore order. In Lebanon however, this was not possible, and henceforth effective and legitimate government could only be assured by a permanent foreign presence. The new system of government established in 1861-4 came as near to assuring it as circumstances allowed. Lebanon was to be a privileged *sanjaq,* with a governor or *mutasarrif* who was to be a Christian chosen from outside Lebanon by the Ottoman government and approved by the Powers; as a Christian he would be acceptable to the Maronites, but, not being a Maronite, being an Ottoman official, and having the support of Europe, he would stand above the aspirations and conflicts of communities. Once a secular principle had thus been restored, it was possible to give a place, although a subordinate one, to the communal principle: the Administrative Council was to be chosen and certain posts to be filled on a communal basis. It was a necessary corollary of the arrangement that the frontiers of the *sanjaq* should be narrowly drawn. If it was to be stable, it could only include those regions where a government of this kind would be accepted as legitimate; it should exclude the Sunni Muslim towns and villages where political consciousness, whether explicit or not, rejected both the idea of local autonomy under the control of the European powers and the principle of communal authority.

The underlying assumption of the new system was that the different communities could live together, but that the Maronites were dominant. This assumption was justified by the changes of the next fifty years. The Christian majority grew, both by natural increase and by emigration of the Druzes to Jabal Druze. The Christian community prospered, as schools were established, trade increased, and emigration to the New World began. In this period, the two concepts of 'Lebanon' and 'the Maronite nation' coalesced, and, for virtually the first time, Maronite writers put forward the idea of Lebanon as an essentially Christian country, destined to govern itself under the perpetual protection of Christian Europe. On the other hand, there gradually developed a sense of political community which cut across the frontiers of communities. Having agreed that the governor should be a Christian, the Ottoman government tried to make sure that he would not be too friendly to Christian separatism. After the first few years the governors tried to restrain and whittle down the privileges of the district, and this led to almost perpetual conflict between them and the Administrative Council. After the Young Turk revolution of 1908 it was suggested that Lebanon should send representatives to the Ottoman Parliament; the suggestion was rejected by the Council, which from this time became the spokesman and defender of Lebanese privileges against the attempts of the Young Turks to impose control. Thus one more constitutive element of modern Lebanon emerges at this time: political activity directed by parties, cutting across the communal boundaries and expressing itself in the elected legislature. The first modern party appears, with the first modern party leader, Salim 'Ammun. It won its first success in 1912, when the Ottoman government agreed, under pressure from Europe, that the Council should have wider powers and be elected on a broader basis.

The arrangement of 1861 once more provided a framework of authority within which the life of Lebanon could develop, but at a price: it widened the gap between the districts inside the framework and those outside. Inside the *sanjaq,* there developed a peasant society of small freeholders cultivating silk for the European market, and a separate political consciousness, moulded by modern education in the mission schools, by the close connection of the Maronites with France, and by emigration to north and south America. Outside there lay country districts where sharecroppers worked for urban landowners, and the great cities of Muslim culture and of a political consciousness bascially Muslim, but now coloured with the new ideas of Ottoman liberalism, pan-Islam and Arab nationalism, all of them embodying in one way or another the ideal of a large, independent, united state in which there would be no place for special autonomies under foreign protection. To some extent the gap was bridged by the formulation of ideas of secular nationalism, 'Syrian' or Arab, in which Muslims and Christians could share alike. But such ideas appealed only to a small educated élite, and could not resolve the underlying tension. This tension was greatest in the growing city of Beirut, which in one sense lay inside Lebanon and in another outside it. Lying officially outside the frontiers of the *sanjaq*, it was nevertheless the cultural and commercial capital of Christian Lebanon. Its life was dominated by Christian merchants and Christian schools, its links with the mountain were growing closer. Lebanon could not be stable and viable unless it included Beirut. But Beirut was the seat of an Ottoman *vali* and the centre of a large Muslim population with a growing educated class; although not economically dominant in the commercial life of the city, the Muslim notables had political influence through their connection with the Ottoman administration, and there was developing among them a different kind of political consciousness, Arab in the manner of the Party of Decentralisation.

In the years before 1914 there was much tension between the Muslim and Christian quarters of Beirut. After 1918, this tension affected the life of Lebanon itself. When the Ottoman army withdrew, Lebanon came under French military occupation and then under French Mandate. The continuity of Lebanese life asserted itself at once. The Administrative Council met again, delegations with clear ideas were sent to the Peace Conference, the Patriarch emerged as the almost unchallenged leader and the one accepted authority of the mountain. This showed that the half-century of restored legitimacy had been fruitful, and that Lebanon existed as a political entity. But the economic needs of the mountain, and the interests of the Mandatory Power, both called for an enlargement of the country, and in 1920 Greater Lebanon was created, including the coastal towns as well as certain country districts. In a sense this was to restate the problem of Lebanon all over again. Within the smaller Lebanon, it would have been possible to give a new form to the arrangement of 1861: a Christian president instead of the Christian *mutasarrif*, drawn from inside instead of outside, and a permanent French presence instead of the Concert of Europe. But Greater Lebanon could not easily accept such an arrangement. The numerical balance had changed: the *sanjaq* had had a Maronite majority, now all the Christian sects together had at best a bare majority. Moreover, half the population of the new Lebanon did not at once accept the legitimacy either of the state or of its form of government. Many Maronites still remained loyal in their hearts to the smaller Lebanon, and did not face the implications of the inclusion in it of Beirut and Tripoli. Most Sunni Muslims were loyal to the idea of an Arab nation and an Arab Syrian state, and were unwilling to accept the change from being part of the political community of the Ottoman Empire to being only one community among others; the Muslims of Tripoli feared that their trade would be strangled—Lebanon did not need two ports of the size of Beirut and Tripoli. Shi'i Muslims derived some benefit from the existence of Lebanon, since for the first time they were recognised legally as a separate community, but they too felt the pull of Arab nationalism. Many of the Orthodox Christians were unwilling to be part of a state where Maronites would dominate and France be always present: their political ideal was either 'Arab' or 'Syrian' (the idea of a secular united Syrian nation, popular among Christians of Beirut in the late nineteenth century, had been carried from there to the emigrant colonies, and was now brought back to Lebanon by the son of an emigrant, who made it the basis of a party which offered an alternative to Lebanese or Arab nationalism).

In this situation there were the seeds of a conflict which might have been no less tragic than that of 1860. The conflict did not break out, and when the French left in 1946 there existed once more a Lebanese state and government which most of the population accepted as legitimate. How did this come about? It is usual to explain it in terms of the communal system: the distribution of offices, from the highest downwards, among the various communities in rough proportion to their numerical strength, and more specifically the allocation of the presidency to the Maronites and the prime ministership to the Sunnis. But by the time the French left the communal system had scarcely been working long enough to become an unchallenged tradition. Formulated in the constitution of 1926 as a provisional arrangement, its implications were not worked out until the 1930s. The first president was not a Maronite but an Orthodox Christian, and when his term of office came to an end there appeared a strong Sunni candidate supported by many Christians; he might have been elected had not the High Commissioner suspended the Constitution. It was only in 1934 that the first Maronite President was elected, in 1937 that there began the virtually unbroken line of Sunni prime ministers, and later still that the Shi'is established their claim to the presidency of the chamber. Even when the system had been created it might have been used in a way similar to that in which the arrangement of 1842 had been used: a president who acted only as a Maronite, a prime minister who acted only as a Sunni, between them could have broken the new Lebanon more irretrievably than the old. To explain why this did not happen, we must look to other factors.

The first of these factors was the development of the legislature. The communal system was retained, but with an all-important difference. From 1926 it was laid down that each deputy represented the whole population, and each was elected by members of all communities. This principle might indeed be regarded as the most important contribution made in the Mandatory period to the political life of Lebanon. It ensured that electoral alliances and programmes should cut across communal divisions. The very existence of a Chamber of Deputies moreover encouraged the development of a common political life. From time to time there were complaints that the system was too expensive, that Lebanon could be governed more simply, but the wisest political thinkers, like Michel Chiha, knew that the existence of an assembly where all matters of common interest could be freely discussed, and where members of different sects might need each others' support, was the necessary condition of the growth of a will to live in common.

Along with this went the development of a certain conception of the role of the president: of a norm, a set of conventions about the relations of the president to his own community and to the other parts of the population. The conventions were extremely subtle, they were not and perhaps could not be fully formulated, but it gradually became clear to the political consciousness of Lebanon what it expected from the president. First of all, it expected that he should stand above the communities, that his authority should be secular, that he should express the unity of the state; or, to put it in other terms, that he should be able to cut across the network of sectarian interests, and make necessary decisions in the light of the national interest. In general, successive presidents were willing to do what was expected of them. Much credit for this goes to the first president, Charles Dabbas, who, not being a member of the dominant Maronite community but of the smaller Orthodox group, carried on, in a way, the tradition of the Christian *mutasarrifs* drawn from outside Lebanon; and credit also must go to Bishara al-Khuri, the first president who was able to use the full power of his office, and whose use of it was controlled by a genuine understanding of the nature of Lebanon.

Behind these two political processes there lay a process of another kind: the growing influence of the city of Beirut. Beirut was prosperous from the transit trade, and there had scarcely begun the development of fruit cultivation with urban capital which was later to restore to the mountain villages some of their prosperity. The population of Beirut was growing; that of the mountains was decreasing because of emigration to the towns, to America and to west Africa. The city was playing an increasingly large part in the life of the Republic, and the political attitude of Beirut, whether Muslim or Christian, was different from that of the villages. Its religious conception was different: in moments of crisis it thought in terms of a sharp opposition of 'Muslims' and 'Christians' rather than of a whole range of sects. This might be dangerous, but on the other side there were certain tendencies towards unity. The educated middle class was growing, and life by its nature was half-secular; people living in the new quarters of the city were not willing to accept the same control by the religious hierarchy as those in the villages. Their education and the ways in which they earned their living led them into some kinds of personal relationships which took no heed of religious differences.

There was one more factor which was necessary before the new Lebanon created in 1920 could come to political life. Political consciousness had developed in the old *sanjaq* within the framework of authority established by the *mutasarrif*, but in opposition to him: in the Lebanese Republic, much the same role was played by France. The French presence guaranteed the framework of government and to some extent compelled the cooperation of all the communities, but, in the event, political unity was precipitated by a common opposition to the Mandate. Perhaps it could not have been otherwise: the Lebanon which had grown up within the French framework could only become aware of its own reality by breaking out. The events of World War II helped this opposition to grow and touch parts of the population hitherto satisfied with the Mandate. The merchant class wanted independence in order to control the machinery of government in its own interests, and to establish close links with countries other than France. Arab nationalists saw in the War, the weakness of France, and the temporary presence of England an opportunity to rid themselves of the Mandate, and they were now prepared to pay the price, which was a recognition of Lebanese independence (although, in their conception, only a conditional one). Some Maronites and Lebanese nationalists, although by no means all, were confident of their ability to stand alone, impatient of mandatory control, and doubtful of the power of France to protect them in the new world. The result of these changes of mood was the 'National Pact', an unwritten agreement between some Christian and some Muslim leaders to accept the independence of Lebanon and preserve the communal system, on condition that Lebanon followed a foreign policy truly independent of France and aligned to that of other Arab states. Opposition to the Mandate and support for independence were encouraged, in part deliberately and in part not, by the presence of British forces in the country after 1941; the old rivalry of England and France in the Middle East played itself out, perhaps for the last time, through the struggles of local political groups, and some of these groups exploited it with skill.

The events of 1943-6 were child's play compared to the struggles through which other nations have won their independence, but they left behind them a fragile sense of unity and of triumph, from which the independent Lebanon and its government could derive something of the revolutionary legitimacy which is the basis of modern nation-states. But already in 1946 a prescient observer could have seen that the process was not yet over, and there were certain forces at work in Lebanese society which might in due time threaten once more the structure of legitimate authority. The 'National Pact' expressed the difference as well as the unity of the sects. All might speak of a Lebanese nation, and of equality between the sects, but they meant different things. For some, Lebanon was still essentially a Maronite national home; for some, a Christian refuge; for some, a secular state based on a scarcely existing national unity; for some, a temporary expedient until a broad, secular Arab state should be ready to absorb it. These concepts expressed themselves in different nationalist movements and parties—Lebanese, 'Syrian' and Arab—but behind them there lay different religious loyalties, still the fundamental reality in Lebanese society.

This clash of political views was taking place in a society in process of rapid change, where the balance of population between Christians and Muslims was shifting, to the advantage of the second, and where the balance between town and countryside was also shifting. Beirut was becoming ever more important in the social and economic life of the country, and while this might make for closer links between men of different faiths who lived and worked together, it might also weaken those links between a man and the district, the village, and the family within which he lived, which had been the basis of the strong solidarity of the old Lebanon. The great, growing, rootless community of the Levantine city might lie open to sudden gusts of political passion springing from a submerged religious feeling.

The very smallness of the country increased the tension. Everyone was involved, at few removes or none, in the political process; the mass of unconcerned private citizens, living remote from political life, which makes the stability of larger states, scarcely existed. A small, weak country, lying in an important position, cannot prevent its internal conflicts becoming the channels through which great powers win influence and pursue their rivalries; by its position and the nature of its population, Lebanon lay open to waves of influence from America, from western Europe, and from the Arab world lying all around.

Against the forces making for dissolution, the country could oppose the frail sense of common citizenship and common interest which existed by this time, and certain no less fragile institutions, the products of its long and continuous development: the Chamber of Deputies, where both the unity and the diversity of Lebanon could express themselves, and the President of the Republic, the keystone of the structure, having power over small things as well as great, standing above communities and able, if he wished, to cut across communal interests and make difficult decisions.

9 Lebanon from Feudalism to Nation-State

Only a few years ago Sir Hamilton Gibb pointed out that there existed 'hardly a single work of genuine historical research into any aspect of the inner historical development of the Middle East in the nineteenth century'. His complaint would be less true now: in the last few years a number of distinguished works have thrown light on this dark and important century, and Dr Salibi's new book is one of the best of them.[1] The latest addition to the admirable 'Asia—Africa series', it is a work of imaginative scholarship, clear in thought and elegant in expression. Dr Salibi is heir to a long tradition of Lebanese historiography, from Salih ibn Yahya in the fifteenth century to 'Isa Iskandar Ma'luf in our own; he has used their material with the skill of a historian trained by the best masters of Islamic history, and in the light of a deep and responsible understanding of the nature of Lebanon.

As we know it today, Lebanon emerged late. The various religious communities of which it is made up have a long history (summarised by the author in a few pages, the ease and clarity of which might lead the reader to overlook their original scholarship); but it was only in the seventeenth century that its 'separate and distinct identity' emerged. That the different communities should have achieved political unity Dr Salibi explains in two ways: first by the emergence of a political authority standing above sectarian loyalties, that of the Ma'ns and their successors the Shihabs; and secondly by the growth among the temporal leaders of the communities of ties which cut across religious frontiers—'feudal chieftains of different religions or sects would formally address one another as brothers, or as cousins', and might 'fight side by side in defence of some common feudal cause, or perhaps of a common homeland'. That there should be an authority standing above the communities, and that communal leaders should have relations with each other based on common interests—these were indeed the two essential conditions for the existence of Lebanon, but once achieved they had to be maintained by constant vigilance; more than once they seemed to have collapsed and had to be re-created in a new form, and it is natural and right that much of Dr Salibi's book should be concerned with the great crises, and above all with the civil wars of 1860 and 1958, those moments of truth when the nature of Lebanon was sharply revealed, and when the threatened balance was restored partly by the intervention of external forces, but also by the will to live in common of the Lebanese people themselves.

The first crisis sprang from the interaction of several processes: the growth of the Christian population, and its spread southwards into districts controlled by Druze chieftains; the emergence of a Christian middle class in the ports and market-towns, created by the trade in European textile goods; the decline and collapse of the authority of the Shihab princes; the centralising policy of the Ottoman reformers; and the growing influence and rivalry of the European powers. The result was the civil war of 1860, the *terminus a quo* from which the oral tradition of the villages still begins and from which all political thinking starts. Until the appearance of this book it had not yet found a worthy historian; at last we have a clear and correct analysis of the connection between religious conflict and social change, and of the way in which the struggle of local forces, no longer held in check by a strong authority, drew in first the Ottoman government and then the European powers. This is perhaps the most important section of the book, and only two criticisms could be made of it. First, Dr Salibi does not seem to have laid sufficient emphasis on one aspect of the crisis, discussed by Dominique Chevallier in an important article[2]: the growth of the Christian middle class, which not only could not be fitted into the traditional structure of feudal society but was even a direct challenge to it, since it tended to establish direct relations with the peasantry and to replace the feudal chieftains as suppliers of agricultural capital and organisers of cultivation. The role of this class in the events of 1860 needs to be investigated further: Dr Salibi mentions in passing a 'Maronite Young Men's League' organised by Bishop Tubiyya 'Awn, but there was something more important than this, a political committee of business-men and clerics in Beirut, which the Turks accused of having played the main part in organising and directing the Maronite attempt to throw off the control of the Druze lords.

Secondly, the British connection with the Druzes was perhaps neither so simple nor so strong as Dr Salibi makes it out to be. It is true, from 1841 the Consulate in Beirut had close relations with the Jumblat family, and it was British intervention which in 1861 prevented the sentences of death on the Druze leaders being carried out; but this does not mean that British policy was to support Druzes against Maronites at all times and in all circumstances. There were British connections with some Maronites and French connections with some Druzes; and if there was a consistent British policy, it was not so much to back Druzes against Maronites as to support the feudal chiefs (more of whom were Druzes than Maronites) against the threat to their traditional supremacy by the Maronite clergy and peasantry. If Dr Salibi has missed some of the nuances of British policy, it is perhaps because he has not used certain sources. He has made full use of various narratives of the civil war—by the Christians Abkarius, 'Aqiqi and Mishaqa, the Druze Abu Shaqra, the English resident Colonel Churchill and the American missionary Jessup—but does not appear to have used the British Blue Books, which give perhaps the most vivid picture of events from 1840 to 1861. His story has the great advantage, however, of being written from within: even if the British were not so wholeheartedly pro-Druze as he maintains, at least the Druzes and Maronites thought they were. A British official, visiting Rashayya soon after the massacre, found that the Druzes

> still entertained the belief . . . that the English Government must be extremely satisfied with what they had done, for they imagine that any diminution of the number of Christians will be acceptable to us as weakening the French influence in the country!

We can see implicit in this the whole tragic relationship between Great Powers and local forces which is the main theme of the political history of the Middle East in modern times.

The balance destroyed in the events of the period from 1840 to 1861 was restored in a new form. By international agreement in 1861, modified in 1864, the authority of a Christian governor appointed by the Porte from outside Lebanon replaced that of the princes, and an Administrative Council in which representatives of the different communities could learn to work together replaced the traditional assemblies and alliances of the chieftains. Dr Salibi's pages on the half-century during which this arrangement lasted are all too brief; but if he does not tell us everything about it, at least he tells us more than we can easily find elsewhere. He seems rather to miss an important process during this period: the growth of genuinely political life within the framework of the new institutions, serving as they did to canalise the political feelings which, during the confused period from 1840 to 1861, had found expression in popular meetings, mass petitions, public proclamations, the emergence of popular leaders *(shuyukh al-shabab)* and peasants' risings. The focus of this political life was the conflict between the governors who, although Christians, were loyal Ottoman officials concerned to prevent Lebanese autonomy becoming too complete, and the Administrative Council which provided a collective political leadership. But Dr Salibi does draw attention to another important process, and one which preserved the continuity of Lebanese life, the emergence from the ranks of the feudal aristocracy of a new 'administrative aristocracy' of high officials.

The last chapter of the book is entitled 'Greater Lebanon', and is a description of the French Mandate and the first years of independence down to the civil war of 1958; it is the best description we have had, written with more insight than the older works of Longrigg and Hourani, and only rivalled by Rondot's *Institutions politiques du Liban*. It records a new phase in the development of the country. Once more the balance had to be re-created because of a change in the relationship of forces: the extension of the frontiers of Lebanon by the French in 1920 brought in a large Muslim population, particularly in the coastal towns, which had never had the same kind of organic relationship with Maronites and Druzes of the mountain as they had had with one another. Once more, the solution was found in a new structure analogous with the old: a new supreme authority, that of the French High Commissioner, and a new constitution providing a framework of institutions within which the communities could learn to live together. Dr Salibi is particularly good on the development of the constitution: the product not of French but of Lebanese political thinking, and in particular of the fertile mind of Michel Chiha, it 'did not attempt to lay down hard and fast principles for cooperation between the various confessions, but preferred to leave the traditional process of give-and-take to operate spontaneously'. Gradually there grew up something rare although not quite unique in the successor states of the Ottoman Empire, a national consensus, a set of generally accepted conventions about how political activity should be carried on. It is a measure of how successful this was that these conventions are now regarded as ancient and unshakeable traditions, although, as Dr Salibi shows, they developed slowly and recently: it was only in 1933 that the first Maronite President was appointed, in 1937 that the first Sunni Prime Minister took office, and in 1943 that the first Shi'i became President of the Chamber. Similarly, the conventions that Parliament should contain six Christian to every five Muslim members, that Christian and Muslim members alike should be elected by all electors in their districts and not by their co-religionists alone, and that posts in government and civil service should be distributed with rough equity between the main sects, only developed gradually by a national debate passing through crises and ending in agreement. So successful indeed was the process that in the end an effective coalition of leaders drawn from different communities, making skilful use of Anglo-French rivalry, was able to replace the French authority by a new indigenous authority, that of the President who, although by this time always a Maronite, was maintained by the pressure of the national consensus in the same supra-communal position as the princes had once had.

But agreement about how institutions should work was not enough once independence had been obtained; it was also necessary to agree about the aims of policy, and this was more difficult. Even those Lebanese who accepted the fact that after 1920 Lebanon could no longer be a 'Christian homeland' sometimes failed to draw out all its implications. The problem after 1945 was not simply that of how Muslims and Christians could live together but that of how the Muslim and Christian conceptions of Lebanon could be reconciled. The 'National Pact' of 1943 was a first attempt, but made in easy circumstances when the two worlds with which Lebanon had links—western Christendom to which the Maronites thought they belonged, and the Arab world to which Muslims gave their final loyalty—were on good terms. What was then attempted had to be re-done a decade later, when the decline of British power in the Middle East destroyed the illusion of a pre-established harmony between the Arabs and the West. The result was the second Lebanese civil war, that of 1958, which ended once more in a reassertion of the national consensus: the presidency, which had been drawn into the civil war, was restored as the final authority standing above sects and factions, leaders of the two sides formed a ministry together, and the subtle balance of power and influence was readjusted so as to meet some of the grievances of the Muslims.

Dr Salibi's account of this train of events is, as always, clear and fair, but it may be that he misses a dimension of it. While understanding that the idea of 'Christian Lebanon' was no longer valid after 1920, he perhaps tends to see the Muslims as non-Lebanese who had to be turned into Lebanese, rather than as people who had something positive to contribute to the process. It is almost unavoidable that someone writing the history of Lebanon should view it as that of the expansion of a mountain community: the princes of south Lebanon extending their rule over the north, the Maronites from the north moving into the south, the north and south united in a single entity absorbing the sea-coast. This may be a correct picture until 1920, but after that the nature of the process changes: the political culture of the mountain-valleys meets the quite different political culture of the coastal cities. The Sunni population of Tripoli, Beirut and Sayda was heir to the political culture of the Ottoman Empire; if it was to enter the Lebanese community, it could only do so by bringing its inheritance with it, and this included a different attitude not only towards the relationship of Lebanon with the outside world but also towards the relationship of spiritual and temporal, of government and society, of leaders and masses.

The difference of political conceptions, as well as of interests and feelings, between Muslim townsmen and Maronite or Druze mountaineers was the more important because of the shift in the centre of gravity of Lebanese life from the mountain down to Beirut. Here we come upon the main lacuna in Dr Salibi's book. He has a most interesting chapter on 'The Lebanese Awakening', with full and rare information in particular about the spread of schools (and if he says rather more than another writer might have done about the schools started by Ilyas and Sulayman Salibi we should not complain, because this illustrates vividly the peculiar cosiness of Lebanese life, based as it is on the strength and stability of the extended family); but there is surprisingly little in this chapter or elsewhere about some of the basic changes in Lebanese society—the emigration to the New World, which meant so much in many different ways, is only mentioned incidentally and in ten lines. Moreover, the chapter ends in 1914, and there is almost nothing on the development of Lebanese culture and society since then; an ignorant reader might imagine that the Arabic culture of Lebanon had flowered suddenly in the nineteenth century and as suddenly died, and even one who knows more than that might miss the significance of the growth of Beirut in the last half-century. What happened was not simply that the population flowed into Beirut from the villages of the mountain, but that influences of many kinds radiated out from Beirut over the countryside, subtly transforming its customs and its opinions. In the mountains, men lived in their closed religious communities, while the new middle class of Beirut found itself involved in a commercial or professional life outside the family and the household and cutting across the frontiers of sects; the mountain peasant regarded the government as something alien or hostile, to be kept as distant as possible, to be paid or obeyed grudgingly, while for the merchants of Beirut, living by the transfer of goods or money, the government was a machine to be controlled or used; in the Christian villages, France might still seem to be the eternal protector, while the merchants wanted first to be free of French control in order to mould policy in the light of their own interests, and secondly to have easy contact with the two poles of their *entrepôt* trade, the factories of the English-speaking world and the markets of Arab Asia; in the mountain the unit of politics was the village, while in Beirut there emerged for the first time in Lebanese history the urban mob (or rather two—Sunnis of the Basta and Armenians of the *bidonvilles*) as an instrument of political action. The most important event in Lebanese history after 1920 was the transformation of an agrarian republic into an extended city-state, a metropolis with its hinterland, and political events can only be understood in this context.

10 Lebanon: Historians and the Formation of a National Image

This paper was written for a conference on Middle Eastern historiography, held at the School of Oriental and African Studies in London in 1958, and published in 1962. Since it was written, the study of Lebanese history, on the basis of the work of its indigenous historians, has been carried further. See in particular D. Chevallier, 'La société du Mont Liban a l'époque de la révolution industrielle en Europe' (Paris, 1971), with a full bibliography; I.F. Harik, 'Politics and Change in a Traditional Society: Lebanon, 1711-1845' (Princeton, 1968); and above all a series of works by K.S. Salibi. These include 'Maronite Historians of Mediaeval Lebanon' (Beirut, 1959), 'The Modern History of Lebanon' (London, 1965), and a number of important articles, mainly in 'Arabica'.

In the last three hundred years the history of Lebanon has been recorded in detail by a series of Lebanese writers of varying skill, but almost all with some historical sense: that is to say, with some awareness of the sequence of cause and effect and the importance of basing their statements upon evidence. There is perhaps no other region of the Arab East, outside some of the great cities, of which this is true; in the mountains of Kurdistan political processes not dissimilar to those of Lebanon found few local writers to record them. There are two reasons for this flowering of Lebanese historiography: first, the development of a literate class, with a good knowledge of Arabic and some of the intellectual interests of the modern age, and secondly the existence of an intelligible and unified subject matter—not only an historical process to be explained but a thesis to be defended.

The first important group of modern Lebanese historians were Maronite and other Uniate priests educated in the seminaries of Rome, and their specific subject was the religious community to which they belonged. The special concern of the Maronites was to defend against other Catholic writers the claim of their Church always to have been steadfastly Catholic and never to have accepted the Monothelite heresy, the imputation of which, even after a thousand years, seemed to them a libel not to be endured. But they were writing at a time when the religious group was also the political community, and they celebrated not only the way in which their ancestors had defended the faith but also that in which they had preserved their autonomy in the valleys of northern Lebanon against the Muslim rulers of the surrounding lands, and established there a separate if fragile political existence. These two lines of thought converged in the work of the Patriarch Istifan al-Duwayhi (1630-1704), the greatest of the Maronite clerical historians. He wrote a number of historical works: a list of the Maronite Patriarchs, a history of the Maronite community, and a general history, the *Ta'rikh al-azmina*.[1] Of these the last is the most important. In form a general history, starting in some manuscripts in 622 and in others with the first Crusade and ending in 1699, it concentrates mainly on the history of Lebanon and its relations with the successive rulers of the surrounding regions, Crusaders, Mamluks, and Ottomans. It is particularly full and important for the last two centuries. Duwayhi was more like a modern historian than his predecessors. He based his work on as wide a collection of sources as possible, and even mentioned them. In his own manuscript copy of the *Ta'rikh* he mentioned some of the earlier historians whose work he used: Ibn Sibat for the Tanukhis, Safadi for Fakhr al-Din, William of Tyre for the Crusades. He gathered material also from Maronite churchbooks and the archives of the Vatican. He made some effort to weigh the value of his sources, although his critical sense broke down when dealing with the early history of the Maronites. Moreover, he had more than an antiquarian's interest in facts for their own sake. Behind his work lies a historical vision; he is concerned with the Maronites not simply as one political group interacting with others, but as the bearers of certain doctrines and of a culture which has grown out of them. The Jacobites who infiltrated into Lebanon in the fifteenth century were, in his view, as much the enemies of the Maronites as were the Mamluk armies all around.

Duwayhi and similar writers did not write history for its own sake alone. Their interest in the Maronite church and its past was one expression only of the new movement of Catholic thought and devotion among the eastern Uniate priesthood. Even within the sphere of history, Maronites looked beyond themselves, and their interest embraced the whole of Arabic history and culture, and the history and literature of all eastern Christendom. Among the Maronite scholars of this time, the family of Assemani were the most famous. A family of priests and scholars, trained in the Maronite College at Rome, they wrote more in Latin for the learned world of Europe than in Arabic for their own people, but they wrote mainly about the thought and life of the eastern Christendom from which they sprang. The greatest of them, Joseph Assemani, Prefect of the Vatican Library (1687-1768), made, in the three volumes of the *Bibliotheca Orientalis*, a survey of the ecclesiastical literature of Maronites, Nestorians and Jacobites.[2] His nephew, Joseph Aloysius, wrote a history of the Chaldean and Nestorian patriarchs,[3] and a third member of the family, Simon, wrote a learned thesis on the influence of Arabic on modern European literature.[4]

When Duwayhi wrote local history, he wrote mainly about northern Lebanon, and indeed for most of the period which he covered north and south were not politically united, nor were they known collectively as 'Lebanon'. The term 'Mount Lebanon' *(Jabal Lubnan)* was used to refer to the northern part of the mountain, inhabited mainly by Maronites, and controlled, beneath the governor of Tripoli, partly by indigenous Maronite *muqaddams*, and partly by Muslim lords placed there by the Mamluks and later by the Ottomans to watch over a population whose loyalty could be doubted. The south, known more often as the mountain of Shuf or of the Druzes *(Jabal al-Shuf* or *Jabal al-Duruz)*, was ruled mainly by Druze chieftains. During the early seventeenth century, however, the whole mountain was unified by Fakhr al-Din II (1585-1635) of the great Druze family of Ma'n, lords of the Shuf district. He finally revolted against the Ottomans and was killed, and his unified principality was dissolved. Later members of his family continued to rule the Shuf, and when the Ma'n family died out in 1697 it was replaced by another, the Muslim family of Shihab. The Shihabs were able to unite southern with northern Lebanon more permanently in the eighteenth century. In principle the Shihab *amir* or prince derived his position from the Ottoman governors of Sayda and Tripoli, who gave him investiture as chief tax-farmer, but in fact he had great freedom of action, and ruled together with a hierarchy of great families, mainly Druze and Maronite, to whom he delegated powers of tax-collection and who had certain rights over the cultivators.

Within this framework there developed a political life which has continued, to some extent, until today: the ruler struggling to maintain his autonomy against encroachments from outside and his authority against the powers and ambitions of the great families; loose associations of great families, Druzes and Maronites alike, competing with each other for land and political influence; religious tolerance masking a religious tension that could be brought to the surface by great political or social changes; a Christian intellectual ascendancy balanced by the political and social predominance of the Druzes; ceaseless efforts by the Turkish rulers of Syria to impose their control, and intervention by France and later by other European powers. The development of this political structure gave a new focus to historiography, and in the eighteenth century there appeared a new class intimately involved in the new political structure and capable of writing its history: families of Christian scholars and writers, mainly laymen but educated in the mission schools and Uniate seminaries, learning the sciences of the Arabic language from Muslim scholars and, because of this knowledge of Arabic, useful to the local rulers as clerks and men of affairs. Towards the end of the century, this group of *literati* began to produce a new sort of history: more exclusively secular and political, and concerned primarily with the struggle for political power, trying not simply to describe but to explain the formation and application of policy, and consciously or not seeing the political process from the point of view of the master whom they served.

Works of this type had indeed been written earlier; Ibn Sibat[5] and Salih b Yahya[6] had written the history of the Tanukhi rulers of the Gharb district, and Ahmad al-Khalidi al-Safadi that of Fakhr al-Din.[7] But in the eighteenth century they increased in number and scope. Since the south was the political centre of Lebanon and the scene of the struggle for power, it was there that most of these works were written, and we know more of what was happening in the south than in the north in this period. There are exceptions to this: for example, Antuniyus Abu Khattar al-'Aynturini, himself one of the *shaykhs* of the northern district of

Bsharri and grandfather of the Maronite national hero Yusuf Bey Karam. His history[8] is particularly strong on the origins of Lebanese families, Maronite church history, and the political history of the northern districts; he gives valuable details, for example, about the expulsion of the Shi'i family of Hamada from the Maronite north. When he deals with general Lebanese history he is interesting because, unlike most of the other historians of his day, he supports the losing side in the political struggles of the time; he is on the side of the sons of Amir Yusuf against Amir Bashir, by whom in fact he was put to death in 1821.

Among this group of works written by Christian scribes in the service of Druze or Muslim rulers of the south, we may mention those written by members of the Sabbagh family about the ruler whom they served, Dahir al-'Umar, who built a petty state in northern Palestine and southern Lebanon and founded the prosperity of Acre; there is a life of him by 'Abbud Sabbagh,[9] and another by Mikha'il,[10] who served in Napoleon's administration in Egypt, fled with the French army to France in 1801, and worked there with the Orientalists of his day until his death in 1816. Of greater interest is Ibrahim al-'Awra's history of the rule of Sulayman Pasha, who succeeded Jazzar as governor of Sayda.[11] 'Awra was a clerk in the *divan* of the provincial government of Sayda (of which the capital had by now been moved to Acre), and a member of a family of clerks. He had been close enough to the centre of affairs to know how decisions were made, and he gives an interesting description of the provincial ruling group founded by Jazzar, which ruled until the Egyptian conquest of 1831: how it was formed, the balance of Mamluk and local, religious and secular, Muslim, Christian and Jewish elements in its composition, the procedure used by officials and the way in which they were paid, the financial and other relations between the province and the central government in Istanbul. 'Awra wrote the book about half a century later (he says that he finished it in 1853), but he has recaptured vividly the events and atmosphere of his youth, and his is one of the few works of Lebanese history in which we can hear the voices of men talking.

The majority of these works of secular history were written by priests or clerks in the service of the Shihab princes or devoted to their interests. Around the Shihabs, and in particular around Bashir II (1788-1840), the last but one and the greatest of them, there gathered almost all the men of letters of the day, who found in the service of the Prince work worthy of their talents (just as, later, the educated Lebanese were to find work in the service of the Khedive and the British in Egypt, and of the British in the Sudan). For this group of men, the writing of history was only one aspect of a multiple literary activity; the clerkly families produced not only the historians of their age, but the fathers of the poetic and linguistic movement of nineteenth-century Lebanon.

Among the outstanding figures of this group was a Greek Catholic monk, Hananiyya al-Munayyir (1756-1832?). He wrote a history of his own religious order, the Shwayrites,[12] a book on the doctrines of the Druzes which was used by Guys and praised by de Sacy, and a general history of Lebanon, or rather of the Shihab family and the Shuf district which was the centre of their power. This last, *al-Durr al-mawsuf fi ta'rikh al-Shuf*,[13] is a political history from 1697 to 1807, based partly on general tradition, partly on his own observations, and partly on diaries and other documents of his own order of monks. Written in a clear and correct style and said to have been revised by the famous writer Shaykh Nasif al-Yaziji, it is for the most part a straight narrative, but it is not difficult to see that the author's sympathies are with Bashir, in his struggle against the encroachments of Jazzar and against the internal opposition led by his kinsmen, the sons of Amir Yusuf.

The most important member of the group, however, was neither a priest nor an official, but a member of the ruling family itself. The Amir Haydar Ahmad Shihab (1761-1835) was a cousin of Bashir II. Unlike Bashir, whose religious allegiance remained in doubt throughout his life, although he died and was buried as a Catholic, Haydar belonged to that section of the Shihab family which had abandoned Islam and become openly Maronite during the second half of the eighteenth century. Bashir employed him on confidential political tasks of some importance, but the greater part of his time was given to pious and learned works, and to gathering around himself a group of scholars and with their help writing the history of Lebanon and of his family. Entitled *al-Ghurar al-hisan fi akhbar abna al-zaman*, it is divided into three parts, each of which was given a separate title by later copyists, but not apparently by the author himself. The first part runs from 622 to the end of the Ma'ni dynasty in 1697, the second from 1697 to 1818, and the third from 1819 to 1827. Haydar appears also to have written a shorter work late in life, dealing specifically with

Amir Bashir and carrying the story almost down to the historian's death.[14]

In accordance with the custom of his own age, Haydar does not refer to his sources in the course of the work, but it is possible to form some idea of them from internal and external evidence alike. For the first part he used the general Islamic histories, in particular al-Tabari, some European sources (William of Tyre and Baronius), and the earlier histories of Lebanon. For the second and third parts also he relied on previous chronicles, but on much else besides. He had at his disposal a large number of official documents—Ottoman firmans, and correspondence between Bashir and Turkish officials—and some of them he quotes in full. Bashir's financial and general administration was carefully documented in accordance with strict rules of procedure, and a large proportion of the documents must have come within Haydar's view in the course of his official work. Most important of all perhaps were his own observations and those of others with whom he was in contact. In a rural community where literacy is rare, where horizons are limited and the supremacy of custom makes it important to remember exactly what happened, a detailed and precise collective memory may go back for several generations. Born in 1761, Haydar would have been able to draw on recollections going back practically to the beginning of the eighteenth century.

The main subject of his book is the policy of the Shihab princes, and the later part of it is dominated by the figure of Bashir. Since Haydar was a member of the ruling family, his history is written not from the point of view of the 'civil service', but from that of the men who made policy and took decisions. The narrative is only rarely suspended for an explanation of motives, but it is clear that Haydar had the political culture, the understanding of the aims, methods and limits of political action, which ruling families develop and transmit. It is clear too that in all the disputes with which he deals he is on the side of his family, and of Bashir. He stands with the Shihabs against Jazzar, with Bashir against Amir Yusuf, and with Bashir also against the challenge of the great Druze family of Jumblat.

He gives also a certain amount of economic and social history (his occasional price-lists might be of interest to an economic historian), and some general history of Syria, although of Damascus and northern Palestine rather than more distant parts. In the early part there are occasional references to European history, and in Part II there is a long account of the French expedition to Egypt, prefaced by a shorter account of the French Revolution—the deposition and execution of Louis XVI, and the rise of Bonaparte. This occupies almost a quarter of Part II—130 pages of the most recent edition. That so much space should be given to the French occupation of Egypt was due primarily to the large amount of material available. Haydar's account is based indeed on a detailed history of the French occupation written by Niqula Turk, a poet and member of Bashir's court, who was sent by Bashir to Egypt to report on the French occupation, and who later wrote what he had learnt and seen in a connected work of which two different versions exist.[15] But Haydar was a self-conscious historian who selected and emphasised his material with a view to what was important; if he decided to use all Niqula Turk's material, it must have been because the Revolution and the expedition to Egypt seemed to him events of quite unusual significance.

We have some information about the way in which Haydar wrote his book. He had a 'workshop' of writers producing material and drafts. They included most of the prominent writers of the time: Faris and As'ad al-Shidyaq, Butrus Karama, Niqula Turk and Nasif al-Yaziji. Some of the material produced by them may have been incorporated without change, but for the most part Haydar himself wrote the definitive version and gave the work its final shape. It is this method of composition which explains why the book exists in more than one form. There are numerous manuscripts of it, some ending earlier than others, and they appear to fall into two distinct groups: those based upon the author's own version, and those derived from a copy made and freely amended by Nasif al-Yaziji. For the same reason, there exist a number of other works clearly based on the same material and having some connection with the main history, some of them ascribed to Haydar himself, others anonymous or ascribed to one of his helpers. They include a history of Ahmad Pasha al-Jazzar[16] recently edited and attributed by its editors to Haydar, and a small work on the political geography and administrative procedure of Lebanon under Bashir.[17]

Of those who worked closely with Haydar and had access to the same material, one was to become a prominent historian in his own right. Tannus al-Shidyaq (1791-1861), the brother of Faris and As'ad, published in 1859, with some assistance from Butrus

Bustani, a large book on the noble families of Lebanon: *Akhbar al-a'yan fi jabal Lubnan*.[18] It is divided into three parts, dealing respectively with the geography of Lebanon, the genealogy and history of its great families, and its recent political history. In the preface, the author gives a list of the sources he has used: they include the earlier chronicles, the personal reminiscences of Druze *shaykhs* and others, a few official documents, and his own memoranda, kept, he tells us, since 1820. Those parts of the narrative where he covers the same ground as Haydar add little, but for later events—the last years of Bashir, the Egyptian occupation and the growth of tension in the 1840s and 1850s—the work is of importance. It gives details about the origin and rise of families which can scarcely be found elsewhere (although sometimes we may suspect him of being too generous in conceding the claims of powerful families to ancient origin); moreover, its very conception is original. His specific subject is not, as with Haydar, a ruler or a ruling family, it is a community, Lebanon itself—the title of the book is itself significant—and he sees Lebanon not simply as a territory unified and ruled by one princely family, but as a whole structure of families each with its own sphere of authority, and all intricately balanced and connected with one another. Those families may be Druze, Maronite, Sunni or Shi'i Muslim, but their authority derives from territorial power rather than religious allegiance, and their common interests give to Lebanon a unity which transcends religious difference. Tannus al-Shidyaq has thus contributed something essential to our understanding of feudal Lebanon.

Feudal Lebanon disappeared in the convulsions of the generation which stretched from 1831 to 1860. In order to impose disarmament and conscription in obedience to the commands of Ibrahim Pasha, Bashir began to play off Christians against Druzes; when Ibrahim was forced to evacuate Syria, Bashir was deposed, and under a weak successor the Shihab princes soon lost their authority and their throne. The Turks began to intervene more and more in order to destroy the autonomy of Lebanon as they had destroyed that of other regions of the Empire; the struggle of Britain and France for influence led the first to establish a relationship with a section of the Druzes, while the second strengthened her old relationship with the Maronites; and the growth of the Maronite community in population, wealth, culture, and solidarity, made them less willing to accept the traditional social leadership of the mainly Druze nobility. It was a combination of these factors which led to the civil war of 1860 and caused it to take on the character of a religious conflict. After the war and the intervention of the Powers, Lebanon was made into a privileged district of the Empire *mutasarrifiyya sanjaq,* under the protection of the Powers and with a political structure laid down in an Organic Law (1861 and 1864) and based on the religious communities. Half a century later, in 1920, it was enlarged and made into the State of Greater Lebanon, which by the Constitution of 1926 was turned into a Republic based on the same principle of equal cooperation between distinct religious communities. These developments gave rise to a third genre of history in addition to the other two.

It is true, these two other genres still continued. Much sectarian history was written; it was still mostly Maronite, and concerned to defend the 'perpetual orthodoxy' of the Maronites and their role in preserving and spreading Catholic faith in the East. The works of Mgr Derian (Daryan),[19] Afram al-Dayrani,[20] Mgr Dib,[21] and Fr Raphael[22] are in the direct line of descent from those of Duwayhi, but Mgr Dib at least brought to the defence of the Maronites the authority of a fully-trained Church historian and theologian. There still continued to be something defensive about this Maronite writing; next to the accusation of heresy, what they most resented was the failure of the Church to recognise the Maronite popular saints, and there is an element of communal pride in the new cult of Mar Sharbal, whose tomb has become a centre of pilgrimage. How sensitive the Maronites are about their distant past was shown when the Vicomte Philippe de Tarrazi published a work (*Asdaq ma kan 'an ta'rikh Lubnan*)[23] to prove that the Jacobites, not the Maronites, were the original inhabitants of Lebanon; this produced a sharp (and convincing) rebuttal from a Maronite scholar, Fr P. Carali (Bulus Qar'ali).[24] Other religious communities were also interested in their own past, and particularly the Greek Catholics, the most cultivated and self-conscious of the Arabic-speaking Christian sects; Frs Q. Basha[25] and Shammas[26] wrote voluminously on their history, and we should mention also H. Zayyat, who in a number of works of profound scholarship cast light on several aspects of the history of Christianity under Muslim rule.[27] Shaykh 'Arif al-Zayn wrote on the history of the Shi'i Muslims in southern Lebanon.[28] That little should have been written about the Sunnis or the Orthodox in Lebanon is not surprising, since for them Lebanon had never been a significant entity, still less the centre of their culture or political life. But the absence of Druze historiography (except for the work of Sulayman Abu 'Izz al-Din)[29] is more difficult to explain.

There still persisted too the tradition of writing histories of powerful families, towns and districts, like Arif al-Zayn's history of Sayda;[30] Mansur Tannus al-Hattuni's history of the Kisrawan district[31] (important for the social disturbances of Kisrawan in the 1850s, the precursor of the civil war of 1860); Nawfal Nawfal al-Tarabulsi's *Kashf al-litham*,[32] which, almost alone among Lebanese histories, seems to have made use of the Turkish historians; and the chronicle of Mikha'il al-Dimashqi dealing with events in Syria from 1782 to 1841, and written by a government official whose identity is uncertain.[33] Of this type of local historian, perhaps the most important is 'Isa Iskandar Ma'luf, who wrote the history of his own town, Zahla,[34] and spent most of his life collecting materials for a vast history of Lebanese and Near Eastern families. He seems to have made some sort of a draft of it, but it was never published as a whole, and probably never completed in publishable form. Some parts of it however were finished and issued separately: a history of the Yaziji family,[35] and a longer work on the Ma'lufs themselves—*Dawani l-qutuf fi ta'rikh bani Ma'luf*[36]—which is far more than its name implies. The Ma'lufs are a large and scattered family, and on to the peg of family history the author has been able to hang a number of learned disquisitions; for example, the family came originally from Hawran, and this makes it possible to write at length about the history of Hawran. What gives importance to all Ma'luf's work is his complete mastery of his sources. He had himself sought out, studied and in some instances copied the manuscripts of the older chronicles, and had a unique, almost textual knowledge of them; he had examined the muniments of monasteries and recorded local traditions stretching back to the eighteenth century. His history of Zahla throws a flood of light on to the growth of the new middle class of the market towns, whose refusal to fit into the feudal structure was one of the causes of the civil war of 1860.

The third type of history which grew up beside these two was fertilised by a new problem. More than ever before there now existed a separate entity called Lebanon; its existence was enshrined in international documents and placed under the protection of the European powers. A new sort of political consciousness grew up, and this gave rise to a new idea, the idea of a community with a continuous historical tradition and worth preserving. Why it should exist, and how it could be preserved, were questions which produced a new sort of historical writing, with a specific purpose—not to defend a church or glorify a prince, but to mould the consciousness of a people.

The historical thought which this writing expressed revolved around two images, one of Lebanon happy and united, and the other of Lebanon in collapse. Much writing was devoted to the periods of happiness and prosperity, and to pointing the moral of them: the need for religious toleration, and for a strong executive power which would hold the balance between the different communities and create ties of common interest between them. This involved the study and analysis of the institution of the princedom, which had given Lebanon its unity and special character, and in particular of the two greatest princes, Fakhr al-Din in the seventeenth century and Bashir in the nineteenth. The basic source for the history of the former, the chronicle of al-Safadi, was published in 1936;[37] and at about the same time Fr P. Carali published two volumes based on documents in the Medicean Archives of Florence (where Fakhr al-Din spent a period of exile), and the Archives of the Vatican and Propaganda in Rome.[38] He prefaced the documents with a long analysis of Fakhr al-Din's character and policy, presenting him as a far-sighted patriot who laid the foundation of Lebanese autonomy. Already in 1934 'Isa Iskandar Ma'luf had written a book in praise of the Ma'ni prince who 'strove with all his might for the independence, expansion and civilisation of his country',[39] and others have followed since. It was less necessary to commemorate the achievements of Bashir, because they are still very much alive in the collective memory of the mountain villages. But he has been much studied; there is a recent analysis of his policy by Asad Rustum.[40] Since his own time he has attracted the attention of many European writers. Their work lies outside our scope, but we should refer to the three volumes of Colonel Churchill,[41] member of a cadet branch of the great English family, who acquired, in the course of a long residence in Lebanon, and through very close relations with the Shihabs (with whom indeed he was connected by marriage) and the Druze nobility, a knowledge of Lebanon so intimate that he may almost be regarded as a Lebanese historiographer. His account of the Druze religion is taken largely from de Sacy, and the older history is based partly at least on Haydar. But he claimed to have seen manuscript records still in the possession of the great Druze and Christian families, and his account of the reign of Bashir is based upon personal knowledge.

Through such works as these the image has been projected of the Ma'ni and Shihabi princes as creators and symbolic embodiments of free Lebanon, but in recent years there has been an attempt by writers of socialist views to create another image, of 'popular' Lebanon struggling against its feudal bonds. Two revolts against heavy taxation in Bashir's reign (the *ammiya* of Antelias and Lahfad) have been regarded as early expressions of the popular will; more plausibly, attention has been directed to the revolt of the Maronite peasants of Kisrawan against their lords of the Khazin family (also Maronites), and the establishment of a 'peasant republic' in 1857. Yusuf Yazbak has published a contemporary chronicle of this event, with tendentious notes.[42]

The image of collapse has been provided by the period between 1840 and 1860, and in particular by the civil war and massacres of 1860. Here too the moral has not been far to seek; the need for mutual toleration, and the danger of foreign intervention making use of communal disputes. Events so unusual and tragic stirred many pens, and a number of the numerous reports by eye-witnesses have been published. Since most of them are written by Christians, a special interest attaches to the one published Druze memoir, that narrated by Husayn Abu Shaqra to Yusuf of the same family.[43] Of all these reports, perhaps the most reliable is that of Mikha'il Mishaqa (1800-88), *al-Jawab ala iqtirah al-ahbab*.[44] Himself a Christian, but a former servant of Bashir and with the outlook of one who serves and respects authority, Mishaqa gives an unbiased analysis of the causes of the outburst, and does not hesitate to blame the Christians for lack of respect for the traditional authority of the nobility. Here also a work by Colonel Churchill should be mentioned; his *Druzes and Maronites under Turkish Rule*[45] is the most vivid and comprehensive account of these events, although perhaps excessively harsh in its view of the Maronite Patriarch.

Within these two poles there has moved a great deal of historical thought: attempts to show, by historical analysis, why Lebanon should exist and how it can survive. Down to 1914, when Lebanon was a privileged Ottoman district with a Christian majority and under the protection of the Powers, the answer to such questions was fairly simple. It was given, for example, by M. Jouplain (the pseudonym of a Maronite, B. Nujaym) in his *La question du Liban*.[46] This work was partly an analysis of the political structure and international position of autonomous Lebanon, partly a detailed history of the years of crisis from 1831 to 1861, based upon documents published by the British and French Governments, and by De Testa in his *Recueil des Traités de la Porte Ottomane*. From his analysis there emerges a clear conception of Lebanon. For him, Lebanon formed part of Syria, but a quite distinctive part. There was a Lebanese nation, with a continuous history since ancient times. It had at times been englobed by great empires, and most recently by the Ottoman Empire, but it had never been absorbed. Since 1861 its existence had been formally recognised, but within boundaries smaller than its natural limits. It was essentially a Christian nation, and looked to France to intervene in order to secure its natural frontiers.

Because Lebanon was still a province within an undivided Empire, because its desire to be free from the Empire found echoes in other provinces, and because the new Lebanese historiography, like the new national consciousness, was linked with a flowering of culture in Arabic, it was possible for Lebanese writers to see the same principles embodied in a larger whole. The idea of 'Syria' as a whole served as an alternative focus of political loyalty and historical thought. Among the histories of 'Syria' in this broad sense produced by Lebanese, we may mention that of Jirji Yanni,[47] an Orthodox Christian of Greek origin, which is important for the history of Tripoli; and the vast history of Syria by the Maronite Archbishop Yusuf al-Dibs (1833-1907).[48] In form a general history of Syria from the earliest times until his own day, with 'Syria' as the explicit subject and with much general Islamic history and history of Arab culture, it tends in the later period to mean 'Lebanon' when it says 'Syria', and is particularly detailed and useful on Maronite ecclesiastical history, for the author had much knowledge of Church literature and documents. The book is typical of a genre of history which became current at this time: its general framework and, in particular, its earlier sections are drawn from European sources, but when it comes to the recent history of Lebanon it changes its character and becomes local history of the traditional sort and based on the local sources.

We may mention, in this connection, another work written by a European so long resident in Lebanon, and so fully identifying himself with its problems, that it may be regarded as belonging to the Lebanese tradition of historical writing: Fr H. Lammens's *La Syrie—précis historique*.[49] Here once more 'Syria' as a natural unit is the subject, but Lebanon is conceived of as having a separate existence inside it. Lammens did not indeed emphasise the existence of something called 'Syria' as an alternative to the idea of 'Lebanon', but as an alternative to that of 'the Arabs'. In his view, the Syrians, and *a fortiori* the Lebanese, were not Arab, and most Maronite writers of his age would probably have agreed with him. But there was a group of writers who, while accepting the existence of a separate entity called 'Syria', would have regarded it as part of a larger whole. The revival of Arabic culture in Lebanon induced some of the historians to look beyond the narrow confines of their mountain. Fr L. Cheikho (Shaykhu) wrote much on Arabic literature,[50] Vicomte Philippe de Tarrazi published several volumes on the history of Arabic journalism,[51] and Jurji Zaydan (1861-1914), in a prolific life as a journalist, published histories of Arabic literature, Islamic civilisation and Egypt, a volume of nineteenth-century biographies, and a score of historical novels, modelled on the Waverley novels but nearer to Henty than to Scott, which have done much to arouse, and not in Lebanon alone, a romantic image of the Arab past.[52]

Since Lebanon became a state, first under French Mandate and then with sovereign independence, there has continued to be an equivocation between the idea of Lebanon and the idea of some larger whole. Most of those who have written about Lebanese history have accepted the thesis of Tannus al-Shidyaq, that there has long existed an entity called 'Lebanon', not simply a religious group nor the estate of a ruling family, but a society; and their problem has not been whether it exists, but what have been, and what should be, its relations with the surrounding world. We can distinguish among recent historians those who lay more emphasis on the separateness of Lebanon and those who emphasise its links with the surrounding world; roughly corresponding with this distinction is another, between those for whom the significance of Lebanon is that it has been a free Christian enclave in a Muslim world, and those who see in it above all a multiple society where men of different faiths have been able to live side by side in peace.

But the distinction is no more than one of emphasis; for most historians Lebanon is both a land of asylum and a place of meeting. Among those who lay their stress on the former, we may mention Michel Chebli, who has published a life of Fakhr al-Din followed by a work on Lebanon under the princes who succeeded him.[53] It is devoted to the glory of the princes who gave Lebanon a good public administration and unity in tolerance; but it is devoted no less to the flowering of Christian culture in Lebanon of the seventeenth and eighteenth centuries. The author had a close connection with the theorist of Lebanese separatism, Michel Chiha, who himself pointed the moral of the book in his preface:

> L'histoire des Chehab est l'histoire d'une résistance. C'est l'histoire d'une communauté nationale, faite de communautés confessionelles établies sur une montagne maritime qui leur sert d'inviolable refuge et unies pour le défense et la préservation de leurs libertés spirituelles et temporelles.[54]

It is significant of the development of modern Lebanon that an historian coming from one of the non-Christian communities should be able to point a similar moral, although his stress is less on the need for Christians to preserve their spiritual liberty than on the need of those who have different beliefs to live together in peace. In 1955 Adel Ismail published the first volume (in French) of a *Histoire du Liban du XVIIe Siècle à nos Jours*.[55] Planned to cover the modern history of Lebanon in six volumes, it will be the most ambitious survey of the subject. This first volume deals with Lebanon in the time of Fakhr al-Din. Ismail follows the example of Fr Carali in going beyond the little group of classical chronicles (Duwayhi, Safadi, Shihab, Shidyaq) on which almost all subsequent work has been based, and trying to find a more secure base in contemporary documents. Whereas Fr Carali used Italian sources, Ismail has made exhaustive use of French documents: the Archives Nationales, those of the Ministry of Foreign Affairs, and the important commercial archives of Marseilles. He is thus able to give a fuller survey of social and economic life than has usually been attempted. On the administration of Fakhr al-Din he does not add much to Carali; but there is a comprehensive view of Fakhr al-Din's foreign policy. Indeed the importance of the Ma'ni prince is clearly brought out, as the man who first gave Lebanon a separate foreign policy. Not in this respect alone, Ismail regards

Fakhr al-Din as the creator of the modern Lebanese nation. He goes further than older writers, and further perhaps than the evidence warrants, in regarding Fakhr al-Din as a conscious nationalist with an articulate grasp of the modern idea of a nation. He had a

> ... conception moderne de la 'nation' ... Tout en restant druse, il sut être musulman, chrétien, maronite, capucin, ou jésuite ... De cette Macédoine de confessions et de rites qu'était le Liban, il fit naître une nation et une patrie dans un Empire ou l'idée de Patrie était inconnue.[56]

That Chebli, Ismail, and others who have written Lebanese history in modern times should be in some sense Lebanese nationalists is not surprising; had Lebanon not been a significant entity for them they would scarcely have cared to write about it. Side by side with them there have been other writers who have devoted themselves to a broader subject. The late nineteenth-century concept of 'Syria' has fallen into the background, banished (although perhaps not for ever) by the march of events, but the concept of 'the Arabs' has become more definite. The works of Philip K. Hitti on Arab history are too well-known to need comment; written in America for an English-speaking audience, they scarcely fall within our scope. His recent work, *Lebanon in History*,[57] is almost the first attempt to treat the whole history of Lebanon from the dawn of history until today, and to place it in the context of Near Eastern history. The chapters on modern history represent one more exploitation of the chronicles, more careful and controlled than that of his predecessors although not different in essence; but there is more on the period from 1861 to 1914, and on the social and intellectual changes of the nineteenth century, than can be found elsewhere.

The history of the Arab national movement, *The Arab Awakening*, has been written by a historian of Lebanese origin, George Antonius.[58] Subsequent historians, working on one or other aspect of the subject, have differed from his interpretation,[59] and Sylvia Haim has cast doubt on his integrity as a historian.[60] But the most of which he can be legitimately accused is that he rarely quoted his sources or explained why, when they conflicted, he preferred one of them to another; and that he laid too much emphasis on the points which he regarded as important. He gives too much importance to the role of the Lebanese Christians, and the American mission-schools in Lebanon, in the formation of Arab nationalism. He regards them indeed as having created the movement; later, 'the ideas which had originally been sown by Christians were . . . finding an increasingly receptive soil among the Moslems'.[61] He says nothing about the influence of the 'Islamic modernists' of Egypt, although Jamal al-Din is briefly mentioned; and while the Syrian members of the Ottoman official and officer class are mentioned as those who became the leaders of the secret societies, the impression is given that they derived their ideas from the Lebanese Christians, not from the professional schools and political atmosphere of Istanbul, and the tradition of their own families. Antonius's very conception of Arab nationalism, as a secular link binding together adherents of different religions, is Lebanese. The first political problem of Lebanon is how to create such a link; in the other Arab countries, where the Christians form a minority, it may be an important problem but it is not the first of all. It is true, Antonius is in no sense a Lebanese nationalist. When talking of Lebanon under the French Mandate, his point of view is that of the Arab nationalists of Damascus, who took it for granted that

> the play of natural forces was bound in time to 'expose' the artificiality of the present frontiers; and that the day would come when the Lebanese themselves would seek a modification, if not the total abolition, of the barriers.[62]

But in this he was typical of the Orthodox Christians of Lebanon of his generation; they felt the attraction of the Lebanese idea far less than the Catholics, and their allegiance was given to the idea of Syria or of the Arabs.

Appendix: the publication of sources

We wish here to draw attention to one of the cardinal virtues of the Lebanese school of historians: their care to base their work on primary sources, and their concern to make those sources available. This quality can be seen as far back as the time of Duwayhi and Haydar Shihab; both of them went to some trouble to collect all the materials they could, and Haydar frequently quoted the text of official documents. But of course they lived before the principles of modern historical enquiry had been made clear, and it is to later writers that we owe the painstaking collection and publication of texts and documents. Before 1914 three important collections were published. Philippe and Farid Khazin published three volumes of diplomatic documents dealing with the policy of the Great Powers in regard to Syria and Lebanon from 1840 to 1910;[63] they were mostly drawn from British and French official publications and from De Testa, although some had not previously been published. T. Anaissi collected important ecclesiastical documents in his *Bullarium Maronitarum*,[64] and Fr A. Rabbath published six fascicles of *Documents inédits pour servir à l'histoire du Christianisme en Orient*.[65] Very few of his documents had been published before; they were drawn mainly from the archives of the Society of Jesus, and also from those of the French Ministry of Foreign Affairs, the Vatican, the eastern patriarchates and bishoprics, and from papers in the Bibliothèque Nationale in Paris. Covering the period of the development of modern Catholic missions, from the sixteenth to the nineteenth century, they deal above all with the splendours and miseries of the missionaries, their struggles with the Orthodox hierarchy, their persecution by the Ottoman authorities and the protection given them by the ambassadors and consuls of France.

In the years since World War I the chronicles of Lebanon have been published or republished in improved editions, mainly through the efforts of a few individuals. Fr P. Carali published, among others, the early chronicle of Ibn al-Qila'i[66] and Haydar's shorter work on Bashir II; his book of Italian documents on Fakhr al-Din has already been referred to,[67] and we may also mention his book on the Syrians in Egypt,[68] based on Church registers. Fr Q. Basha edited the chronicles of Mikha'il Sabbagh[69] and Ibrahim al-'Awra;[70] the first-named was part of a series of *Documents inédits pour servir à l'Histoire des Patriarches Melkites*. A. Rustum and F.A. Bustani published, under the auspices of the Lebanese Directorate (subsequently Ministry) of Education and Fine Arts, al-Safadi's history of Fakhr al-Din,[71] and the second and third parts of Haydar's chronicle.[72] These were intended to be the first two in a series which should include all the basic Arabic sources for the history of Lebanon. World War II intervened and the series went no further, but in the last few years more official series have been started, one by the Lebanese University[73] and one by the Department of Antiquities in the Ministry of Education.[74]

Much of the work of publishing chronicles, biographies, and memoirs was done by periodicals, some of them comparatively short-lived, like *al-Manara*,[75] *al-Masarra*,[76] *al-Majalla al-suriyya*,[77] and its continuation *al-Majalla al-batriyarkiyya*,[78] and the recently established *Awraq lubnaniyya*,[79] others with a longer history and a solid reputation. Two have been particularly important: Shaykh 'Arif al-Zayn's *al-'Irfan*,[80] which has published much work on Shi'i doctrine and antiquities in the last half-century, and the Jesuit periodical *al-Mashriq*[81] which has naturally laid most emphasis on Christian Lebanon and Eastern Christendom in general. In the last few years it has printed a new and complete edition of Duwayhi's *Ta'rikh al-azmina*,[82] and the chronicles of 'Aynturini[83] and Munayyir.[84] With these, the publication of the important chronicles is virtually complete, except for the work of Ibn Sibat.

There has been a tendency among Lebanese historians to base their work simply upon what previous historians have written, and in particular upon the four or five major chronicles. In recent years, however, the importance of going beyond chronicles to official and other documents has been more fully recognised. Some types of document are comparatively scarce in Lebanese historiography; for example, the memoirs, diaries and private letters which are so important a source for modern European political history. Official documents, however, exist in abundance, and the first man to collect them systematically was A. Rustum, who published two large collections dealing with the history of Lebanon and Syria under Ibrahim Pasha (1831-41). The first is a collection of Arabic sources,[85] drawn from family papers and the archives of the religious courts (the only important archives for the Ottoman period which seem to exist in the Arab provincial towns); of particular importance are the long extracts from the register of the *majlis* set up by Ibrahim Pasha in Aleppo, which throw a flood of light on Ibrahim's methods of administration and on the social and economic life of Syria at that time. The second work is a calendar of papers in the Egyptian archives relating to Syria:[86] an exhaustive list with text or full summaries of the more important documents. These two works will be of fundamental importance for anyone who wishes to write the history of Syria and Lebanon during these crucial years. It is a pity that Professor Rustum himself has not yet had an opportunity to write the work of synthesis for which he is uniquely qualified. He has, however, published several short works on specific points.[87]

It is partly due to his efforts, and partly to those of the Director of Antiquities (Amir Maurice Shihab, himself a member of the former ruling family) that the National Archives of Lebanon have been created in the last few years. The basis of these are two collections of family papers; those of the Khazins, the Maronite lords of Kisrawan, and those of the Muslim Bayhums, one of the leading merchant families of Beirut. Recently, there have come to light, in the palace of Bteddin, a large number of documents of the period of Bashir II, and others from that of the *Mutasarrifiyya* (1861-1915). Microfilms have been made of all important documents dealing with Lebanon in the French archives, and it is hoped to do the same for the British and Ottoman archives. All these papers are now being arranged and classified, and some of them are already available to historians.[88] They will provide the necessary foundation for the history of one of the two poles of Lebanese life, the government in its successive forms—the princedom, the *Mutasarrifiyya,* the independent Republic. There is another pole, the Maronite Patriarchate; its archives are well-preserved but have only been spasmodically open to scholars, and perhaps they too will some day become readily available.

11 Ideologies of the Mountain and the City: Reflections on the Lebanese Civil War

In 1963 a group of historians and political scientists held a conference at the University of Chicago to discuss the working of the Lebanese political system, and their papers were later published in a book edited by Leonard Binder, *Politics in Lebanon*.[1] Anyone who has turned to that book during the last months of civil war in Lebanon, in the hope that it would help him to understand what was happening, must have felt that something had been left out of it.

The idea which seems to have moulded the papers and discussions is that of a self-contained political society seeking and finding its own equilibrium, by a series of successful adjustments to changing circumstances. Throughout the process of change, it was suggested, there could be seen a basic continuity: from the emergence of the 'principality' in the seventeenth and eighteenth centuries, through the various changes in the middle years of the nineteenth, down to the creation of Greater Lebanon in 1920, the Constitution of 1926, the National Pact of 1943, and the reaffirmation of unity after an earlier civil war, that of 1958.

The lessons of this successful process of adjustment seemed clear. For Lebanon to maintain its separate existence, there had to be some kind of authority (that of the prince, the *mutasarrif* or the president) which, whatever its origins, stood above the interests of particular communities; a habit of discussion and alliance on lines which cut across the frontiers of communities; an agreement on the sharing of power between them; and some measure of agreement also on the purposes for which that power should be used, in particular in relation to the surrounding states.

This analysis may well be valid as far as it goes, and nothing which has happened in the last few months has disproved it. It may be, however, that the discussions which led to the book, and others like them, concentrated too much on one problem, that of the balance between religious communities, and failed to give due importance to other factors which have helped to determine the ways in which the system works and limit the extent to which it is self-sustaining and can find its own equilibrium. Not enough emphasis was laid, for example, on the smallness and fragility of Lebanon; it was clear from the time of the National Pact, or at least from that of the civil war of 1958, that Lebanon could not easily follow a policy opposed to that of its Arab neighbours, in regard to the problem of Israel, or in its relations with the great powers, but it was not so clear that the surrounding states would have an interest in making use of any kind of inner fragmentation for their own purposes. Again, the degree to which the various communities had really been drawn into the political system may have been exaggerated. Some groups remained precariously inside or virtually outside it: the Orthodox Christians, who controlled much of the wealth of Beirut but played only a minor part in its political life; the Armenians, who were only marginally involved in it; the Shi'is, who had been formally drawn in by being given the third office of state, that of the President of the Chamber, but who had needs and aspirations which were only just beginning to be formulated; above all, the Palestinians, who scarcely existed as a separate political force in 1963.

Perhaps the most important factor, which was not so clear then as it is now, is that the 'communities' are not, beyond a certain limit, solid bodies having a single interest or attitude, and the division into religious communities is not the only division which can be made of the population of Lebanon, and in some ways may not be the most significant. We can now see that it is necessary to ask, exactly who in each community profits from the position it has in the political system? In general, it would be true to say that those who have profited have been, on one level, the commercial and financial groups whose interests have been served by the policy of openness to the outside world which was implicit in the 'National Pact', and that of *laissez faire* in internal matters which followed necessarily from the agreement that government should be carried on by a balancing of interests between the various communities; and on another, the political leaders, to whom the system, based as it was on a process of bargains and alliances at the top, guaranteed the exercise of patronage and thus the possibility of maintaining their own systems of clients. By and large, there was close agreement between the interests of the leaders and those of the commercial and financial class, and this became more significant and dangerous as the economic and social system changed, first with the growth of Beirut and the extension of its power over the hinterland, and then, in the last few years, with the growth in and around Beirut of a depressed world of rural immigrants and Palestinian refugees, not sharing in the profits of trade and finance and affected by inflation.

In such discussions as those embodied in Binder's book, the solidarity of each community was exaggerated, and so too therefore was the extent to which it had accepted the Lebanese political system. If there was a basic agreement amongst most of the leaders about the way in which the system should work, this did not necessarily mean that there was deeper or wider agreement about the nature of Lebanon or the purposes for which its political system should be used, or, in other words, that there really existed a Lebanese political society.

Much of the political writing about Lebanon seems to assume that the history of Lebanon has been that of the gradual expansion of the political tradition of the Christian parts of the Mountain, and the gradual conversion of Druzes, Sunnis and Shi'is to a political idea which had grown up among the Maronites. What happened in fact, however, was different; it was a broadening agreement between political élites, each of which controlled its community in its own way and in the name of its own political ideologies. To the extent to which they entered the Lebanese political alliance, they did so with their own modes of action and their own traditions.

It has been customary to refer to the heads of these élites as za'im's,[2] but this term covers at least three different modes of political activity. First, there is the 'feudal' mode: that of the great lords of those parts of the countryside where large estates and traditional lordships exist (among Druzes and Shi'is in the south, Shi'is in the Biqa', and Sunnis in 'Akkar). Their power rests on their position as landowners, often of ancient lineage, their use of strong-arm men, and their ability to give protection and patronage. Secondly, there are the 'populist' politicians of the mainly Christian regions in the northern half of the country, where smallholdings are common, and leadership has less of a solid base of socio-economic power, and is derived on the one hand from the use of powers of protection and patronage to maintain political 'clans', on the other from some kind of ideology or programme of action. Thirdly, there are the leaders of the Muslim populations of the coastal cities; they also obtain and retain leadership by ideological appeal and the exercise of patronage, but add to these a third source of power, the manipulation of the urban masses, mobilised for them by the 'strong arm' men of the popular quarters, the *qabaday's*.[3]

Of these three kinds of leader, therefore, two have to appeal in terms of ideologies and programmes, and cannot simply rely on primordial loyalties or allegiances. It is here that the differences between the political traditions which have come together to form Lebanon are relevant. We can distinguish two kinds of tradition, which we may call those of the mountain and those of the city, and within each of them a number of sub-divisions can be made.

The 'ideologies of the mountain' are specifically ideologies of the Maronite community; other communities in the mountain villages had a solidarity no less strong, but did not, for a number of reasons, express it in articulate political ideas from which programmes of action could be drawn. They have at least three aspects, connected with different phases in the history of the Maronites.[4] The idea which emerged earliest was that of a compact community, the Maronite church, living by itself under its own hierarchy, protecting itself from attack by the Muslim rulers of the cities and plains, and also against the more insidious attacks of Jacobites and other 'heretics'. This idea is already present in the histories of the Patriarch Istifan Duwayhi in the seventeenth century, and forms a permanent strand in Maronite self-consciousness. Maronites are aware of themselves as the only Catholic 'nation' in the Middle East, and indeed of Asia, and are therefore sensitive to any doubts cast on their Catholicism; the idea of the 'perpetual orthodoxy' of the Maronites, and Leo X's description of them as 'a rose among thorns', have been themes of Maronite writers. At the same time, however, they have strongly defended their position as a Uniate Church against encroachments by Rome; the failure of the Catholic church as a whole to canonise some whom the Maronites accept as saints has also been a theme of Maronite writing.

At a rather later stage a second idea emerged, that of this

'nation' as living within a broader political framework, that established and maintained by a hierarchy of leading families, associated with each other as a political élite. Implicit in this idea was a certain religious pluralism, for the leading families were Sunni as well as Druze and Maronite, and the alliances between them cut across religious divisions. This idea can be found, explicitly or by implication, in the work of some historians of the nineteenth century, such as Haydar Shihab and Tannus Shidyaq. It could scarcely have emerged earlier, because it was only in the eighteenth century that the northern, mainly Maronite, parts of the mountain were absorbed into the area controlled by the prince, and only in the later part of that century that the dominant section of the princely family of Shihab became Maronite and so provided a focus for Christian loyalty.

After the abolition of the princedom in the 1840s there began a campaign, supported by France, for the restoration of a Maronite Shihab. In the work of a political writer of the time, Nicolas Murad, we can see both these ideas present: the Maronites are a separate religious group, a perpetually orthodox part of the Catholic church, but they are also ethnically distinct, descendants of the 'Mardaites', a mysterious people mentioned in the history of the early Islamic period. From this time onwards there is an attempt to give historical depth to the idea of a separate and virtually independent political entity. Emphasis is placed upon the role of the Druze prince of the seventeenth century, Fakhr al-Din II, as the creator both of Lebanese independence and of the principle of communal alliance. This idea owes much to the historical work of the Maronite Bulus Qar'ali, but has been given full expression by another historian, Adel Ismail, a Sunni from one of the few Sunni villages in the mountain.[5]

In the troubled years of the mid-nineteenth century a third strand appears, that of 'populism', a new kind of appeal made by a new kind of claimant to leadership. Such an appeal could be made in the Christian villages of the north more easily than in the east or south. The northern part of the mountain had not had a highly developed 'feudal' structure, because since Mamluk and early Ottoman times it had been under more direct control by a governor of Tripoli; further south, in Kisrawan, there was a lordly family, that of Khazin, but in the 1850s the small cultivators were able to throw off its domination in a popular movement encouraged by the Church; to the south and east, there were mainly Christian market towns of recent growth—Zahla and Dayr al-Qamar—which had grown up in regions dominated by Druze lords but were reluctant to accept their control. In all these regions, Christians in villages and small towns were open to the appeal of 'populist' leaders: Tanyus Shahin who led the little revolt of Kisrawan, Yusuf Karam who led the forlorn hope of the Maronites against the compromises involved in the Organic Law of 1861-4, and the members of the Administrative Council who opposed attempts by the *mutasarrif* to limit the special privileges granted in the Organic Law of 1861. In a sense, the Phalanges of today can be seen as the heirs of this tradition.

Implicit in this mountain populism was a certain distrust of the city, an expression of that tension between countrymen and city-dwellers which has been described by Baroja as one of the 'ancient commonplaces' of Mediterranean society.[6] For the villager, rural society is created by God, urban by man; the life of the fields is 'natural' life in all its purity. This image of a pure and natural way of living was carried by the emigrants to the cities of the New World, strengthened and perhaps distorted there by nostalgia, and reflected back from them onto Lebanon itself.

The Lebanon of the eighteenth and nineteenth centuries did not include the larger towns of the coast. Lebanese claims and French policy had led to their incorporation into 'Greater Lebanon' in 1920, and in the next half century one of them, Beirut, became a great centre of international trade and finance, of services and communications. It became not only a part but the dominant part of the country, and from it there came other ideas of what Lebanon was or should be. Implicitly or explicitly, the urban idea of Lebanon was neither of a society closed against the outside world, nor of a unitary society in which smaller communities were dissolved, but something between the two: a plural society in which communities, still different on the level of inherited religious loyalties and intimate family ties, coexisted within a common framework.

This idea begins to emerge in the second half of the nineteenth century, partly as a reaction to the civil troubles of 1860, partly as a reflection of the policy of the *tanzimat* in the Ottoman Empire as a whole, but basically as the expression of the interests of a commercial city, where men must meet in peace in order to do business, and doors should be open to the outside world. It was this idea, rather than those of the mountain, which guided the political development of Lebanon from 1920 onwards, that is to say, from the time when Beirut was incorporated in it.

There was more than one way, however, in which it could be expressed and explained. On the one hand, the idea of a plural Lebanon could be a kind of transplantation and modification in the city of the idea of the Christian mountain. This can be seen in the writings of Michel Chiha, who was not only a theorist of Lebanese nationalism but one of its creators, for he played a large part in drafting the constitution of 1926.[7] His writing is Christian in its cultural content rather than its explicit ideas. His ideal is that of a pluralist and non-sectarian state, and he accepts communalism with reluctance, and as a temporary expedient: in the words of the Constitution, it should be accepted *à titre transitoire*. When he writes about Palestine there is an Arab element in what he says, which is far from the strict neutralism of the Maronite mountain, and is perhaps connected with his acceptance of the weakness of Lebanon and its need to lie open to the world around it; the Lebanese are 'by vocation and necessity, the friends of the masters of the world'. At this point however the essential tension of Lebanon's existence appears: 'we are not disposed to resign ourselves to the decline of Europe'. Between Arab and European affinities, the tension can only be resolved in a concept which can include them both, that of a common 'Mediterranean civilisation', the source of all belief in a supernatural world.[8]

A more extreme and less influential version of a similar idea was put forward in the same period by a number of men of letters, and by Charles Corm in particular. Lebanon is seen as the heir of Phoenicia. The modern Lebanese are descendants of the Phoenicians. Their distinctive culture, although expressed in modern languages and styles, reveals 'the atavistic forms of the national sensibility'. Like Phoenicia, Lebanon is part of the world of classical Mediterranean civilisation and can only live by immersion in it. But this vision is suffused with a Maronite romanticism; Lebanon is not only the heir of Phoenicia, it is the child of the Church, the only Christian country in Asia.[9]

There was, however, a second type of urban conception of Lebanon, not a transplantation of the ideas of the mountain, but a transplantation of later Ottoman ideas. For those Muslims who, in the 1930s and 1940s, came to accept the existence of Lebanon, it was an embodiment of the ideal formulated, in different ways, by the statesmen of the *tanzimat* and their Syrian supporters, and then by the Ottoman liberals and their allies in the Arab cities, the Party of Decentralisation and the Beirut Reform Committee of 1913. It should be carefully non-sectarian, with a national concept embracing all but suffused with a memory of the Arab, and therefore the Muslim, past. Lebanon should be a separate part of a broader unity, conceived not in terms of classical Mediterranean classical civilisation but of that of the Arabs.[10] A variation of this idea was that put forward by the *Hizb al-Qawmi*, the Parti Populaire Syrien, in the 1930s, the idea of a territorially limited and strictly non-sectarian Syrian nation, child of another late Ottoman idea, current in Beirut towards the end of the nineteenth century, carried from there to the emigrant community in Brazil and brought back to Lebanon by the son of an emigrant. Although it had a special appeal to some Lebanese, in particular those who were neither Maronite nor Sunni Muslim, it was by its nature an idea which challenged the separate existence of Lebanon, not one which underpinned it.[11]

It was such urban ideas which formed, so to speak, the 'official' ideological basis of the Lebanese state. The events of recent months have shown how fragile that basis was. In political terms, it laid its main emphasis on the institution of the Presidency, standing above religious communities and political 'clans', and on the possibility of an alliance between Maronite and Sunni leaders (one of the first Sunnis to accept the existence of Lebanon, Khayr al-Din Ahdab, stated in 1932 that 'we demand the Presidency for the Muslims or the Maronites, to the exclusion of the minorities');[12] and it assumed that the common interest of the commercial and financial classes would give strength to this alliance. But the Presidency could never liberate itself from political clans, and, at moments of deep division between communities, it could not easily stand aside. The alliance of Christian and Muslim politicians did not necessarily imply a merging of the communities in whose names they spoke; on the contrary, the new immigrants into the cities seemed to be more conscious of sectarian differences than those living in the countryside.[13] What is most important, the civil war has shown how much of Lebanon has not been fully drawn into the political community: the Sunni urban leaders can no longer speak in the name of the Muslim part of the population; and the Phalanges and other Maronite political groups have won their main support among Maronites newly settled in the cities or

178   *The Emergence of the Modern Middle East*

living within their expanding sphere of social influence, not fully at home in them, and uneasy with the compromises of the existing political system.

12 Middle Eastern Nationalism Yesterday and Today

Early in the nineteenth century, there began in the Middle East a change from one system of social thought to another. The old system started from the idea that there is some principle which stands above the state and society, guiding and judging the life of society and the actions of governments; it found this principle in the teachings of a revealed religion, Islam. The new system also believed that a principle existed, but it thought it could be found by human reason. From this idea it derived a programme of action which could, in some circumstances, be one of revolution: if the institutions of society are not what reason says they should be, men are not obliged to obey them; rather, they should replace them by others more rational and remake the social world in the light of their image of perfection.

This is the obvious way of describing the change, but in fact it has gone deeper. In the Middle East as elsewhere, men's minds have moved not only from the idea that the principles of social action are religious to the idea that they are rational, but also from the idea that there *are* such principles, standing above society, to the idea that society is its own judge and master, that the principles by which it should live are generated within itself and change as it changes, and that its own interest is the supreme principle.

To put it crudely, the first change—the formation of the idea that there are eternal truths about society to be discovered by reason—was the work of the eighteenth century. The second was the work of the nineteenth, and was the product of many factors: the desire of thinkers to 'close the revolutionary age,' to find a principle which would justify necessary change without establishing the tyranny of abstract ideas; the philosophy of Hegel and the great sciences and half-sciences to which it gave an impetus—

historiography, mythology, anthropology, sociology; the exploration of the world, revealing the variety of human beliefs and practices; the study of geology and biology; the effect of such changes on religious beliefs—the growth of a discipline of biblical criticism, the emergence of doubts about whether revelation could be literally accepted in the light of what science was thought to say about the origin and development of the world.

From such sources came the characteristic idea, almost the religion, of the nineteenth century—the belief in cosmic process or activity. The essence of the universe was thought to be change or process; this change tended in a certain direction—from less to more complex forms, unconsciousness to full self-consciousness, the externally determined to the self-determined—and it contained within itself its own efficient and final causes, was moved by an inner force towards a goal which was not beyond itself but its own highest stage. This belief could form the basis of a conservative theory of politics and society, and such indeed was its appeal to those who feared above all the revolutionary spirit released into the world in 1789. But it could also carry with it a programme of revolutionary action, and inspire men to destroy those institutions which no longer expressed the spirit of the age and to replace them by others, in the conviction that they were helping the forward movement of the universe.

In Europe and America, of course, such ideas did not arise suddenly or erupt into a stable society organised on different principles. They came as companions to a vast social change which was already taking place, the growth of industry and the city. But when they first came to the Middle East it was to a society not yet touched by the change and sheltered by a different system of thought. At the beginning of the nineteenth century, those in the Middle East who thought about society and government believed for the most part in the primacy of revelation—in the existence of an ideal system of social morality derived from Islam. During the first Islamic centuries most Muslims had accepted the authority of the caliph, the successor of Muhammad, not indeed as prophet but as ruler of the Muslim community, holding temporal authority with a religious sanction and ruling in accordance with revealed law. But Islam too had had its revolutionary age; the authority of the caliph had weakened, the political unity of Islam had broken up, and orthodox beliefs and laws had been put in question by new ideas. This age had ended with the growth of a new social and political system. The Mamluk state of Egypt and Syria and its successor the Ottoman Empire were very different from the caliphate of earlier days. They were based on force and the solidarity of a professional or ethnic group—in the Mamluk state a group of military freedmen from the Caucasus, in the Ottoman state a military and official class, of Turkish language but, in the great days, largely of slave origin.

The older political theories of Islam had grown up around the institution of the caliphate, but with these new states came a new type of thought. From the revolutionary age, later Muslim thinkers derived a lasting horror of chaos. Anarchy and disorder must be avoided to preserve the fabric of Islamic society. All governments should therefore be obeyed, but that did not mean that all were alike. Some of them were just. But what did it mean to be a just government? Those who thought seriously about it knew that the universal caliphate of earlier times had ended. But something else remained, the *shari'a*, the system of social morality and law derived by rational process from the Qur'an and the traditions of what Muhammad and his companions had done and said; and it was by their attitude towards the *shari'a* that governments could be regarded as just or unjust. If the ruler upheld it, did nothing which went clearly against it, respected and consulted the *'ulama,* the men learned in religious sciences and law, his rule was just, no matter how it had begun, and Muslims should obey and cooperate actively with it. But if the ruler were unjust the devout should show their disapproval, by exhortation or silent withdrawal, although not so as to disturb the public peace.

Behind this doctrine lay a belief in an invisible order which would reverse the injustices of the world. By the eighteenth century most devout Muslims belonged to one or other of the brotherhoods of mystics, and the mystics believed in the existence of an invisible hierarchy of saints by whose intercession with God the order of the world was maintained. This belief in an invisible order of perfection might be interpreted in a revolutionary way, and there was in popular Islamic thought a revolutionary strain—the belief in a *mahdi,* a man sent by God to overturn the kingdoms of the world and open the final age of peace and justice. But in spite of occasional outbursts the political influence of the orders of mystics was in the direction of quietism and patient acceptance rather than revolt.

This was so because, while Muslims might disapprove of

specific acts of Ottoman rulers, and even depose one sultan and replace him by another, they did not doubt that the Ottoman state was a just Islamic state. The sultans respected and consulted the *'ulama,* supported the courts where Islamic law was dispensed, organised the pilgrimage to the Holy Cities, protected the more orthodox of the orders of mystics. Under the sultans, the adherents of other religions, the Christians of various kinds and the Jews, had religious freedom under their own spiritual heads and a civil position which was usually bearable and sometimes favoured. There was thus a certain harmony between the political system and the prevailing political ideas. This left no room for new ideas to penetrate from Europe.

These ideas did not begin to have influence until there took place a change in the position of the Ottoman Empire: its growing weakness in face of Europe's growing strength. That the Empire could not defend itself against the forces of a European power was shown during the Russo-Turkish war of 1768-74, when a Russo-Greek fleet sailed the eastern Mediterranean and carried out landings in Greece and at Beirut. A generation later a French force occupied Egypt at the heart of the Muslim world and was dislodged only with the help of another European power. A generation later still the Greek subjects of the sultan revolted and, with the support of Europe, a Greek national state was established. Other subject peoples were encouraged by this to hope that what the Greeks had done they could do too, and the Ottoman government saw that, if it were to prevent this, it must reform itself. During the next century a not unsuccessful attempt at reform was made. A new army and administration were created; a new system of laws, derived from those of Europe, was set up beside the *shari'a* and implicit in it was a new principle—that all citizens, whether they were Muslims or not, had equal rights and were full members of the political community.

To administer the new laws and institutions a new class had to be created—of officials, officers and technicians. In Istanbul and in two Arab provincial centres, Cairo and Tunis, where practically autonomous governments carried out a similar policy, professional schools were set up and students were also sent to Europe to study. From those who acquired a European education there sprang the first groups of modern thinkers, Turks and Arabs, in the generation which flourished roughly from 1830 to 1870. A little apart from them stood another group, Arabic-speaking Christians of Lebanon and Syria educated in French and American mission schools.

To some extent the purpose of all these groups was one: they wanted to explain why Europe was strong and the East was weak. They tended to give the same explanation—one cast in terms of modern science and invention but also of moral factors, of the political freedom and justice which Englishmen, Frenchmen and Americans enjoyed. But when they asked how the Middle East could become strong a certain difference appeared. The older thinkers were at heart Islamic conservatives and thought that the necessary reforms could be introduced from above by benevolent autocracy; but a little later there began a call for constitutional rule, and a short-lived constitution was granted in Tunisia in 1864 and an Ottoman constitution in 1876. There was a difference also between the Muslim thinkers and the Lebanese Christians. Christian writers tended to support secularisation but Muslims on the whole did not; their aim was rather to show that the characteristic institutions of modern Europe—democratic government, patriotic loyalty, legal reform—were permitted by Islam, if only Islam were rightly understood.

The writers of this age thought of liberal Europe as an ally in the work of reform, but soon a time came when they had also to think of her as a danger. In the next generation, stretching roughly from 1870 to 1900, the position of the Ottoman countries grew worse. In the eastern crisis of the 1870s the centre of the Empire was threatened by European power; at the fringes, France occupied Tunisia in 1881, Britain occupied Egypt the next year, the Russians advanced in central Asia. First the Bulgarians and then the Armenians revolted in the hope that Europe would intervene to help them, and the Bulgarians at least succeeded. Such events gave strength to the desire for reform.

By now there was a new generation of thinkers more European in their culture, and among them two new intellectual movements arose. The Young Turks, and those Arabs who thought like them, believed that what the Empire needed was political change: a revival of the constitution, the spread of real equality and Ottoman patriotism. But there were others who maintained that political reform by itself would do nothing, and what alone could save the Empire and the Muslim peoples was Islam itself. To some extent those who talked of Islamic revival and Pan-Islam were really talking about politics, and wanted to create a political movement of defence against the advance of Europe. But a few of them meant something different: a real revival of Islam as a religious system.

Here we come on a strange figure, that of Jamal al-Din al-Afghani, who in a life of incessant movement and activity left a deep mark on the Muslims of his generation. In his political activity, his calls for unity against British aggression, he may seem like a modern nationalist, but there is something also which recalls an older type of political action. He was not a democrat or constitutionalist on principle; what he wanted was rather the typical Islamic combination of a religious reformer and a strong ruler. He was modern, however, in his thought about the direction of reform. Muslims should become part of the modern world, and the modern world had two bases, reason and worldly activity aiming at progress. In his view these were of the essence of the true Islam, which taught the primacy of reason and the duty of activity in pursuit of the goods of this world and the next. By returning to the truth of their religion Muslims would acquire the sources of strength in the modern world.

Such ideas were given a serious theological basis by his disciples: Muhammad 'Abduh and the Syrian Rashid Rida in Egypt, and others in other countries. Their work was intended to convince Muslims with a modern education that they could still be Muslims, and to save them from having to live in two worlds at once, one derived from the principles of Islam and the other from those of European thought. In some ways they changed the emphasis of Jamal al-Din's thought. Thus his idea that Islam meant activity was developed into a criticism of the mystical orders as causes of intellectual sloth and political quietism. More than a century earlier there had been a violent movement of protest against mysticism and return to the early faith—the Wahhabi movement in Arabia, which exerted continuing influence.

But the weakening of the hold of the brotherhoods may have helped to weaken the link between the educated class and the people. Such thinkers as 'Abduh tried also to define the role of reason in religious law and the changes which should be made to adapt the *shari'a* to the needs of modern life. Their aim was to create a modern unified *shari'a* and prevent the growth of a gap between two parts of social life, one where religious law ruled and one where secular law ruled. But here again their work had an unforeseen effect. By reducing the dogmas of Islam to a simple system they also reduced the difference between Islam and other religions, or even between Islam and the high-minded agnosticism of Victorian Europe; and by justifying the idea of legal and social change, without being able to provide principles clear enough to control the change, they opened the way to new and more effective principles drawn from the advanced thought of Europe.

II

This was the way taken by thinkers of the next generation which came to maturity in the years after 1900: Egyptians like Ahmad Lutfi al-Sayyid, Turks like Ziya Gökalp. They were Muslims—in education to some extent, and certainly in tradition, feeling and intention. The Egyptian group at least would have called themselves disciples of 'Abduh and said that their aim was his: to reform Muslim society in accordance with the true spirit of Islam. But they had had a different education and had a wider grasp of European thought, and they lived in an age when the inexorable development of law, of administration and of economic life was bringing about a *de facto* separation of the religious and secular spheres. What they thought they were doing was to take the principles of the true Islam as they conceived it and apply them to the problems of society—to improving the position of women, reforming the schools, laying the foundations of democratic government and creating national industries. But the basis of their thought had changed, whether they quite knew it or not. When they talked of the rights of women or the importance of democracy they could point to verses of the Qur'an or traditions of the prophet which justified the changes they suggested, but that was not the reason why they suggested them. They had all been influenced by the European idea that there is a sphere of religion and a sphere of secular life, and the principles they appealed to for the reform of secular life were human, rational ones—individual rights, civilisation, social utility.

Among the principles which they appealed to were those of national unity and independence. They did not, of course, invent nationalism; as soon as Middle Eastern statesmen and thinkers began to ask what was the secret of Europe's power, they noticed the national unity of European states and the strength of national loyalties, and this factor became ever more important in their minds as the Balkan Christian subjects of the Empire obtained their national independence. But the idea did not become an important political force in the Muslim parts of the Empire until the first part of this century, with the rise of Egyptian opposition to British rule and Persian opposition to Russian influence, the growing division between Turks and Arabs after the Young Turk revolution of 1908, the collapse of the Ottoman Empire after World War I, the emergence from its ruins of the independent state of Turkey, the establishment of British and French mandatory rule in the former Arab provinces, and the increase of Zionist immigration into Palestine.

Since the idea of nationalism came in from outside it was not always clear what it meant. In the years between 1900 and 1940 there were two different types of national idea (which could, however, live together in any particular national movement). On one side stood the nationalism which was linked with a specific piece of land, and on the other that which was linked with a group possessing some kind of cultural, ethnic or racial unity. In general, the Persian, Turkish, Egyptian and Lebanese nationalisms of this period belonged to the first type, Arab nationalism to the second. But to say this is to simplify too much. It was only slowly that modern Turkish nationalism emerged from a movement of the second type, Pan-Turanism; and by 1940 Egyptian territorial patriotism was changing into Arab ethnic nationalism. Arab nationalism itself took its present form only gradually. Behind it, in the nineteenth century, lay a 'Syrian' patriotic movement of the first type, and signs of this still existed in the 1930s. Few of the Arab nationalist writers of the time would have included in the Arab nation all who spoke Arabic—Egyptians, Sudanese, North Africans; with some exceptions, they identified the Arab nation with a specific territory—Syria in the geographical sense, Iraq and the Arabian peninsula.

Modern nationalism enshrines a secular principle, but in this generation the nationalism of the Middle East was not wholly secular. To evoke a distant past is a way of revolting against the immediate past, and in most nationalist movements there was a tendency to go back beyond Islam to an earlier period: Turks looked back to the Hittites, Egyptians to the Pharaohs, Lebanese to the Phoenicians. But for the most part this was a passing phase. Even the violent secularism of Turkey in the time of Atatürk did not dissolve the link between the Turkish nation and Islam, and to be a Turk still meant to be a Muslim. In the apparently stable countries like Turkey, Egypt and Iran, based on territorial patriotism, there was a submerged religious feeling not coterminous with the nation, which could emerge at moments of crisis. In Turkey in the 1950s there was a burst of revolutionary activity expressing itself through a religious order, the Tijaniyya; and in Egypt there grew up a religious movement, the Muslim Brotherhood, which, although not anti-nationalist, maintained that beyond an Egyptian's duty to Egypt there lay his allegiance to Islam and his loyalty to the Muslim people.

The position of Arab nationalism was more complicated. The tendency to secularism was strong, all the more so because Arab Christians had played a part in the formation of modern ideas. They laid their emphasis on such factors as language, which united them with their Muslim neighbours; and Muslim Arab nationalists too wanted a national idea which could include the Christians. But the religious foundation of Arab nationalism was strong. The sense of the past which lies at the heart of any national movement could not, among the Arabs, be anything but a sense of the Islamic past. Few Arab Muslims would have made a separation between religion and nation so complete as that made by Atatürk, and even Arab Christians who became Arab nationalists often did so through identifying themselves with the Islamic past, in the sense that Islam was what the Arabs had done in history. By no means all Arabic-speaking Christians took this path, however. The Islamic basis of Arab nationalism made many of them uneasy, and led them to try to create a separate Lebanese state where Christians would not have to make the compromises all minorities must make.

In another sense, too, the nationalism of this period was not completely secular. In the Middle East as in Europe, it had grown in a certain intellectual soil, as one of a number of ideas closely linked with each other. For most thinkers of the time, national independence was not the final aim; the nation was the servant of something universal. They might express it in different ways. Rashid Rida justified his nationalism in religious terms—an Arab revival was necessary for an Islamic revival; Atatürk would not have used such words, but he, too, saw Turkish independence as a step towards something else—the creation in Turkey of a modern civilisation based on rational principles. The nationalist movements of this time had a content derived for the most part from the thought of liberal Europe: to be a nationalist meant to believe in constitutional government, universal education, the rights of women and intellectual freedom. At the heart of the national idea there lay an idea of individual virtue, as the foundation of the strength of states and the final cause of their existence.

III

The years before 1939 seem in retrospect to belong to a different age of history. This is not only because of the end of European domination of the world, although that by itself would be important enough to mark the passing of an age. There are other changes which have taken place all over the world, and which are themselves in a sense the final product of European power. They can be described in many ways. We can point, for example, to the growth of population and of the industrial city, with its problems of people living close together and far from their roots; to the growth also of the educated population, claiming to take an active part in the political process and open to the power of abstract ideas; to the acquisition by Middle Eastern states of real independence. Independence has often led to instability, and that for various reasons: because of the absence of a political tradition, which encourages the army to take power as the only force standing above sectional interests; because, once independence is achieved, the relations of social forces with each other and with the government have to be redefined; because of the absence of the restraining and stabilising power of an imperial government; and, in some Arab countries, because of a discrepancy between the frontiers of the state and those of the dominant national idea.

All this needs no further explanation, but what deserves analysis is the growth of a new type of political and social thought relevant to such problems of the new age. Its characteristic problem is no longer that of the difference between 'East' and 'West'. The 'West' may be thought of as technically more advanced, or as a political danger, but it is no longer thought of as having a 'secret' which Asians and Africans must learn if they are to make progress; our new concepts of 'developed' and 'developing' peoples are different from the older concepts of 'East' and 'West.' 'progressive' and 'stagnant', 'civilised' and 'barbaric'. The tension between tradition and modernity, which underlay the thought of 'Abduh and his disciples, has either disappeared from the mind of educated men or changed its form. They may be conscious of their own national or religious tradition, anxious to preserve its culture or its social forms or what they regard as its private virtues; but they would not regard it as able to teach them how to organise a government or an army, an industry or a school. The idea of a specifically Islamic government is put forward more rarely. There have been and still are Islamic political movements, from the Pan-Islamic movement of the nineteenth century to its successors today; but in practice they are modern not traditional movements, and their aim is not so much to restore the rule of virtue and religion as to mobilise feeling in order to defend or achieve a position of power. In our days we have seen an attempt to create an Islamic republic in Pakistan, but it has been no easier there than elsewhere to establish a form of government based on Islam and capable of meeting the needs of modern life.

The idea of a specifically Islamic society, moreover, seems to have lost its hold on many educated people. They are no longer conscious of a tension between how modern thought says they should live and how the *shari'a* says they should live. The hold of the *shari'a* over society has grown weaker. Already in the nineteenth and early twentieth centuries new civil, criminal and commercial codes were introduced in Egypt, the Ottoman Empire, British India and elsewhere, and the hold of the *shari'a* was confined to matters of personal status. In the last generation there have been inroads even in this sphere. Turkey abolished the Muslim law of personal status in the 1920s; Tunisia forbade polygamy a few years ago; Egypt has absorbed the religious courts into the general legal system. (But the change should not be exaggerated. There is a distinction in Muslim jurisprudence between acts of worship and social acts, and no government, however strong, could introduce changes in the first without meeting strong opposition. This was shown in 1960 when the Tunisian Government tried to discourage Muslims from fasting during Ramadan. The fast is one of the essential acts of devotion, and one in which the Muslim world becomes conscious of its unity and its links with the past, and the government's action aroused much criticism.)

In these states and societies in the process of modernisation, the universal language is that of nationalism. But nationalism is not by itself a system of principles by which a state or a society can be organised; for that it must depend on the other ideas it can attract and absorb. Here too there has been a change in the last 20 years. When a man in the Middle East says he is a nationalist today he does not necessarily mean, as he would probably have done a generation ago, that he believes in constitutional government and the rights of individuals. Not that he would positively disbelieve in them, but his attention has shifted to other aims which he would regard as more urgent. He might well describe them in terms of 'socialism', 'neutralism' and 'unity', and know more or less clearly what he meant by them. By 'socialism' (or some other term roughly equivalent to it) he would mean the extension of schools and social services, reform of land ownership, and the rapid development of industry under control of the government—for only the government, with its authority and its access to foreign capital, could industrialise the country as quickly as he wishes.[6] By 'neutralism' he would mean, essentially, that he would not wish his country, having achieved independence, to fall into a new sort of political or economic dependence; neutralism is an expression of the difference between the ways in which a weak state and a great power look at the world. By 'unity' an Arab would mean not simply that a number of states if united would be stronger than any one of them by itself (which is indeed a doubtful proposition). He would be talking not about strength but about legitimacy: he would not regard the state as having an unconditional claim upon him unless it could call itself an Arab state.

Until a few years ago, most Middle Eastern countries were the scene of a deep conflict between these ideas and another, older conception of nationalism: monarchic and hierarchic in political views, pro-Western in foreign policy, more cautious and traditional in social matters, more individualist in economic policy. Egypt, Syria, Iraq, Yemen, Sudan, Tunisia and Algeria have each had a national revolution, and although many changes may be expected it seems unlikely that any of them will return to the old political system. In Jordan, Saudi Arabia and the smaller states of the Arabian peninsula the conflict continues, but it seems probable that it will end in the same way. In Israel and Turkey, faced with rather different problems, the ruling elements have each in their own way achieved a certain underlying unity, based on overriding common interests, the pressure of an enemy on the frontier, and the existence of a common concept of society. In Lebanon, a deep division between different parts of the population, in regard to relations with the West and to the internal structure of the country, is precariously bridged by a general will that the state should survive as an independent country, and by reluctance to push differences to the point where another civil war like that of 1958 might break out.

There remain Iran and Morocco, where the conflict is still raging and it is difficult to see how it will end. In both countries, the monarchs have shown some skill in keeping control of the government and leadership of part of the nationalist forces; but they have paid the price of being drawn into the heart of the conflict, so that any movement against the régime shakes the throne and the structure of the state.

Beneath the surface there are grave weaknesses in the Middle Eastern bodies politic. The new content of nationalism provides a programme of action but not a moral ideal by which actions can be judged—an ideal of political virtue and its concomitant, an idea of individual rights. Partly this is due to the new and necessary emphasis on social and economic development. When it organises a large part of economic life and wants to bring about very rapid economic change, the government is apt to regard the individual as a statistical unit and all forms of private association as obstacles to its plans. In an age of planning, there is a danger that the state will come to control everything, and the need is great for some principle on which individual rights can be securely based, or for some institution which can defend them. This can scarcely be found in the Middle East today, partly because of the decline in the influence of the *shari'a*, but also because of the absence of stable political institutions; for in an age which on the whole is not one of fervent, unquestioned religious faith, a system of old, tried, accepted institutions, of ways in which power is exercised and limited, is a school of political virtue and a shield for the individual.

There is another danger which in the end may be even greater. While there is broad agreement within a large section of the ruling and educated class, there is also perhaps a greater gap between them and the mass of the people than once there was—a gap in power and in education. In most countries of the Middle East, although in some more than others, there is growing up a new ruling élite isolated by power and education from the mass of the people. The movement of economic and social development, in its first stage at least, may strengthen the position of this limited class; it may improve their standard of living faster than that of the people, and will certainly give them a vast power over the life of society. For their part, the mass of the people may find in the policy and nationalist ideas of this class neither a real profit nor an ideal which satisfies the human desire for justice. If this happens, there may rise to the surface a new type of revolutionary spirit; there were signs of it in Iraq after the *coup d'état* of 1958. Up to a point this new spirit may find old channels of expression. The idea of the Muslim community is still alive in the popular mind; the mystical orders are still alive, although not among the educated; and inherent in this popular Islam is an ideal of revolutionary justice and of human virtue. To some extent the new revolutionary governments try to appeal to this religious spirit and its ideals, and if they do so it is not only for purposes of propaganda but because of something still present in the minds of the rulers; but it is not certain that the kind of secular nationalist programme which they offer will in the long run keep the allegiance of the masses.

Marxism, too, has its idea of revolutionary justice, of the nation and the state. Among the educated class Marxist ideas have had some success in the last few years. It is difficult to say how much, because to a great extent the process takes place underground; so far as open manifestations are concerned, Marxism seems to have spread mainly in the diluted form which has become part of the semi-official ideology of Egypt and other countries. This is compatible with nationalism and indeed gives it part of its present content. But between a full Marxist system and the new nationalist system of ideas there is conflict not only on principles but in regard to policy. This was seen in the Algerian war; it has been seen in Iraq in the last few years in regard to land reform and Kurdish policy. Wherever Marxism and nationalism have been in conflict, so far it is the latter which has proved to be the more successful. But its victory is fragile at best. In Iraq the balance of forces is still precarious; in Iran, should the present régime be overthrown, it is not certain that the nationalist groups would be able to lead and control the forces which revolution would unleash. Even in countries where the present régime seems strong, it may be we have not seen the end of the matter.

13 'The Arab Awakening Forty Years After'

George Antonius was born in 1891 of Lebanese Christian parents who had settled in Alexandria. He studied at Victoria College, the English school in Alexandria, and then at King's College, Cambridge, where he obtained first-class honours in the Mechanical Sciences Tripos. After working during World War I in the censorship department of the Egyptian Expeditionary Force, he served in the British Mandatory Administration in Palestine, in the Education Department, 1921-7 and the Secretariat, 1927-30. He then left official service and began a new career as Middle Eastern associate of the Institute of Current World Affairs, an American organisation of which the aim was to spread understanding of what was happening in the outside world by the circulation to subscribers of confidential newsletters; it had been founded by Charles Crane, a Chicago business man who had himself played some part in the Middle East as a member of the King-Crane Commission, sent to the region by President Wilson in 1919. In 1938 he published his only book, *The Arab Awakening: the Story of the Arab Nationalist Movement,* and dedicated it to Mr Crane. He died in 1942.[1]

Why, it may be asked, should a book published forty years ago, and dealing with an early phase in the history of a national movement which has taken more than one new direction since then be taken seriously enough for a study to be devoted to it? There must be some intrinsic merit or significance in it to make it still deserving of serious study and consideration. In answer to such a question, at least three claims may be made for the book without much fear of contradiction.

First of all, most readers would agree that *The Arab Awakening* has literary merit of a high order. It is written in an excellent narrative style, precise, vivid, highly coloured, at times moving, carrying the reader easily and swiftly from one episode to another, and compelling belief as he reads it, even if some doubts may come later; its explanations are clear even if not always profound or sufficient. There is no extended analysis of ideas, but there are sharply expressed depictions of human personalities. Here is what he says of Mark Sykes:

> His mind was both perceptive and quick, and at the same time strangely inattentive and undiscerning; and, in his nature, he had something of the improvidence as well as all the warmth of the enthusiast. He knew a good deal about the Arabs at first hand, but his knowledge was as remarkable for its gaps as for its range, and his judgments alternated between perspicacity and incomprehension, as though his mental vision were patterned like a chessboard . . . This placed him at a disadvantage in the game of diplomatic bargaining . . .[2]

Here again is his memory of King Husayn in old age:

> . . . ill at ease, in an armchair far too large for his small frame, shrunken with paralysis, his beautiful face blanched by the pallor of death, his eyes suddenly glowing from the vacancy of resignation to flashes of controlled passion . . . his mind seemed less flexible and the mannerisms of expression which were a feature of his conversation obtruded themselves with greater frequency, as though habit had begun to steal upon reasoning. His old craving for justification had become an obsession.[3]

His judgement of T.E. Lawrence, once more, is perceptive:

> . . . that very inconsistency which pervades his revelations and causes him to appear unreal, now as a man of vision and then as a victim of self-delusion, alternating between candour and affectation . . . There are errors and misfits in [his book], which cannot be disposed of as mere lapses or defects of knowledge or memory and point rather to some constant psychological peculiarities. It seems as though Lawrence, with his aptitude to see life as a succession of images, had felt the need to connect and rationalise his experiences into a pattern; and in doing so had allowed sensations to impinge upon facts.[4]

This was indeed almost the first attempt to break away from the picture of Lawrence propagated by his friends on the basis of what he had himself told them, and at that time generally accepted almost as an article of faith. Antonius was taken to task by at least one of Lawrence's friends; since then, others have tried to answer the questions he posed—Richard Aldington, Sulayman Musa, John Mack[5]—but we still lack what Antonius suggested that we needed, a study of *Seven Pillars of Wisdom* as a work of the imagination in which events are transmuted into myths.

It cannot, secondly, be doubted that the book had a great impact at the time when it appeared. It came out near the end of 'Britain's moment in the Middle East',[6] that strange interlude in Middle Eastern history, when the region was not, as it had for so long been and was to become again, the point where the interests of all the Great Powers met in concert or in rivalry, but was under the effective domination of one of them. Russia, Germany and Austria-Hungary had collapsed or withdrawn at the end of World War I, the United States was not yet involved in more than a marginal way. France was, indeed, present in the Middle East, but as a nation weakened both politically and economically by the War and its aftermath. Final power over most of the area lay with Great Britain, but that power was now being challenged, by the growth of German and Italian influence, by the emergence of nationalist movements, in Egypt, Iran and the Arab countries of Asia, and by the posing of questions, inside England itself, about the legitimacy of rule over other nations. To these questions a certain answer was being given, that it was possible to respond to the challenge of nationalism and give a moral basis to the retention of final power, by establishing a new relationship with the peoples ruled by Great Britain, and one which offered them the ultimate prospect of independence: Ireland had been given independence, within certain limits, in 1921; the Government of India Act of 1935 had provided for a certain transfer of responsibility from British to Indians; the Anglo-Iraqi Treaty of 1930, and the Anglo-Egyptian Treaty of 1936, had also led to such a transfer, although within limits imposed by a continuing British presence. On the other hand, there had now appeared another problem which could not easily be resolved in this way. Jewish immigration into Palestine, under the pressure of events in Europe, had aroused among Palestinian Arabs a mass reaction, of an order different from the political opposition to foreign rule in Syria or Iraq; Jews all over the world and Arabs in the countries surrounding Palestine were being drawn into the conflict, which threatened to have repercussions upon British interests and policies all over the world. The report of the Royal Commission, proposing the partition of Palestine, had been published, accepted in principle by the British government, and then virtually abandoned because of the difficulties of carrying it out, and Great Britain seemed to be moving towards another kind of solution.

It was in this context that Antonius's book appeared. It was written quickly and urgently, and was indeed a shortened and altered version of another book he had intended to write, a detailed historical study of the origins and early development of the Arab movement; and it was written for a particular audience at a particular moment in time. The readers to whom it was addressed were primarily British, politicians, diplomats, officials, journalists and scholars, members of the élite of a few thousand people who were seriously concerned about imperial policy and in a position to exercise some influence upon decisions. It provided them with historical information, and with an explanation of political attitudes; it gave the clearest exposition which had ever been given of the Arab fears in regard to Palestine (Antonius had given evidence to the Royal Commission when it was in Palestine in 1937, and had deeply impressed members of it). It strengthened the sense, which by now was widespread among British officials, that some serious errors of policy had been made, but at the same time appeased it by suggesting a way out.

There is no doubt that it had a great and immediate influence. Documents studied recently by Elie Kedourie bear witness to its influence among civil servants, although by no means all of them accepted its version of events. When the 'Round Table Conference' was held at St James's Palace in 1939, Antonius was chosen as Secretary-General of the Arab delegations, apparently at the suggestion of the British Government.[7] He played an important part in drafting documents submitted by the Arab delegations to the conference, and a dominant one in the committee set up to consider the meaning of the various letters exchanged and agreements made during World War I; it was largely because of his advocacy that the British members of the committee admitted that there was more force to the Arab contentions than had appeared hitherto, an expression which came as near as any great government does to agreeing that it had been mistaken.[8] During World War II, before his early death, he continued to have some influence on British officials in the Middle East, and here again his persuasive tongue and pen seem to have helped to incline them to the belief that some kind of Arab unity, and some concessions to the Arabs in regard to Palestine, would be in harmony with British interests.

Thirdly, there is no doubt that *The Arab Awakening* has had a great influence (although not everyone, as we shall see, would think it a good one) on academic studies of the modern Middle East, in both England and the United States. It stands in fact near the beginning of the development of these studies. Before Antonius and a few others of his generation wrote, those who wished to know about the modern history of the Middle East did not have much to rely on. There were books by travellers and memoirs of former officials, studies of the 'eastern question' and of colonial policy. The former tended to be superficial or partial, the latter might be more solid but had a certain limitation which by then was becoming apparent. Writers on the 'eastern question' studied the relations of the European Powers with each other, within a framework of generally accepted conventions about the ways in which those relations should be carried on, and in regard to the problems posed by the weakness of the great Islamic states of early modern times, Morocco, Iran and the Ottoman Empire. They tended to look on those states as passive bodies over which the Powers argued, quarrelled and agreed, not as active parties, however weak, in the process; it is only in recent years that such work as that of Thomas Naff and Allan Cunningham has begun to change this view.[9] Books on colonial policy tended to base themselves on the writings of officials or the archives of colonial governments, and to accept that what happened was what governments or officials thought was happening or wanted to happen. Once again, it is only in recent years that a view of British rule derived from Lord Cromer's apologia in his *Modern Egypt* has been modified by such work as that of Afaf Lutfi al-Sayyid, Alexander Schölch and Jacques Berque; the Egypt of the time can now be seen not as the matter on which Lord Cromer imposed form, but as one party in a relationship (even if it was one of unequal power) in which each party had its own motives and direction of change.[10]

Seen in retrospect, *The Arab Awakening* was one of two books published in the period between the two wars which played an important part in preparing the way for such changes of view.

The other was Arnold Toynbee's *The Western Question in Greece and Turkey*,[11] a book less well-known than his later *Study of History,* but which contains in embryonic form some of the ideas later expounded there, about contacts between civilisations, and in particular about the relationship of unequal strength between Great Powers and small states or nationalist movements, and the nature of conflicts between powers which are fought out not directly but by means of client states and movements:

> ... the illusions of local nationalities have been utilised by the Western diplomats in order to save something from the wreck of their schemes ... Greeks and Turks can be swayed and stampeded by visions of 'The City', 'Ionia', 'The Abode of Felicity' or the Holy Sepulchres of Edirné ... a kind of 'Juggernaut' national personality can be conjured into existence and induced, by offerings attractive to its divinity, to drive over its worshippers' bodies. On the international chess-board such pieces make excellent pawns ... [But] the trap in which the victims have been caught in order to be exploited was not cunningly hidden. They rushed into it because they could not resist the bait ... They did not suspect how quickly pawns in distress become an embarrassment, or how little the players care if they disappear from the board.[12]

Implicit in statements like this is an understanding of the tragic nature of such relationships. Great powers are primarily concerned with their relations with other great powers; their clients must fit into this framework, but often forget this, and in doing so may draw their patrons into conflicts they do not desire, or find too late that their patrons abandon them at the moment of crisis, in order to avoid a conflict. In an age when the 'shadow of the West' falls across the whole world, and takes the shape of nationalist movements, this process may end by the disruption of ancient communities and the dissolution of ancient ties of neighbourliness. The episode which Toynbee studied in this book ended with the destruction of the Greek communities of Asia Minor: Greeks and Turks, who had lived together in city and countryside for centuries, faced each other as strangers and enemies.

Although Toynbee and Antonius knew each other, there is no evidence that Antonius had read *The Western Question* or been influenced by it, but his book points much the same moral. At the heart of it there lies a detailed account of the dealings of one Great Power with one nationalist movement, and it ends with a fear that, under the shadow of British policy, what had happened between Greeks and Turks in Asia Minor might happen between Arabs and Jews in Palestine.

Since *The Arab Awakening* was published, interest in the Middle East has grown, and has moved in a direction to which it is relevant. It has had a major impact on later scholars, and one might say that it is the point from which many of them have started. It is still used by students, and liked by many of them, and still present in the minds of later writers on the same range of subjects, most of whom find it necessary to define their areas of agreement and disagreement with it. Even if this were not true, it would still have played an important part in the growth of a certain field of study, and that is as much as can be said for most works of scholarship of a past generation. Since it *is* true, however, we must ask how far the book can be regarded as a permanent and valuable contribution to our knowledge of its subject. Some later writers have expressed serious doubts about this, and to some extent Antonius himself must be held responsible for this. His book is a slightly uneasy combination of two different kinds of writing. It is a work of historical narrative, but also of political advocacy. This is clear from the style, which moves from one register to another, and from the intrusion of moral judgements, sometimes strongly expressed. We are forced therefore at least to pose the question, to what extent his own political feelings and convictions determined his principles of selection and emphasis. Moreover, it is difficult to judge the depth and range of the documentation on which the book is based, because there is almost none of the apparatus of scholarship; there are few footnotes and no bibliography. This may be explained partly by the haste with which it was written, but also perhaps in another way: the book was not primarily addressed to scholars, but to the kind of reader who might have been put off by too great a display of learning. Antonius may have judged his readership well, for he was addressing himself to the kind of Englishman who, in that generation, might have had a certain cult of the amateur and a suspicion of anything which might appear to be 'showing off'.

Antonius's own correspondence makes it clear that the book was in fact based on wide reading. He had worked in the Public Record Office in London, at a time when the fifty years' rule was in force and documents were not available beyond the 1880s; he had been allowed to see some papers of the Foreign Office and the Committee of Imperial Defence; he had been given access to the private papers of D.G. Hogarth, Sir Gilbert Clayton and Sir Mark Sykes. In the United States he had seen documents in the State Department and some private papers, those of Colonel House and Professor Westermann.[13] The extent of his Arabic documentation is more difficult to judge. He certainly made use of newspapers, and of printed works containing documents, like Amin Sa'id's *al-Thawra al-'arabiyya al-kubra*,[14] and he appears to have had access to documents in the possession of the Hashimite family, some of which seem to have disappeared since then.[15] Above all, the book is based on many conversations and interviews with those who had taken an active part in the Arab movement.

Since he wrote, many more documents have become available. In particular, those in the Public Record Office are now open for the whole period with which the book deals, and have been studied by a number of later writers. In the course of time, too, concerns and convictions have changed, and no writer today perhaps would place the emphasis exactly where Antonius did. We must therefore ask at least two questions: how far have the documents now available shown that Antonius's narrative or interpretation is erroneous, and how far did his personal convictions lead him to distort the story, even within the limits of the materials which were available to him? These questions have clearly been present in the minds of such later writers as Elie Kedourie and Sylvia Haim, A.L. Tibawi, Z.N. Zeine and C.E. Dawn.[16] On the whole, they express considerable disagreement and disquiet. Some at least of these are justified, but it may be that certain parts of the book have greater and more lasting value than others.

The book falls into three parts, all rather different from each other in both matter and style. The first of them narrates the early development of the Arab nationalist movement down to the outbreak of war in 1914; the second studies in detail the relations between various Arab groups and the British government during the War and the subsequent period when questions raised during the War were being settled; and the third describes the development of the Arabian Peninsula, and of the successor states of the Ottoman Empire placed under British and French mandate, in the 1920s and 1930s.

Of these three parts, the first may have seemed to most readers to be the most valuable and original when it was first published. It provided information about some aspects of the modern history of the Middle East which, although not completely new, must have been unfamiliar to most English and American readers: for example, it was one of the first accounts in English of the Lebanese literary movement. In one respect at least it was almost wholly new: its description of the origins and nature of the Arab societies of the Young Turk period was based to a great extent on information given by former members of them, and it still appears to be substantially accurate so far as it goes, although Majid Khadduri and others have corrected it in detail.[17] When we pass from facts to explanations, however, a sharp criticism has been made, and with some reason, by Zeine, Dawn, Tibawi and others.

Such criticism is directed towards Antonius's view of the nature of Arab nationalism in that early period. It can best be approached by asking three kinds of question. First, who were the nationalists and why did they become nationalists? Antonius gives the impression that they were men of differing origins, Lebanese, Syrians and Iraqis, Muslims and Christians, who had one thing in common: they had been moved by the rediscovery of the Arabic language and its literature, and 'the contemplation of its beauty'[18] revived in them the consciousness of being Arabs, and gave birth to a resolve to recreate a society in which Arabs could live together and rule themselves. Once this seed had been planted, it had to grow in a certain way: a reform of the Ottoman Empire, of such a kind as to enable the Arabs to continue living in it, was impossible, for it was based on the idea of an 'unnatural alliance of Turks and Arabs'.[19]

Because the alliance of Turks and Arabs was in fact dissolved, we may easily assume that it had to be; but it was not so obvious at the time as Antonius implies. In fact, those who joined the societies before 1914, and who later emerged as members of the ruling élite of the Arab successor states of the Ottoman Empire, were men who on the whole came from a certain milieu, and who became nationalists gradually, reluctantly, and to some extent unconsciously. There were among them a few members of the new educated Christian class of Syria, Lebanon and Palestine, and a few members of the traditional Muslim learned class, in particular those who had been brought within the range of the ideas of 'Islamic modernism' put forward by Rashid Rida in his periodical *al-Manar*. For the most part, however, they were members in some sense of the Ottoman ruling élite; or, to be more precise, members of those great families in the cities of the Arab provinces who had a tradition of learning and social leadership, had always played a part in the Ottoman system of local government, and from the late nineteenth century were being drawn more fully into the Ottoman service as officers or civil servants.

C.E. Dawn has the credit of being the first scholar to draw attention to this fact. His thesis is that the rise of Arab nationalism in the years before 1914 can be explained in terms of an 'inter-élite conflict defined in terms of ideologies': the real conflict was not one of ideas, it was one of personal, family and factional rivalries, the purpose of which was to obtain or keep office or influence within the Ottoman system of government.[20] This is a good starting point, but it may be that Dawn's view needs to be further refined.

It is true, to begin with, that such families had always been linked with the Ottoman system of government. The failure to make this clear is indeed one of the most serious defects in Antonius's book. He missed the framework of institutions within which the Arab movement arose. At the time when he wrote, little work had been done in the Ottoman archives, and the dissolution of the Empire was still a recent memory, so that it was possible for Arabs, as for the peoples of the Balkans, to think of the Ottoman government as an alien despotism which had held its subject-peoples back until they broke away from it. It is common for nationalist movements to think of the immediate past with revulsion, and to appeal against it in the name of some more distant past, real or imagined. In the last generation, however, views have changed. Study of the Ottoman archives, both by western scholars and by the new school of Turkish historians, has thrown new light on the institutions of government; this has recently been described, so far as the classical period is concerned, in Halil Inalcik's book, *The Ottoman Empire: the Classical Age 1300-1600*.[21] More recently there have been some studies of the Arab provinces which take Ottoman documents into account, such as those of Raymond and Shaw for Egypt, and Rafeq, Cohen and Barbir for the Syrian provinces.[22] Such work makes it possible to look at Ottoman rule in Syria in a light different from the familiar one. The eighteenth century, which is usually regarded as a period when Ottoman power was seized by local despots, was one in which that power in fact was reasserted in a new way, by

'Ottoman governors with local roots'.[23] It was at this time that certain notable families in cities like Aleppo and Damascus consolidated their social power by means of their links with the Ottoman government: they held local offices or in other ways had access to the rulers, and were sensible of the prestige of Ottoman culture, whether expressed in the literature of the ruling élite or in the Hanafi legal code which was the code officially recognised by the government. In the nineteenth century, during the earlier period of Ottoman reform, the balance of local power between Ottoman governors and local notables moved for a time in favour of the second, but towards the end of the century it moved back in the other direction: the Ottoman policy of administrative centralisation began to succeed, and some of the local families began to send their sons to the professional schools in Istanbul and from there into the Ottoman army or civil service.

After the Young Turk revolution of 1908, new conflicts began to appear within such families, and in particular among those members of them who had taken service in army or administration, but it would be best not to take Dawn's view to extremes and think of these conflicts as being simply struggles for position or power, nor to accept Antonius's distinction between those who became Arab nationalists by passion and conviction (the 'suffering idealists',[24] as he calls them) and those who clung to the 'unnatural alliance between Turks and Arabs'. Intermingled with the struggles for position, there were genuine differences of opinion and conviction, but for the most part these were local forms of certain differences which existed throughout the Empire, and concerned the problem of what should be done if the Empire was to survive: there was a difference between those who wished it to remain an Islamic autocracy within the bounds of the *shari'a*, and those who wanted it to be a constitutional state on the western European model, and also between those who supported the Young Turk policy of centralisation and those who wanted a greater measure of decentralisation. A few individuals apart, the idea that the Arabs should break away from the Empire scarcely arose until two events brought it to the surface: the entry of the Empire into the War in 1914, at a moment when Arab-Turkish relations were strained; and the collapse of the Empire in 1918, which faced everyone, and in particular the members of the ruling élite, with an inescapable choice.

The second kind of question we need to ask concerns the ideas in terms of which these differences of opinion were expressed. In so far as they were expressed in 'Arab' terms, what exactly were they and where did they come from? Here again there is no doubt that Antonius gave too simple an answer. The Lebanese Christian literary movement was not a major factor. No strong line of descent can be traced from Nasif al-Yaziji and Butrus al-Bustani to the nationalists of the next generation; curiously enough, Antonius does not mention the one writer of this kind who can in some ways be considered a precursor, Ahmad Faris al-Shidyaq. Two other lines of thought were more important. One was a certain development of the 'Islamic modernism' of the Salafi school. Re-interpreting Islamic law in the light of what the 'pious elders' were believed to have done and said, it naturally laid more emphasis on the period of Arab domination in Islamic history. At some point the Islamic community had taken a wrong turning; this was connected with the ascendancy first of Persians and then of Turks in the Muslim world, and the conclusion was drawn that the centre of gravity must move back to the Arabs—the advocacy of an Arab caliphate was one aspect of this. Secondly, and perhaps more important, there were ideas picked up by Arab students in the professional schools of Istanbul or by officers and officials in Ottoman service: ideas which were the commonplaces of the Ottoman ruling élite, drawn from French books or German military instructors, and which were restated in an 'Arab' idiom by some students, officers and officials, perhaps under the stress of a sense of exclusion from the inner circle of the élite, which remained largely Turkish. (In the same way, at much the same time, Jews, Armenians and Turks in the Russian Empire, who had gone far enough on the road of assimilation to have absorbed the ideas of the Russian intelligensia, had restated these ideas in their own idiom as Zionism, Armenian nationalism and Pan-Turanism.)

Why was it, thirdly, that such ideas in their Arab form began to attract members of the ruling élite, and what difference did they make to their actions? Here once more it would be best to take a middle path between the explanation suggested by Antonius and a contrary opinion. Antonius seems to be saying that certain Arabs experienced a kind of sudden conversion, moved as they were by the beauty of their language and the memory of their ancestors. On the other hand, it is sometimes suggested that Arab nationalism was little more than a form of words, which indicated at most some changing fashion of the imagination, but did not serve as a guide to action: the reality behind it was either the desire of individuals to secure power and office, or the desire for political domination which, according to such formulations, is intrinsic to Islam, at least in its Sunni form.

A change of words and images must, however, be significant of something beyond itself. In all communities, there is a kind of rhetoric which is used at moments of high tension, as a spur to action. In stable communities it tends to express ancestral pieties; an example of this has been given by the sociologist Robert Bellah in his essay on 'The civil religion of America', in which he analyses the language used by Presidents in their inaugural addresses.[25] If this language changes, if it expresses the past in some different way or turns away from the past towards an imagined future, this may be a sign of some other kind of change: some fundamental, rapid and unexpected change in the social order, of such a kind that old beliefs, symbols and rituals can no longer serve as guides to social action. The point has been well expressed by Clifford Geertz:

> In politics firmly embedded in Edmund Burke's golden assemblage of 'ancient opinions and rules of life', the role of ideology is marginal. In such truly traditional political systems the participants act as ... men of untaught feelings ... which do not leave them 'hesitating in the moment of decision, sceptical, puzzled and unresolved' ... But when ... those hallowed opinions and rules of life come into question, the search for systematic ideological formulations flourishes. The function of ideology is to make an autonomous politics possible by providing the authoritative concepts that render it meaningful.[26]

Such changes were indeed taking place in Ottoman society in the late nineteenth century, and by the end of the century were having a deep effect on the life of the provinces and the minds of the educated class. Ottomans, whether Turkish or Arabic-speaking, found themselves living under a different system of administration and law; their wealth and social position were affected by changes in patterns of production and trade; faster communications gave them a different relationship with other parts of the Empire and with the outside world; new media of expression made it possible for ideas and news to be spread and discussed widely; and the shadow of European power lay over all of them. It is in this context that we should try to understand the significance of the new ideology of 'Arabism'. It had by no means driven out other ideologies, those of Ottomanism and Pan-Islamism, nor had it replaced, throughout society, something far older, the acceptance of the rule of a just Muslim sultan. That it was emerging and spreading at this time, however, indicates that for some at least of the Arabic-speaking Ottomans neither the traditional idea of authority nor the other ideologies could provide a guide to social action. The analysis of 'Arabism' as an ideology, with all that this implies, is missing from *The Arab Awakening,* but it is also missing from the work of most of its critics.

We come now to the second part of the book, which deals with World War I and the peace settlement after it. There is evidence here of wide reading of documents not generally available at the time it was written, and of information drawn from personal contacts. Antonius gives us a clear description of Arab participation in the Arabian and Syrian campaigns, and one of special interest to Middle Eastern historians because they can see in it almost the last example of a recurrent process in the history of the region, before modern technology changed the world. He shows us how a new dynasty emerged, springing as usual from an urban initiative. An urban family, that of the Hashimite Sharifs of Mecca, created around itself a combination of forces, partly by the formation of a small regular army but even more so by making alliances with rural leaders, and it was able to do this by providing both a leadership which could be regarded as standing above the different groups in the alliance, and an aim which could persuade them to rise above their divisions. The combined forces move along a line of communications linking a chain of oasis-settlements and market towns, towards a great city; but—and here is the difference from the traditional process—it fails at the moment of victory to establish its control over the city by allying its interests with those of the urban population, because circumstances have changed, the strength it has been using is not its own but borrowed from a more powerful patron which in the end has abandoned it.

There is, however, a point of weakness in the narrative. Antonius tends to ascribe to this fragile combination of forces around the leadership of the Hashimites a unity and solidity which it did not possess. The rural leaders, in particular those of pastoral groups, could not be subjected to discipline beyond a certain point,

The Arab Awakening Forty Years Later

and, what was more important, there were differences of conception and purpose between the two forces which composed the 'Arab movement' at that time: the nationalist societies, formed mainly of Syrians, with their centres of activity in Damascus and Cairo, and the Hashimite family whose power was rooted in the Hejaz. The relationship between them, and between each of them and the British authorities in Cairo and Khartoum, was shifting and unstable. It passed through at least three different stages. In the first year or so of the War, there was a concentration of Arab elements in the Ottoman army in Syria, and the British were thinking of a possible landing on the Syrian coast at Alexandretta; this explains the rather mysterious negotiations with the Arab Ottoman officer al-Faruqi, who claimed to speak on behalf of the nationalist societies but had also some contact with the Sharif Husayn, and the sense of urgency with which they were conducted by the British. Then, after the end of the Dardanelles campaign, there seemed to be a possibility of a Turco-German advance from Syria, westwards against the Suez Canal and southwards in western Arabia; in these circumstances, an agreement with the ruler of Mecca became more important for the British, and he for his part was afraid that such an advance would mean an extension of direct Ottoman control in the Hejaz. Finally, in 1917 and 1918, there came the successful British advance from Egypt into Palestine and Syria. The British needed to make decisions about the future of the conquered territory, and to achieve some kind of balance in their relations with all parties concerned, Hashimites, Syrians, Zionists and French; and tensions between Syrians and Hashimites, and even within the Hashimite family itself, began to come to the surface. Antonius must have been aware of all this, given his unusual contacts with all parties, but he tended to obscure it, partly because his main information came from the Hashimites, and partly perhaps because, throughout the book, his main emphasis was on the underlying unity of the Arab movement. A reader may be conscious here of some confusion between historical explanation and political advocacy. It should be said, however, that apart from C.E. Dawn,[27] other writers too have tended to underrate the importance and independence of the Syrian nationalists.

Together with the description of the campaign there went an analysis of the network of discussions and agreements which surrounded it. This shows a political sense which is rare among historians. Much modern history is written on the level of the higher civil service; Antonius himself had been a civil servant, but by temperament he was more of a politician, and understood how politicians think and make decisions. Although, for example, in the last part of the book he drew a contrast between what he regarded as the failure of French policy in Syria and the success of British policy in Iraq, he had a complete understanding of the reasons why French policy was as it was: the overriding concern to do nothing in the Middle East which might affect the French position in North Africa, and the sense of weakness which Frenchmen in the Middle East felt *vis à vis* the British, so that French policy was really a sequence of tactical replies to what appeared to be British threats to French interests.[28]

To take an even more striking example, Antonius gave perhaps the first cogent explanation of the reasons for which the British Government issued the Balfour Declaration of support for the establishment of a Jewish National Home in Palestine. It was issued, he suggests, primarily because the British Government and the Zionists found they had a common interest: the British wished to prevent any potential rival acquiring a position of power in Palestine, so close to the Suez Canal, while the Zionists wanted a powerful patron. They were thus able to reach an agreement, by which Great Britain would support the Zionist idea and the Zionists would ask for British protection.[29] Antonius's suggestion must have been more than a guess, it was surely based on documents to which he had access, interpreted by his fine sense of the way in which political negotiations take place. It has been in general confirmed by the most careful and judicious study made since the opening of the relevant British archives, that of Mayir Vereté in his article on 'The Balfour Declaration and its makers'.[30]

In other ways, however, his treatment of the war-time agreements has been exposed to much criticism. It is inevitable that much of what he says should be out-dated. He first provided some of the essential documents in an easily accessible form, but in the last decade or so many more have become available and been studied: by Sulayman Musa and A.L. Tibawi, by I. Friedman, J. Nevakivi and R. Adelson, and most recently by Elie Kedourie in his *In the Anglo-Arab Labyrinth*.[31] A vast construction of scholarship and argument now exists, and no attempt will be made to add to it. It is necessary, however, to ask where Antonius stands on the main points at issue, and whether his stand is a tenable one.

Antonius was concerned to make three essential points: in the Husayn-McMahon correspondence of 1914-15, the British Government gave certain undertakings to the Arab nationalists in order to induce them to revolt against the Ottoman government; in the Sykes-Picot Agreement of 1916, the British made concessions to the French which were incompatible with the undertakings given to the Arabs; in the Balfour Declaration of 1917, the British gave an undertaking to the Zionists which was no less incompatible with those given to the Arab nationalists.

Some later writers have denied all these claims. Elie Kedourie maintains that no undertakings were given to the Arabs, and that such hopes as they might have conceived on the basis of badly drafted letters were not incompatible with the precise undertakings given to France, undertakings which were in any case explained to the Sharif Husayn.[32] I. Friedman for his part claims that Palestine was never included in whatever pledges were given to the Arabs, and the Balfour Declaration was therefore compatible with those pledges.[33]

The evidence which they and others have produced, however, can be regarded as pointing in the direction of conclusions different from theirs. There seems no doubt that in the letters sent by McMahon, expressions were used which Husayn could legitimately regard as constituting pledges, and they were so used not because of bad draftsmanship, since in fact they were drafted by an official of high intelligence, Gilbert Clayton, and approved at every stage by the Foreign Office, but because they expressed British policy and intentions at that time. Once they were used, they were regarded by the British government as constituting binding engagements. Very few of those who studied the documents at that time had any doubt of this: that is true not only of comparatively junior officials like Arnold Toynbee and Harold Nicolson, but of the Foreign Secretary, Sir Edward Grey. It was stated forcefully by a later Foreign Secretary, Arthur Balfour, in his famous memorandum of August 1919, and by the Prime Minister, Lloyd George, in a conversation with Husayn's son Faysal in September of that year.[34]

If George Antonius is right on this, however, he appears to be on less safe ground when he maintains that the pledges given to the Arabs were incompatible with those given to the French. It seems clear now that the intention of the British government, when it made the Sykes-Picot agreement, was to reconcile the interests of France with the pledges given to the Sharif Husayn, and the agreement can be regarded as having reconciled them, if it is interpreted in a certain way, but not if it is interpreted in another. Once more, there is no question of inept draftsmanship; if the agreement was ambiguous, it was not because it was badly expressed, but because it was a war-time agreement. Such agreements were made in a hurry and under stress, and for an immediate purpose: not to decide what should happen once the War was ended, but to achieve the minimum of agreement without which campaigns could not be fought in common. In a difficult negotiation, when there is an urgent need to reach agreement, it is natural and legitimate to try to devise a formula which can be interpreted in more than one way, and to leave the question of which interpretation should prevail to be decided by the balance of strength when the war was over.

Ambiguous agreements secretly arrived at can cause difficulties for historians fifty years on, but still more at the time, for they do not end the discussion, they provide a new basis for it to be carried on. Each party sets himself to ensure that his interpretation should prevail, either by argument or by trying to obtain a position of power. It was not only British, French and Arabs who could interpret pledges and agreements in different ways. British officials seem to have given different interpretations when talking to the other parties, and such differences of interpretation may have reflected different views of policy. When talking to Husayn or the Syrian nationalists, there seems no doubt that British officials did all they could to persuade them that their government accepted the Arab interpretation. When Sir Mark Sykes met Husayn in May 1917, Professor Kedourie maintains that he gave Husayn full information about the Sykes-Picot agreement; but the evidence he produces appears to show that Husayn may only have been told of 'the principle of the agreement as regards an Arab confederation or state', and that he may have been encouraged to believe that even on the Syrian coast, where France was to be free, according to the Agreement, to set up any administration she wanted, she would in fact act as favourably to Arab aspirations as the British had recently proclaimed they would act in that part of Iraq where they too would be free to do as they wanted.[35] Similarly, in June 1918, the British High Commissioner in Egypt, Sir Reginald Wingate, told Husayn's agent in Cairo that the Sykes-Picot Agreement was 'merely a record of old conversations and of a provisional understanding'.³⁶ A little later, in November 1918, an Anglo-French declaration gave the most unequivocal support for Arab independence, and Antonius is surely right to lay stress upon it.³⁷ It is difficult, therefore, to blame the Arab nationalists for having been encouraged to believe that the Sykes-Picot Agreement meant one thing, only to discover after the War that the French meant by it something else. (In the same way, Sykes tried to reassure the Zionist leaders when he met them in February 1917; they seem to have had some kind of information about the recent Anglo-French Agreement and asked him whether the British Government had given any pledge to its allies in regard to Palestine. The Agreement in fact provided for an international administration of Palestine, but Sykes assured them that 'with great difficulty the British Government had managed to keep the question of Palestine open'.³⁸)

As for the third question, that of whether Palestine was excluded from the area in which the Arabs were given hopes of independence, the balance of the evidence seems to be that, at the time of the Husayn-McMahon letters, the British probably did extend to exclude Palestine, not for the absurd reason later advanced that it could be regarded as part of the area lying to the west of Damascus, Homs, Hama and Aleppo which could not be regarded as being wholly Arab, but on the ground that it was part of the area within which Britain was not 'free to act without detriment to the interests of her ally France'. That phrase was intended to apply specifically to the region west of the four Syrian cities, but it might have been intended to apply generally to Palestine as well.³⁹ It was a vague phrase of uncertain extension, and Husayn was willing to leave it as such, because he was aware of the complexity of international interests in Palestine, and because he needed British support against the French in Syria, and was willing as the price of such support to leave aside the question of Palestine, or to recognise Britain's special position there. The question of Zionism had not yet arisen, and his acquiescence in possible British claims did not imply acceptance of Zionist claims. When the Balfour Declaration was made, the Syrian nationalists soon reacted against it, but Professor Kedourie may well be right in saying that the Hashimites did not oppose it strongly until after Britain withdrew its support for Faysal in Syria.⁴⁰

The argument about the interpretation of these agreements is one which is impossible to end, because they were intended to bear more than one interpretation. If later historians have tried to end it by supporting one or other of the possible interpretations, it is partly because those interpretations have a significance beyond themselves, as symbols of certain attitudes or policies, and historians, whether or not they know it, are carrying on the political discussion which began with the agreements. This is true of Antonius himself, writing as he did at a time when the questions of French policy in Syria and the implications of the Jewish National Home were burning political issues about which he had strong convictions; it is equally true of more recent writers, since the end of 'Britain's moment in the Middle East' is recent enough to generate controversy about the success or failure of British policy, and the question of Palestine is still with us.

About the last part of the book there is less to say. It gives a clear account of events from the peace settlement to the time when it was written, and makes certain suggestions about British policy in Palestine and French in Syria. It is important for another reason than its explicit content, however. A text can be read for what it tells us about the author and his times, and from these pages there emerges an image of the colonial relationship in the penultimate phase of British and French domination of the world. It was a relationship of unequal strength, and in such situations the weaker party, being unable to compel the stronger to change its policy, must try to use arguments, and persuade it of an identity of real interests between the two. In pages such as those of Antonius there is no idea of revolutionary change, of a victorious liberation which creates another kind of human being, but rather of a peaceful resolution of conflict by agreement between men of reason and goodwill, searching for points of common interest and smoothing the transition to independent rule. In such a process of persuasion, the production of documents and the attempt to interpret them precisely has a special place.

The relationship is also one of cultural dependence. The weaker party tries to assure the stronger that its essential interests will be safe even if its power is surrendered, and does so by demonstrating its own mastery of the culture and values of the stronger, and showing therefore that the transition to independence can take place without shock, and will not appear as a radical change. The experience of the last thirty years, indeed, has shown that the first phase of independent rule, in many countries, has been almost like a continuation of the last phase of colonial rule; the real shock of change has come later.

In such situations, there is a need for intermediaries who can explain each party to the others, and find and express their points of common interest. George Antonius was exceptionally good at such work, and his career in fact contained a series of successful mediations. Thus in 1925 he helped Sir Gilbert Clayton on his official mission to negotiate with 'Abd al-'Aziz Ibn Sa'ud about recognition and frontiers. His role was to talk persuasively to the king's officials and advisers, and he was very successful in this: 'I am quite convinced I could not have succeeded without him', Clayton declared.[41] In 1926 he went with Clayton on a similar mission to Yemen, and in 1928 on a second one to Ibn Sa'ud. In 1927, while on vacation in Egypt, he helped the Egyptian Government and the British High Commissioner, Lord Lloyd, to resolve a crisis which had arisen in regard to the Egyptian army, by finding a formula which both could accept. In 1929, during the crisis over the Wailing Wall in Jerusalem, he was the member of the Secretariat who maintained liaison with the Arab political leaders. After 1930, when he left the government's service, he was free to undertake a wider range of activities. In 1932 his correspondence shows him to have been engaged almost at the same time in at least half a dozen negotiations. He was involved in the controversy within the Orthodox Christian community over the Patriarchal election, and discussing it with the different candidates, the Greek consul-general, the Fraternity of the Holy Sepulchre and leaders of the laity. He was talking to leaders of the Islamic conference recently held in Jerusalem about the future of Islam, and to Nallino and other orientalists about a project for a new Arabic lexicon. He was discussing with the Prime Minister of Egypt, Sidqi Pasha, the vexed question of tariffs on Palestinian oranges, and with Chauvel, the *chef de cabinet* of the French High Commissioner for Syria and Lebanon, the more difficult question of Syrian nationalism; and all the time he was talking to the British High Commissioner in Palestine about British policy there.[42]

Anyone who reads *The Arab Awakening* now may end it with a certain feeling of sadness. This is partly a reflection of the anxiety which the author himself felt and expressed. Already by 1938 a shadow of what was to come had fallen across his pages: a new age of mass-politics, when issues would be determined otherwise than by delicate negotiations between men who understood and trusted one another. In his final section on the problem of Palestine, he makes clear that what is at issue is not simply the question of who should have sovereignty, but that of physical possession of the land. He records the beginning of mass action: the Palestine revolt continuing as he wrote was not, he insisted, inspired or manipulated by urban politicians but a genuine rural upheaval. Once more, recent research by T. Bowden has confirmed his view.[43]

There is another cause of sadness, however. Contemplation of the life of George Antonius will reveal how difficult is the path of the intermediary; he may so easily fall into the chasm he is trying to bridge. His official career showed that he was too large and complex for the kind of intermediate position which was all that was available to an Arab in the mandatory administration; he was squeezed out of the Education Department in a way which reflected little credit on his colleagues. There was, at that time, no other government or institution to which he could give all his talents and devotion. His personal tragedy was that of someone who could not fit easily into any of the moulds available to him at a time when, with the disintegration of ancient societies and systems of government, and the rise of nationalism, men were being forced to define their identities in new and narrower terms. In the last analysis, he belonged to an earlier world: he was a citizen of Alexandria in the last phase of Franco-Ottoman civilisation, the city where all men could be at home, all could be more than one thing, and all matters could be resolved by delicate compromise. He belonged to a world lost and irrecoverable, but embalmed for ever in the poems of Cavafy—in such a poem as that which portrays a Syrian eager to serve his country:

> I am young and in excellent health.
> I have a wonderful mastery of Greek
>
> (Aristotle, Plato, I know them forwards and backwards:
> And orators, and poets, and anything you mention).
> Of military matters I have a notion,
> And I have friendships with leaders of the mercenaries,
> I have plenty of entries to administrative things too . . .
>
> Wherefore I believe that I fill the bill,
> Marked out to be of service to this country,

My own dear land of Syria.

Whatever work they put me to I will endeavour
To be of use to the country. That is my purpose.
If on the other hand they hinder me . . .
it isn't my fault . . .

The almighty gods ought to have seen about
Creating a fourth man and an honest one.
I should have been delighted to work with him.[44]

Notes

INTRODUCTION

1. W. L. Langer, *European Alliances and Alignments* (New York, 1931) and *The Diplomacy of Imperialism*, 2 vols (New York, 1935).
2. A. J. Toynbee, *A Study of History*, 12 vols (London, 1934–61).
3. A. J. Toynbee, *Survey of International Affairs 1925*, vol 1 *The Islamic World since the Peace Settlement* (London, 1927).
4. George Antonius, *The Arab Awakening* (London, 1938).
5. A. H. Hourani, *Syria and Lebanon: a Political Essay* (London, 1946) and *Minorities in the Arab World* (London, 1947).
6. H. A. R. Gibb, *Mohammedanism: an Historical Survey* (Oxford, 1949), *Modern Trends in Islam* (Chicago, 1947), and 'The structure of religious thought in Islam' in *Studies on the Civilization of Islam* (London, 1962).
7. London, 1962.
8. H. A. R. Gibb and H. Bowen, *Islamic Society and the West*, vol. 1 *Islamic Society in the Eighteenth Century*, part 1 (London, 1950) and part 2 (London, 1957).
9. A. H. Hourani and S. M. Stern (eds), *The Islamic City* (Oxford, 1970). See Chapter 2 in this volume.
10. C. Geertz, *Islam Observed: Religious Development in Morocco and Indonesia* (Chicago, 1968).
11. J. Berque, *L'Egypte, impérialisme et révolution* (Paris, 1967), Eng. trans., *Egypt, Imperialism and Revolution* (London, 1972).
12. I. M. Lapidus, *Muslim Cities in the Later Middle Ages* (Cambridge, Mass., 1967).
13. See in particular André Raymond, *Artisans et commerçants au Caire au XVIIIe siècle*, 2 vols. (Damascus, 1973–4).

CHAPTER 1

1. J. J. Rousseau, *Du Contrat social*, book IV, ch. 8.
2. (J. H. Newman), *Lectures on the History of the Turks* (Dublin, 1854) p. 105.
3. B. Lewis, *The Arabs in History*, revised edition (London, 1958) p. 147.
4. R. M. Adams, *Land behind Baghdad* (Chicago, 1965).
5. B. Lewis, 'The Mongols, the Turks and the Muslim polity' in *Transactions of the Royal Historical Society*, 5th series, vol. 18 (1968) p. 64; reprinted in Lewis, *Islam in History* (London, 1973) p. 194.
6. T. W. Arnold. *The Caliphate*, new ed. (London, 1965) p. 203.

CHAPTER 2

1. This essay formed the introduction to A. H. Hourani and S. M. Stern (eds), *The Islamic City* (Oxford, 1970), the papers of a colloquium held at Oxford in 1965. In the notes which follow, references are to papers in that volume, unless they are specifically attributed to other books and periodicals.
2. E. Pauty, 'Villes spontanées et villes créées en Islam' in *Annales de l'Institut d'Études Orientales*, 9 (1951) pp. 52–75.
3. J. Sauvaget, *Alep*, 2 vols (Parish, 1941).
4. For a summary of the results of such work, see D. and J. Sourdel, *La civilisation de l'islam classique* (Paris, 1968) ch. 9. See in particular R. Le Tourneau, *Fès avant le protectorat* (Casablanca, 1949), R. Mantran, *Istanbul dans la seconde moitié du XVIIe siècle* (Paris, 1962) and A. Raymond, *Artisans et commerçants au Caire au XVIIIe siècle*, 2 vols (Damascus, 1973–4).
5. W. Marçais, 'L'Islamisme et la vie urbaine' in *Articles et Conférences* (Paris, 1961) pp. 59–67; G. Marçais, 'La conception des villes dans l'Islam' in *Revue d'Alger*, 2 (1954-5) pp. 517–33, and 'L'urbanisme musulman' in *Mélanges d'Histoire et d'Archéologie de l'Occident Musulman* (Algiers, 1957) pp. 219–31. Cf. G. E. von Grunebaum, 'The structure of the Muslim town' in *Islam, Essays in the Nature and Growth of a Cultural Tradition* (London, 1955) pp. 141–58.
6. L. Massignon, 'Ṣinf' in *Encyclopaedia of Islam*, 1st edn, 4, pp. 436–7.
7. J. Sauvaget, *Alep*; 'Esquisse d'une histoire de la ville de Damas' in *Revue des Études Islamiques*, 8 (1934) pp. 421–80; 'Le plan de Laodicée-sur-Mer' in *Bulletin d'Études Orientales*, 4 (1934) pp. 82–114.
8. M. Weber, *The City*, trans. by D. Martindale and G. Neuwirth (Glencoe, Ill., 1958) p. 88.
9. N. Elisséeff, 'Damas à la lumière des théories de Jean Sauvaget', p. 157.
10. C. Cahen, 'Y a-t-il eu des corporations professionnelles dans le monde musulman classique?', p. 51.
11. S. M. Stern, 'The constitution of the Islamic city', p. 25.
12. J. Aubin, 'Elements pour l'étude des agglomerations urbaines dans l'Iran médiéval', p. 65.
13. J. Gernet, 'Note sur les villes chinoises au moment de l'apogée islamique', p. 77.
14. For the culture of the bourgeoisie, see O. Grabar, 'The illustrated maqāmāt of the thirteenth century: the bourgeoisie and the arts', p. 207.
15. E. Ashtor-Strauss, 'L'administration urbaine en Syrie médiévale' in *Rivista degli Studi Orientali*, 31 (1956) pp. 73–128, and 'L'urbanisme syrien à la basse-epoque' in *Rivista ...*, 33 (1958) pp. 181–209.
16. I. M. Lapidus, 'Muslim urban society in Mamluk Syria', p. 95.
17. In addition to the papers by Cahen and Lapidus in this volume, cf. C. Cahen, 'Mouvements populaires et autonomisme urbain dans l'Asie musulmane du moyen age' in *Arabica*, 5 (1958) pp. 225–50, and 6 (1959), pp. 25–56, 223–65; I. M. Lapidus, *Muslim Cities in the Later Middle Ages* (Cambridge, Mass., 1967).

18. J. Lassner, 'The Caliph's personal domain: the city plan of Baghdad re-examined', p. 103; S. A. El-Ali, 'The foundation of Baghdad', p. 87.
19. J. M. Rogers, 'Samarra: a study of medieval town-planning', p. 119.
20. A. Raymond, 'Essai de géographie des quartiers de résidence aristocratique au Caire au XVIIIème siècle' in *Journal of the Economic and Social History of the Orient*, 6 (1963) pp. 58–103.
21. L. Massignon, 'Explication du plan de Kufa (Irak)' in *Opera Minora* (Beirut, 1963) 3, pp. 35–60.
22. G. T. Scanlon, 'Housing and sanitation: some aspects of medieval public service', p. 179.
23. 'Mouvements populaires . . .' in *Arabica*, 6, pp. 255–60.
24. R. Brunschvig, 'Urbanisme médiévale et droit musulman' in *Revue des Études Islamiques*, 15 (1947) pp. 127–55.
25. L. Torres Balbás, 'Les villes musulmanes d'Espagne et leur urbanisation' in *Annales de l'Institut d'Études Orientales*, 6 (1942–7) pp. 5–30.

CHAPTER 3

1. S. J. Shaw, *Financial and Administrative Organization and Development of Ottoman Egypt 1517–1798* (Princeton, 1962).
2. A. K. S. Lambton, *Landlord and Peasant in Persia* (London, 1953).
3. N. Itzkowitz, 'Eighteenth century Ottoman realities' in *Studia Islamica*, 16 (1962) pp. 73–94.
4. D. Ayalon, 'Studies in al-Jabarti I. Notes on the transformation of Mamluk society in Egypt under the Ottomans' in *Journal of the Economic and Social History of the Orient*, 3 (1960) pp. 275–325; P. M. Holt, *Egypt and the Fertile Crescent 1516–1922* (London, 1966), chapters 5, 6; Shaw, *Financial and Administrative Organization*. See now A. Raymond, *Artisans et commerçants au Caire au XVIIIe siècle* 2 vols (Damascus, 1973–4), in the light of which this account of the relationship between *beys*, leaders of military corps and merchants needs to be revised.
5. See now L. C. Brown, *The Tunisia of Ahmad Bey 1837–1855* (Princeton, 1974).
6. G. Baer, *Egyptian Guilds in Modern Times* (Jerusalem, 1964).
7. G. Baer, 'The Settlement of the Beduins', 'The Dissolution of the Village Community', 'The Village Shaykh 1800–1950', all in *Studies in the Social History of Modern Egypt* (Chicago, 1969) pp. 3–61.
8. A. Schölch, *Ägypten den Ägyptern: die politische und gesellschaftliche Krise der Jahre 1878–1882 in Ägypten* (Zurich, 1973) now throws new light on this.
9. S. Mardin, *The Genesis of Young Ottoman Thought* (Princeton, 1962).
10. U. Heyd, 'The Ottoman 'ulemā and westernization in the time of Selim III and Mahmud II' in Heyd (ed), *Studies in Islamic History and Civilization* (Jerusalem, 1961) pp. 63–96.
11. Iliya Qudsi, 'Notice sur les corporations de Damas', in *Actes du VIème Congres des Orientalists* (Leiden, 1885).
12. D. Chevallier, 'Aspects sociaux de la question d'Orient: aux origines des troubles agraires libanais en 1858' in *Annales*, 14 (1959) pp. 35–64.

CHAPTER 4

1. 'Ottoman Reform and the Politics of Notables' in W. R. Polk and R. L. Chambers (eds), *The Beginning of Modernization in the Middle East* (Chicago, 1968) p. 41f. Chapter 3 in the present volume.

CHAPTER 5

1. A. Hourani, *Arabic Thought in the Liberal Age* (London, 1962).
2. Muhammad Rashīd Ridā, *Ta'rīkh al-ustādh al-imām al-shaykh Muhammad 'Abduh*, vol I (Cairo, 1931) p. 130.
3. For the life of Baha' al-Din Naqshband, see D. S. Margoliouth, 'Nakshband' in E.I., 1st edn, vol 3, p. 841: Ahmad Taşköprüzade, *al-Shaqā' iq al-nu'maniyya fi 'ulamā' al-dawla al-'uthmāniyya* (margins of Ibn Khalliqān, *Wafāyāt al-a'yān* (Bulaq, A.H. 1299), vol 1, p. 378f, German trans. by O. Rescher (Istanbul, 1927) p. 165; W. Barthold, *Histoire des Turcs d'Asie centrale* (French adaptation, Paris, 1945) p. 161: A. Vambéry, *Travels in Central Asia* (London, 1864) pp. 194–6.
4. 'Abd al-Majīd al-Khānī, *al-Hadā'iq al-wardiyya fi haqā'iq ajillā' al-naqshbandiyya* (Cairo, A.H. 1308) p. 6. This is a collection of biographies of those connected with the order. There is a more recent one most of which follows al-Khānī's book very closely: Muhammad al-Rakhāwī, *al-Anwār al-qudsiyya fi manāqib al-sāda al-naqshbandiyya* (Cairo, A.H. 1344).
5. Muhammad ibn Sulaymān, *al-Hadīqa al-naddiyya* (on margin of *Asfa al-mawārid*—see note 19 below) p. 15.
6. M. Molé, 'Quelques traités naqshbandis' in *Farhang-e Iran Zamin*, 6 (1337, 1958/9) p. 273f.: 'La version persane du traité de dix principes de Najm al-Din Kubra' in same vol., p. 38f; 'Autour du Daré Mansour: l'apprentissage mystique de Baha' al-Din Naqshband' in *Revue des Études Islamiques*, 27 (1959) p. 35f.; *Les Mystiques musulmans* (Paris, 1965). See also F. Babinger, 'Zur Frühgeschichte des Naqschbandiordens' in *Der Islam*, 17 (1923) p. 105f.
7. H. Algar has now begun to publish a series of articles which seem likely to make necessary a revision of Molé's ideas: see 'Some notes on the Naqshbandi tarīqat in Bosnia' in *Welt des Islams* N.S. 13 (1972) p. 168f; 'Bibliographical notes on the Naqshbandi tariqat' in G. F. Hourani (ed), *Essays on Islamic Philosphy and Science* (Albany, N.Y., 1975) p. 254f; 'The Naqshbandi order: a preliminary survey of its history and significance' in *Studia Islamica* 44 (1976) p. 123f.
8. Molé, *Mystiques*, p. 40.
9. Molé, 'Autour du Daré Mansour', p. 66.
10. *Ibid.*, p. 45.
11. C. J. Edmonds, *Kurds, Turks and Arabs* (London, 1957) p. 204.
12. A. S. Husseini, 'Uways al-Qaranī and the Uwaysī Sūfīs' in *Muslim World*, 57 (1967) p. 103f.
13. M. Habib, 'Some Notes on the Naqshabandī Order' in *Muslim World*, 59 (1969) p. 40f.
14. For the order in India, see K. A. Nizami, 'Naqshbandī Influence on

Mughal Rulers and Politics' in *Islamic Culture*, 39 (1965) p. 41f: K. A. Nizami, 'Early Indo-Muslim Mystics and their Attitude towards the State' in *Islamic Culture*, 22 (1948) p. 387f, vol 23 (1949), pp. 13f, 162f, 312f, 24 (1950) p. 60f; I. H. Qureshi, *The Muslim Community of the Indo-Pakistan Sub-Continent* (The Hague, 1962) p. 150f; S. M. Ikram, *Muslim Civilization in India* (New York and London, 1964) p. 166f; A. Ahmed, *Studies in Islamic Culture in the Indian Environment* (Oxford, 1964) p. 182f. See now Y. Friedmann, *Shaykh Ahmad Sirhindī* (Montreal, 1971), which casts doubt on some of the claims made for Shaykh Ahmad by Muslim writers in the sub-continent.

15. E. J. W. Gibb, *A History of Ottoman Poetry*, vol II (London, 1902) p. 374; J. P. Brown, *The Dervishes: or Oriental Spiritualism* (London, 1968) pp. 57, 127f; H. A. R. Gibb and H. Bowen, *Islamic Society and the West*, vol I, part ii (London, 1957) p. 197f; H. J. Kissling, 'Die soziologische und pädagogische Rolle der Derwischorden im osmanischen Reiche' in ZDMG, 103 (1953) p. 18f, Eng. trans. in G. E. von Grunebaum (ed), *Studies in Islamic Cultural History* in *The American Anthropologist*, memoir no. LVI (1956) p. 23f.

16. F. W. Hasluck, *Christianity and Islam under the Sultans* (Oxford, 1929) vol I, p. 356f.

17. Muhammad Khalīl al-Murādī, *silk al-durar fī a'yān al-qarn al-thānī 'ashar* (Cairo, 1291–1301) vol 3, p. 31.

18. al-Murādī, vol 1, pp. 25, 145f, vol II, p. 70f, vol 3, p. 219f, vol IV, pp. 114f, 129f. See also H. A. R. Gibb, 'al-Muradi' in E.I., 1st edn, supp., p. 155.

19. Biographies of Khālid in 'Uthmān ibn Sanad al-Wa' ilī, *Asfa-al-mawārid min silsāl ahwāl al-imām Khālid* (Cairo, A.H. 1313); Ibrāhīm Faṣīḥ alrḤaydārī, *al-Majd al-tālid fī manāqib Mawlānā Khālid* (Istanbul, A.H. 1316); Muhammad ibn Sulaymān, *al-Hadīqa al-naddiyya fī abād al-tarīqa al-naqshbandiyya wa'l-bahja al-khālidiyya* (on margins of the above); al-Khānī, *al-Hadā'iq*, p. 223f; al-Rakhāwī, *al-Anwār*, p. 224f; 'Abd al-Razzāq al-Bīṭār, *Ḥilyat al-bashar fī ta'rīkh al-qarn al-thālith 'ashar* (Damascus, 1961) vol I, p. 570f; Muhammad Jamīl al-Shaṭṭī, *Rawd al-bashar fī a'yān Dimashq fi'l-qarn al-thālith 'ashar*, 2 vols (Damascus, 1940–48) p. 80f; Khayr al-Dīn al-Ziriqlī, *al-A'lām* (2nd ed, n.p., 1954) vol 2, p. 334; 'Umar Ridā Kaḥḥāla, *Mu'jam al-mu' allifīn*, vol 4 (Damascus, 1957) p. 95.

20. Haydar al-Shihābī, *Lubnān fī 'ahd al-umarā' al-shihabiyyīn*, vol 2 (Beirut, 1933) pp. 524–6; Mikha' il al-Dimashqī, *Ta'rīkh hawādith al-Sham wa Lubnān* (Beirut, 1912) p. 20f; Ibrāhīm al-'Awrā, *Ta'rīkh wilāyat Sulaymān bāshā al-'ādil* (Saydā, 1936) pp. 94–5.

21. al-'Awrā, p. 94.

22. al-Khānī, p. 230.

23. C. J. Rich, *Narrative of a Residence in Koordistan* (London, 1836) vol. I, pp. 140–1, 320–1.

24. Edmonds, pp. 73, 77.

25. Muhammad Amīn Zakī, *Ta'rīkh al-Sulaymāniyya* (Baghdad, 1951) p. 218.

26. al-Khānī, pp. 245–6

27. Muḥammad ibn Sulaymān, p. 51.

28. *Ibid.*, pp. 56–7.
29. List in al-Khānī, p. 256, and Algar, 'Bibliographical notes...', p. 258.
30. 'Abbās Mahmud al-'Azzāwī, *'Ashā' ir al-'Irāq*, vol. II (Baghdad, 1947) p. 225f.
31. al-Khānī, p. 259; Mahmud Shukrī al-Alūsī, *al-Misk al-adhfar* (Baghdad, 1930) p. 82f. See also L. Massignon, *Mission en Mésopotamie 1907–8* in *Mémoires de l'Institut français d'Archéologie oriental*, XXXI (1912) vol. 11, pp. 64–5.
32. Muhammad ibn Sulaymān, pp. 54, 73.
33. S. Mardin, *Genesis of Young Ottoman Thought* (Princeton, 1962) p. 214.
34. al-Khānī, p. 281
35. C. Snouck Hurgronje, *Mekka in the latter part of the 19th century* (English trans., Leyden, 1931) pp. 176f, 215f, 241f.
36. Hasluck, vol. II, p. 567; J. K. Birge, *The Bektashi Order of Dervishes* (London etc. 1937) p. 78.
37. W. E. D. Allen and P. Muratoff, *Caucasian Battlefields* (Cambridge, 1953) p. 47f.
38. H. Carrère d'Encausse, *Réforme et révolution chez les musulmans de l'empire russe* (Bukhara, 1966) p. 66; 'Organizing and colonizing the Conquered Territories' in E. Allworth (ed); *Central Asia: a Century of Russian Rule* (New York and London, 1967) pp. 167–9; L. Krader, *Peoples of Central Asia* (Bloomington, Indiana, and The Hague, 1966) p. 106.
39. Muhammad Rashīd Ridā, *al-Manār wa' l-Azhar* (Cairo, 1934) p. 148f. See Chapter 6 in the present volume.

CHAPTER 6

1. C. C. Adams, *Islam and Modernism in Egypt* (London, 1933); H. Laoust, 'Le réformisme orthodoxe des "Salafiya"' in *Revue des Etudes Islamiques*, 6 (1932) p. 175f. See also H. A. R. Gibb, *Modern Trends in Islam* (Chicago, 1947).
2. M. R. Ridā, *al-Manār wa'l-Azhar* (Cairo, 1934) pp. 171–2. Translation in A. Hourani, *Arabic Thought in the Liberal Age* (London, 1962) p. 225, and J. Jomier, *Le commentaire coranique du Manar* (Paris, 1954) p. 29.
3. For 'Abduh's attitude to Sufism, see M. R. Ridā, *Tarīkh al-ustādh al-imām al-shaykh Muhammad 'Abduh*, vol. 1 (Cairo, 1931) p. 106. For Ridā's attitude, see Jomier, p. 236f.
4. On Sufism in general, see, among much else, L. Massignon, *Essai sur les origines du lexique technique de la mystique musulmane* (Paris, 1954); M. Molé, *Les mystiques musulmans* (Paris, 1965); A. M. Schimmel, *Mystical Dimensions of Islam* (Chapel Hill, N.C., 1975); M. N. C. Hodgson, *The Venture of Islam* (Chicago, 1974) vol. 1, book II, ch. 4, vol. 2, book III, ch. 4.
5. Schimmel, p. 103.
6. On *karāmāt*, see L. Massignon, *La passion d'al-Hosayn-ibn-Mansour al-Hallaj*, 2 vols (Paris, 1922) vol. 1, p. 137f.; *Encyclopaedia of Islam*, 1st edn, vol. 1, p. 744 (D. B. Macdonald), and 2nd edn, vol. 4, p. 615 (L. Gardet).

7. H. Laoust, *Essai sur les doctrines sociales et politiques de Takī-d-Dīn Ahmad b. Taimīya* (Cairo, 1939) p. 89f.
8. G. Makdisi, 'The Hanbali school and Sufism' in *Humaniora Islamica*, 2 (1974) p. 61f; 'Ibn Taimīya: a Sūfi of the Qādiriya order' in *American Journal of Arabic Studies*, 1 (1973) p. 118f.
9. Laoust, *Essai sur . . . Ibn Taimiya*, p. 506f.
10. For the Naqshbandiyya, see H. Algar, 'Bibliographical notes on the Naqshbandi tariqat' in G. F. Hourani, ed, *Essays on Islamic Philosophy and Science* (Albany, N.Y., 1975) p. 254f and 'The Naqshbandi order: a preliminary survey of its history and significance' in *Studia Islamica*, 44 (1976) p. 123f; M. Molé, 'Quelques traités naqshbandis' in *Farhang-i Irān-zamin*, 6 (1337 solar/1958-9) p. 273f and 'Autour du Daré Mansour: l'apprentissage mystique de Bahā' al-Dīn Naqshband' in *Revue des Etudes Islamiques*, 27 (1959) p. 35f. See also Chapter 5 in the present volume. For Sufism in the modern world, see F. Rahman, *Islam* (London, 1966) p. 205f; C. Geertz, *Islam Observed* (New Haven, Conn. 1968); M. Gilsenan, *Saint and Sufi in Modern Egypt* (Oxford 1973); E. Gellner, *Saints of the Atlas* (London 1969); J. Abun-Nasr, *The Tijaniyya: a Sufi Order in the Modern World* (London 1965); E. E. Evans-Pritchard, *The Sanusi of Cyrenaica* (Oxford 1949); J. vans Ess, 'Libanesische Miszellen. 6. Die Yasrutiya' in *Welt des Islams* 16 (1975) p. lf.
11. Y. Friedmann, *Shaykh Ahmad Sirhindi* (Montreal, 1971).
12. See Schimmel, p. 365.
13. Massignon, *La passion . . .*, vol. 2, p. 796f on *chasteté de regard*; see also Schimmmel, p. 289.
14. *Tafsīr al-Qur' ān al-karim*, vol. 9 (Cairo, 1347/1928) p. 415f on *awliyā' Allah*; *Ta'rīkh . . .*, vol. 1, p. 106f; *al-Manār* on *karāmāt al-awliyā'*, 2 (1316-17/1898-99) pp. 401, 417, 449, 481, 545, 657, 5 (1320/1902) p. 938f, 6 (1321/1903) pp. 12f, 54f, 109f, 184f; *al-Manār wa' l-Azhar*, p. 146f, reproduced in S. Arslān, *al-Sayyid Rashīd Ridā aw ikhā' arba' īn sana* (Damascus, 1937) p. 47f.
15. *Tafsīr*, vol. 9, p. 427f.
16. See references to *al-Manār* and *al-Manār wa' l-Azhar* in note 14.
17. *al-Manār wa' l-Azhar*, p. 156; *Tafsīr*, vol. 9, p. 448.
18. See R.J. McCarthy (ed), al-Bāqillānī, *Kitāb al-bayān* (Baghdad/Beirut, 1958).
19. *al-Manār wa' l-Azhar*, p. 140.
20. See F. W. Hasluck, *Christianity and Islam under the Sultans*, 2 vols (Oxford, 1929); F.J. Bliss, *The Religions of Modern Syria and Palestine* (Edinburgh, 1912); I. Goldziher, 'Veneration of saints in Islam' in *Muslim Studies*, vol. 2 (London 1971) p. 255f.
21. *al-Manār wa' l-Azhar*, p. 178.
22. *Ibid.*, p. 160f.
23. *Ibid.*, p. 172.
24. *Ibid.*, p. 179.
25. *Ibid.*, p. 173; *Tafsīr*, vol. 7 (1346/1927 p. 331f.
26. *Ta'rīkh . . .* vol. 1, p. 106. For 'ālam al-mithāl, see F. Rahman, 'Dream, imagination and *'alam al-mithāl'* in G. E. von Grunebaum and R.

27. *al-Manār*, 4 (1318-19/1901-2) p. 259f.
28. *al-Manār*, 22 (1339-40/1920-1), p. 177; *Ta'rīkh* ..., vol. 1 pp. 115, 124.
29. *Ta'rīkh* ..., vol. 1, pp. 113, 133.
30. *al-Manār*, 2, p. 401; 6, pp. 116, 195.
31. *al-Manār*, 4, p. 259.
32. *Ta'rikh* ..., vol. 1, pp. 108, 126.
33. *al-Manār wa' l-Azhar*, p. 148; *Tafsīr*, vol. 9, pp. 420, 445.
34. *al-Manār*, 22, p. 178.
35. *al-Manār wa' l-Azhar*, pp.131-2.
36. Abun-Nasr, *Tijaniyya*, p. 39.
37. *al-Manār wa' l-Azhar*, p. 134.
38. *al-Manār*, 4, p. 259.
39. J. Abun-Nasr, 'The Salafiya movement in Morocco: the religious bases of the Moroccan nationalist movement' in A. Hourani (ed), *St. Antony's Papers 16: Middle Eastern Affairs* 3 (London, 1963), p. 90f.
40. Gilsenan, *Saint and Sufi* ..., p. 188f.
41. I am grateful to Professor G. Makdisi and Dr. G. Böwering, both of the University of Pennsylvania, for reading this paper and making some useful criticisms and suggestions.

CHAPTER 7

1. The transliteration of Arabic names is not quite consistent; some of the Syrian families lived so much through the medium of the French language that it seems preferable to give their names in the form they themselves used.
2. 'Abd al-Raḥmān al-Jabartī, *'ajā'ib al-āthār fi'l-tarājim wa'l-akhbār* (Būlāq 1207/1879-80) vol. 3, p. 194.
3. Jabartī, vol. 4, p. 164.
4. The treatment of the eighteenth century needs now to be reconsidered in the light of A. Raymond, *Artisans et commerçants au Caire au XVIIIe siècle*, 2 vols (Damascus, 1973-4).
5. Most of this is based on Girard, 'Mémoire sur l'agriculture, l'industrie et le commerce de l' Égypte' in *Description de l'Égypte* (2nd edition, Paris, 1821-29), vol. 17. A few details are taken from De Chabrol, 'Essai sur les moeurs des habitans modernes de l'Égypte' in *Description*, vol. 18 i, and Jomard, 'Description de la ville et de la citadelle du Caire' in *Description*, vol. 18 ii. See also R. Clement, *Les Français d'Égypte aux XVIIe et XVIIIe siècles* (Cairo, 1960).
6. C. Brockelmann, *Geschichte der arabischen Literatur* 5 vols (Leiden, 1937-49) vol.2, p. 645.
7. Jabartī, vol. 2, p. 90.
8. Most of this information comes from B.Qar'alī, *al-sūriyyūn fī miṣr*, vol. 1 (Cairo, 1928), a work based mainly on church registers and other documents of religious communities.
9. Jomard in *Description*, vol. 13 ii, pp. 127-8.

10. F. Mengin, *Histoire de l'Egypte sous le gouvernment de Mohammed-Aly*, 2 vols (Paris, 1823) vol. 2, p. 275.
11. Information kindly supplied by Mr. A. Raymond. See also Jomard in *Description*, vol. 18 ii.
12. See in particular Qar' alī, vol. 2 (Bayt Shabāb, 1933), and also Jomard in *Description*, vol. 18, p. 329.
13. Villoteau, 'Description historique, technique et littéraire des instrumens de musique des Orientaux' in *Description*, vol. 13, p. 554.
14. S. J. Shaw, *The financial and administrative organization of Ottoman Egypt, 1517–1798* (Princeton, N.J., 1962) p. 322. Since Copts and Greeks are specifically referred to, I am assuming that *Nasāra* refers to the Syrians.
15. Girard in *Description*, vol. 17, *passim*; Mengin, vol.2, p. 272f; for Kūsa, see Qar'alī, vol. 2, p. 20.
16. C. F. Volney, *Travels through Syria and Egypt* (English trans., Dublin, 1793) vol. 1, p. 140; Girard in *Description*, vol. 17, p. 375; Estève, 'Mémoire sur les finances de l'Egypte' in *Description*, vol. 12, p. 148; Qar'alī, vol. 1, p. 85; Jabartī, vol. 2, pp. 90, 158; Shaw, p. 100f.
17. S. Runciman, *The Great Church in Captivity* (Cambridge, 1968) p. 178.
18. Jabartī, vol. 1, p. 188.
19. Qar'alī, vol. 2, p. 18f.
20. Q. Bāshā, *Ta'rīkh usrat Āl Fara'urn* (Harissa, 1932).
21. Bāshā, p. 110; F. Charles-Roux, *Bonaparte, Governor of Egypt* (English trans., London, 1937) pp. 12–13; A. Cherfils, *Bonaparte et l'Islam* (Paris, 1914) pp. 92, 94.
22. C. Bachatly, 'Un membre oriental du premier Institut d'Egypte: Don Raphael (1759–1831)' in *Bulletin de l'Institut d'Egypte*, 17 (1934–35), pp. 257–60.
23. N. Turk, *Mudhakkirāt*, G. Wiet (ed) (Cairo, 1950) p. 50.
24. G. Guémard, 'Les auxiliaires de l'armée de Bonaparte en Égypte' in *Bulletin de l'Institut d'Egypte*, 9 (1926–7), pp. 1–17.
25. Jabartī, vol. 3, pp. 22, 37; Turk, p. 82; Cherfils, p. 92; Qar'alī, vol. 1, p. 89.
26. Jabartī, vol. 3, p. 70.
27. Jabartī, vol. 3, pp. 14, 23, 44, 59, 78.
28. Jabartī, vol. 3, p. 45.
29. Jabartī, vol. 3, p. 132.
30. Bachatli, p. 257; A. Clot Bey, *Mémoires*, J. Tagher (ed) (Cairo, 1949 pp. 76, 93; Bāshā, p. 128.
31. Heyworth-Dunne, *An Introduction to the History of Education in Modern Egypt* (London, 1938), pp. 106, 109; A. Radwān, *Ta'rīkh matba'at Būlāq* (Cairo, 1953) p. 56.
32. 'Awra, *Ta'rīkh wilāyat Sulaymān bāshā* (Sayda, 1936) pp. 76, 90, 129–30; M. Mishāqa, *Muntakhabāt min al-jawāb 'alā iqtirāh al-ahbāb*, Rustum and Abū Shaqrā (eds.) (Beirut, 1955) pp. 39, 42–4.
33. Jabartī, vol. 4, p. 303.
34. For the role of Ḥanna Baḥri and other Syrian officials in the Egyption administration of Syria, see A. Rustum, *al-Mahfūzāt al-malikiyya al-miṣriyya*, 4 vols. (Beirut, 1940–43) *passim*.

35. Jabartī, vol. 4, p. 280.
36. A. Clot Bey, *Aperçu general sur l'Égypte*, 2 vols (Paris, 1840) vol. 2, p. 144.
37. J. Bowring, *Report on Egypt and Candia* in *Parliamentary Papers 1840*, vol. 21, no. 277, pp. 80–2.
38. Mengin, vol. 2, p. 38lf.; H. Rivlin, *The Agricultural Policy of Muhammad 'Ali in Egypt* (Cambridge, Mass., 1961) pp. 164–65.
39. E. W. Lane, *The Manners and Customs of the Modern Egyptians* (London, 1936) p. 23; Clot, *Aperçu*, vol. 1, pp. 164, 245, vol. 2, p. 144.
40. A. Mubārak, *al-Khiṭaṭ al-tawfīqiyya al-jadīda* 20 parts, (Bulaq 1304–1306/1887–89) part 2, p. 68, part 3, pp. 74, 81, part 6, p. 71.
41. Egypt, Ministère de l'Interieur, *Recensement général de l'Égypte 1882* (Cairo, 1884) vol. 1, table 16.
42. Egypt, Ministère des Finances, *Recensement général de l'Égypte 1897* (Cairo, 1898) vol. 1, table 46.
43. Egypt, Ministère des Finances, *Annuaire statistique de l'Égypte 1910* (Cairo, 1910) p. 26f.
44. Egypt, Ministry of Finance, *Census of Egypt 1917* 2 vols (Cairo, 1920–21) vol. 2, p. 482f.
45. Egypt, Ministry of Finance, *Census of Egypt 1927* (Cairo, 1931) vol.1, pp. 38f, 181f, 192f.
46. M. Clerget, *Le Caire*, 2 vols (Cairo, 1934) vol. 1, p. 187f.
47. D.M. Wallace, *Egypt and the Egyptian Question* (London, 1883) p. 284; G. Baer, *A History of Landownership in Modern Egypt 1800–1950* (London, 1962) p. 36.
48. D. Landes, *Bankers and Pashas* (London, 1958) p. 149, where however they are wrongly described as Greeks. For the founding of the company see A. Sāmī, *Taqwīm al-Nīl*, 3 vols (Cairo, 1916–36) vol. 3 ii, pp. 483, 585. For other details about the family see Y. Sarkīs, *Mu'jam al-matbu'āt al-'arabiyya*, 2 vols (Cairo, 1928–31), vol. 2, p. 1035.
49. J. Zaydān, *Tarājim mashāhīr al-sharq fi'l-qarn al-tāsi' 'ashar* 2nd ed., 2 vols (Cairo, 1910–11) vol. 2, p. 166 for Salīm Bustrus, p. 311 for As'ad Trad.
50. Egypt, Ministère de l'interieur, *Statistique de l'Égypte 1873* (Cairo, 1873) p. 59.
51. International Federation of Master Cotton Spinners' and Manufacturers' Associations, *Official Report: Egypt and the Anglo-Egyptian Sudan 1912* (Manchester, 1913) p. 185.
52. F. Charles-Roux, *La Production du coton en Egypte* (Paris, 1908), p. 395f.
53. Zaydān, *Mashāhīr*, vol. 1, p. 326f.
54. British Chamber of Commerce of Egypt, *List of Financial, Manufacturing, Transport and other Companies established in Egypt* (Alexandria, 1901); E. Papasian, *L'Egypte économique et financière* (Cairo, 1926) p. 97f.
55. *Recensement ... 1882*, vol. 1, p. 223f.
56. *Recensement ... 1897*, vol. 1, p. 172f.
57. *Ibid.*
58. For the investment boom during these years, see E. R. J. Owen, *Cotton and the Egyptian Economy 1820–1914* (Oxford, 1969) p. 280f.
59. Baer, p. 96.

60. *Hadīqat al-akhbār*, 18 June 1859. I owe this reference and that in the next note to Mr B. Abu Manneh.
61. *Taqwīm*, vol. 3 ii, p. 579; *Hadīqat al-akhbār*, 24 October 1864.
62. *Taqwīm*, vol. 3 iii, p. 1527.
63. *Taqwīm*, vol. 3 ii, p. 607; vol. 3 iii, p. 1527.
64. *Taqwīm*, vol. 3 iii, p. 1404.
65. Wallace, p. 143; Lord Cromer, *Modern Egypt*, 2 vols (London, 1908) vol. 2 p. 213f.
66. C. E. Coles, *Recollections and Reflections* (London, 1918 pp. 164–5).
67. For Sābā, see A. Wright (ed), *Twentieth Century Impressions of Egypt* (London, 1909) p. 192; for Ṣfayr, see C. Boyle, *Boyle of Cairo* (Kendal, 1965) p. 159.
68. Cromer, col. 2, p. 213f.
69. Boyle, p. 60.
70. Cromer, vol. 2, pp. 216–7; A. S. White, *The Expansion of Egypt under Anglo-Egyptian Condominium* (London, 1899) p. 153.
71. C. Ayoub Sinano, 'The Levant' in P. Jullien, *The Snob Spotter's Guide* (London, 1958) p. 109f.
72. For the Surūr family, see Mishāqa, p. 21; A. Kayat, *A Voice from Lebanon* (London, 1847) p. 78.
73. *Mercure égyptien 1914* (Cairo, 1914) p. 35f.
74. Heyworth-Dunne, p. 449f.
75. Heyworth-Dunne, p. 374.; *Taqwīm*, vol. 3 iii, pp. 1085, 1204.
76. *Egyptian Gazette*, 23 March 1900. I owe this reference to Dr. E. R. J. Owen.
77. For May Ziyāda, see Y. Dāghir, *Masādir al-dirāsāt al-adabiyya*, part 2 (Beirut, 1955) p. 435.
78. For Mārūn Naqqāsh, see M. Y. Najm, *al-masrahiyya fi'l-adab al-'arabī al-hadīth* (Beirut, 1956) p. 31f.
79. Najm, pp. 94f.; J. Taghir, 'Les débuts du theatre moderne en Egypte' in *Cahiers d'Histoire Egyptienne*, 1 ii (1948) p. 200f.
80. Najm, p. 152f.; J. Berque, *L'Egypte: impérialisme et révolution* (Paris, 1967) p. 359. The following paragraphs owe much to this book of Professor Berque.
81. For the history of Arabic newpapers, see I. 'Abduh, *Tatawwur al-ṣihāfa al-miṣriyya*, 3rd edn (Cairo, 1951); F. de Ṭarrazī, *Ta'rīkh al-ṣihāfa al-'arabiyya*, 4 vols (Beirut, 1913–33).
82. For Arabic periodicals, besides the work of Ṭarrazī listed above, see J. Zaydān, *Ta'rīkh adāb al-lugha al-'arabiyya*, vol. 4, 2nd edn (Cairo, 1937).
83. For the Syrian Christian journalists and writers, besides the works of Ṭarrazī and Zaydan listed above, see A. Hourani, *Arabic Thought in the Liberal Age 1798–1939* (London, 1962) chapters 4 and 10. There is an unpublished thesis by the late Mrs N. Farag, on *Al-Muqtataf 1876–1900: a Study of the Influence of Victorian Thought on Modern Arabic Thought* (D. Phil, Oxford, 1969). For bibliographical details see the works of Brockelmann, Sarkīs and Dāghir listed above, also G. Graf, *Geschichte der christlichen arabischen Literatur*, 5 vols (Vatican, 1944–53) vols 3 and 4.

84. Mishāqa, p. 62f.
85. For this famous incident see Hourani, p. 249; also Farag pp. 24f, 69f, 254f.
86. Hourani, chapter 9; J. Jomier, *Le commentaire coranique du Manar* (Paris, 1954).
87. C. Issawi, *Egypt in Revolution* (London, 1963) p. 89.

CHAPTER 9

1. Review of Kamal S. Salibi, *The Modern History of Lebanon* (London, 1965).
2. 'Aspects sociaux de la question d'Orient: aux origines des troubles agraires libanais en 1858' in *Annales*, 14 (1959) pp. 35–64.

CHAPTER 10

1. Rashīd al-Shartūnī (ed), *Silsilat batārikat al-ṭa'ifa al-mārūniyya* (Beirut, 1898, second ed. enlarged 1902). Rashīd al-Shartūnī (ed), *Ta'rīkh al-ṭa'ifa al-mārūniyya* (Beirut, 1890). *Ta'rīkh al-azmina:* partly included in the above, but edited in full by F. Tawtal (Beirut, 1951).
2. 4 vols (Rome, 1719–28).
3. *De catholicis seu patriarchis Chaldaeorum et Nestorianorum commentarius historico-chronologicus* (Rome, 1775).
4. *Se gli Arabi ebbero alcune influenza sull' origine della poesia moderna in Europa* (Padua, 1807).
5. Ḥamza b. Aḥmad b. Sibāṭ al-Gharbī: *Ta'rīkh*, MS. in American University of Beirut.
6. L. Shaykhū (ed), *Kitāb ta'rīkh Bayrūt wa-akhbār al-umarā' al-buḥturiyyīn* (Beirut, 1927).
7. F. A. Bustānī and A. Rustum (eds), *Lubnūn fī 'ahd al-amīr Fakhr al-Dīn* (Beirut, 1936).
8. Fr. I. T. al-Khūrī (ed), *Kitāb mukhtaṣar ta'rīkh jabal Lubnān* in *al-Mashriq*, 46–7 (1952–3).
9. *al-Rawḍ al-zāhir fī ta'rīkh Ḍāhir.* Extracts are published in the following work.
10. Fr. Q. Bāshā (ed), *Ta'rīkh al-shaykh Ḍāhir al-'Umar al-Zaydānī* (Harissa, 1927–8).
11. Fr. Q. Bāshā (ed), *Ta'rīkh wilāyat Sulaymān bāshā al-'ādil* (Sayda, 1936).
12. *Ta'rīkh al-rahbana al-ḥanawiyya al-mulaqqaba bi'l-shuwayriyya* in work cited, n.16.
13. Fr. I. Sarkīs (ed) in *al-Mashriq*, 48–51 (1954–7).
14. All three parts of *al-Ghurar al-hisān* were published in an unsatisfactory edition by N. Mughabghab (Cairo, 1900). Fr. B. Qar'alī published, in *al-Majalla al-sūriyya* (later *al-Majalla al-batriyarkiyya*), 2–7 (1927–32), an anonymous history of Bashīr II which may incorporate Haydar's shorter work. A. Rustum and F. A. Bustānī published a definitive edition of parts II and III of *al-Ghurar al-hisān*, under the title *Lubnān fī 'ahd al-umarā' al-shihābiyyīn* (Beirut, 1933). They follow the author's own MS.; where it ends, in 1827, they add the narrative for the years 1828–32 from the work published by B. Qar'alī.

15. Niqūla Turk, *Histoire de l'expedition des Français en Egypte*, trans. by A. Desgranges (Paris, 1839). Nicolas Turk, *Chronique d'Egypte, 1798-- 1804*, ed and trans by G. Wiet (Cairo, 1950).
16. Amīr Haydar Ahmad Shihāb: *Ta'rīkh Ahmad bāshā al-Jazzār*, A. Shiblī and I. A. Khalīfa (ed), (Beirut, 1955).
17. Published several times in Arabic and European languages. The fullest version is that published by Fr. Q. Bāshā in *al-Masarra*, 22 (1936).
18. Beirut, 1859. There is a recent reprint.
19. *Lubab al-barāhīn al-jaliyya 'an haqīqat amr al-tā'ifa al-mārūniyya* (Beirut, 1911).
20. *Kitāb al-muhāmāt 'an al-Mawārina wa-qiddīsihim* (Beirut, 1899).
21. 'Maronite (Eglise)' in *Dictionnaire de Théologie Catholique*, vol. x, part I (Paris, 1928).
22. *Le rôle des Maronites dans le retour des Églises Orientales* (Beirut, 1935); Arabic version, Aleppo (1936).
23. 3 vols (Beirut, 1948).
24. *al-Mawārina fī Lubnān* (Jounieh, 1949).
25. *Ta'rīkh ta'ifat al-Rūm al-malikiyya* (Sayda, part I 1938, part II 1939-45).
26. Yūsuf Shammās, *Khulāsat ta'rīkh al-kanīsa al-malikiyya*, 3 vols (Sayda, 1947-52).
27. They include: *al-Salīb fī'l-Islām* (Harrissa, 1935); *al-Rūm al-malikiyyūn fī'l-Islām* (Harissa, 1953).
28. *Mukhtasar ta'rīkh al-Shī'a* (Sayda, 1914).
29. *Ibrāhīm bāshā fī Suriyya* (Beirut, 1929).
30. Sayda, 1913.
31. *Nabdha ta'rīkhiyya fī' l-muqāta'a al-kisrawāniyya* (n.d., n.p.; probably Beirut, 1884. There is a recent reprint).
32. *Kashf al-lithām 'an muhayya al-hukūma wa'l-ahkām*, MS. in American University of Beirut. The author was writing it in 1883.
33. *Ta'rīkh hawādith al-Shām wa Lubnān*, ed. L. Ma'lūf (Beirut, 1912).
34. *Ta'rīkh madīnat Zahla* (Zahle, 1912).
35. *al-Ghurar al-ta'rīkhiyya fī'l-usra al-yāzijiyya*, 2 vols (Sayda, 1945).
36. Ba'abda, 1907-8.
37. See p. 229, n.7 above.
38. Vol. i: P. Carali, *Fakhr al-Din II ... e la Corte di Toscana* (Rome, 1938). Vol. ii, containing Arabic introduction and sources: B. Qar'ali, *Fakhr al-Dīn al-Ma'nī al-thānī* (Rome and Harissa, 1938).
39. *Ta'rīkh al-amīr Fakhr al-Dīn al-Ma'nī al-thānī* (Jounieh, 1934).
40. *Bashīr bayn al-sultān wa' l-'azīz*, 2 vols (Beirut, 1956-57).
41. C. Churchill, *Mount Lebanon*, 3 vols (London, 1853).
42. Antūn Dāhir al-'Aqīqī, *Thawra wa fitna fī Lubnān*, ed. Yūsuf Yazbak (Beirut, 1938). English translation by Malcolm H. Kerr, *Lebanon in the last years of feudalism, 1840-1868* (Beirut, 1959).
43. *al-Harakāt fī Lubnān*, told by Husayn Abū Shaqrā to Yūsuf Abū Shaqrā, ed 'Ārif Abū Shaqrā (Beirut, 1952).
44. An unsatisfactory edition of this was published under the title *Mashhad al-a'yān bihawādith Sūriya wa-Lubnān*, ed M. K. 'Abduh and A. H. Shakhāshīrī (Cairo, 1908). There is a better edition by A. Rustum and S. Abū Shaqrā, *Muntakhabāt min al-jawāb 'alā iqtirāh al-ahbāb* (Beirut,

1955). This, however, stops at the year 1841. Manuscripts of the complete work, including the later sections, are numerous; there is one in the library of the American University of Beirut. See now Y. Porath, 'The peasant revolt of 1858–1861 in Kisrawan' in *Asian and African Studies*, 2 (1966) pp. 77–157.
45. London, 1862.
46. Paris, 1908.
47. *Ta'rīkh Sūriyya* (Beirut, 1881).
48. *Ta'rīkh Sūriyya*, 8 vols (Beirut, 1893–1905). The material on the Maronites is separately published also in *al-Jāmi' al-mufaṣṣal fī ta'rīkh al-Mawārina al-mu'aṣṣal* (Beirut, 1905).
49. 2 vols (Beirut, 1921).
50. Including *al-Ādāb al-'arabiyya fi'l-qarn al-tāsi' 'ashar*, 2 vols (2nd ed. revised, Beirut, 1924–6).
51. *Ta'rīkh al-ṣiḥāfa al-'arabiyya*, 4 vols (Beirut, 1913–33).
52. *Ta'rīkh adāb al-lugha al-'arabiyya*, 3 vols (Cairo, 1914). *Ta'rīkh al-tamaddun al-islāmī*, 5 vols (Cairo, 1902–3). *Ta'rīkh miṣr al-ḥadīth*, 2 vols (Cairo, 1911). *Mashāhīr al-sharq*, 2 vols. (Cairo, 1902–1902).
53. *Fakhreddine II Maan, Prince du Liban* (Beirut, 1946); *Une histoire du Liban a l'époque des Emirs, 1635–1841* (Beirut, 1955). Among other works written broadly from a Lebanese nationalist point of view, note: A. Rustum and F. A. Bustānī, *Ta'rīkh Lubnān* (Beirut, 1946); and Yūsuf Mazhar, *Ta'rīkh Lubnān al- 'āmm*, 2 vols (n.d., n.p.).
54. *Histoire du Liban*, preface, p. 11.
55. Vol. i: *Le Liban au temps de Fakhr al-Din II (1590–1633)* (Paris, 1955). There has now appeared also vol. iv: *Redressement et déclin du féodalisme libanais 1840–1861* (Beirut, 1958).
56. Vol. i, pp. 167–8.
57. London, 1957.
58. London, 1938.
59. E. Kedourie: *England and the Middle East* (London, 1956), Z. N. Zeine: *Arab-Turkish relations and the emergence of Arab nationalism* (Beirut, 1958) and *The struggle for Arab independence* (Beirut, 1960). Also now C. E. Dawn, *From Ottomanism to Arabism* (Urbana, Illinois, 1973) and E. Kedourie, *In the Anglo-Arab Labyrinth* (Cambridge, 1976).
60. ' "The Arab Awakening", A Source for the Historian?' in *Die Welt des Islams*, N. S. vol. 2 (1952) p. 237.
61. p. 95.
62. p. 385.
63. *Majmū'at al-muḥarrarāt al-siyāsiyya wa' l-mufawwadāt al-duwaliyya 'an Sūriya wa-Lubnān*, 3 vols (Jounich, 1910–11).
64. Rome, 1911.
65. 2 vols 6 fascicles (Fasc. I–V, Paris, 1905–11; Fasc. VI, ed F. Tournebize, Beirut, 1921).
66. *Ḥurub al-muqaddamīn* (Bayt Shabāb, 1937).
67. See p. 236, n. 38 above.
68. *al-Sūriyyūn fī Miṣr*, vol. i (Cairo, 1928).
69. See p. 229, n.10 above.
70. See p. 229, n.11 above.

71. See p. 229, n.7 above.
72. See p. 231, n.14 above.
73. *Manshūrāt al-jāmi'a al-lubnāniyya, qism al-dirāsāt al-ta'rīkhīyya.*
74. *Mudīriyyat al-āthār, nuṣūṣ wa wathā'iq ta'rīkhiyya.*
75. Jounieh, 1930-50.
76. Harissa, 1910-.
77. Cairo, 1926-9.
78. Jounieh then Beirut, 1930-.
79. Hadath, 1956-.
80. Sayda, 1909.
81. Beirut, 1898-.
82. See p. 226, n.1. above.
83. See p. 229, n.8 above.
84. See p. 230, n.13 above.
85. *al-Usūl al-'arabiyya li ta'rīkh Sūriyya fi 'ahd Muḥammad 'Alī bāshā,* 5 vols in 4 (Beirut, 1930-3).
86. *al-Maḥfūẓāt al-malikiyya al-miṣriyya,* 4 vols (Beirut, 1940-3).
87. They include: *The Royal Archives of Egypt and the Origins of the Egyptian Expedition to Syria, 1831-1841* (Beirut, 1936); *The Royal Archives of Egypt and the Disturbances in Palestine, 1834* (Beirut, 1938); *Bashīr bayn al-sulṭān wa' l-'azīz, 1804-41,* vol. i (1956), vol. ii (1957).
88. For a partial exploration of the Archives, cf. Dominique Chevallier, 'Aspects sociaux de la question d'Orient: aux origines des troubles agraires libanais en 1858', in *Annales* (January-March 1959) i, 33-64. For a description of them, see now M. C. Chehab, 'Les archives historiques du Liban' in J. Berque and D. Chevallier (eds), *Les Arabes par leurs archives* (Paris, 1976) p. 55.

CHAPTER 11

1. L. Binder (ed), *Politics in Lebanon* (New York etc. 1966); see also M. Hudson, *The Precarious Republic: Political Modernization in Lebanon* (New York, 1968) and K. S. Salibi, *The Modern History of Lebanon* (London, 1965).
2. A. Hottinger, 'Zu'ama in historical perspective' in Binder, p. 85f.
3. A. Blok, *The Mafia of a Sicilian Village 1860-1960* (Oxford, 1974).
4. I. F. Harik, *Politics and Change in a Traditional Society: Lebanon, 1711-1845* (Princeton, N.J., 1968); K. S. Salibi, *Maronite Historians of Mediaeval Lebanon* (Beirut, 1959); Salibi, 'The Traditional histriography of the Maronites' in B. Lewis and P. M. Holt (eds), *Historians of the Middle East* (London, 1962) p. 212f; A. H. Hourani, 'Historians of Lebanon' in Lewis and Holt, p. 226f.
5. P. Carali (B. Qar'alī), *Fakhr al-Din II e la Corte di Toscana,* 2 vols (Rome, 1938) and *Fakhr al-Dīn al-Ma'nī al-thānī* ... (Harissa, 1938); A. Ismail, *Histoire du Liban,* vol. 1, *Le Liban au temps de Fakhr al-Din II (1590-1633)* (Paris, 1955).

6. J. C. Baroja, 'The city and the country: reflexions on some ancient commonplaces' in J. Pitt-Rivers (ed), *Mediterranean Countrymen* (Paris, 1963).
7. P. Rondot, 'The political institutions of Lebanese democracy' in Binder, p. 127f.
8. M. Chiha, *Essais*, 2 vols (Beirut, 1950-2), particularly vol. I, p. 202 and vol. II, p. 200; A. Hourani, *Arabic Thought in the Liberal Age* (London, 1962) p. 319f.
9. C. Corm, *L'art phénicien: petit répertoire* (Beirut, n.d.) p. 39.
10. E. E. Ramsaur, *The Young Turks: Prelude to the Revolution of 1908* (Princeton, N.J., 1957); R. I. Khalidi, *British Policy towards Syria and Palestine, 1906-1914* (London, 1980), chs. 4 and 5.
11. L. Zuwiyya Yamak, *The Syrian Social Nationalist Party: an Ideological Analysis* (Cambridge, Mass., 1966).
12. Rondot in Binder, p. 136.
13. F. I. Khuri, 'Sectarian loyalty among rural immigrants in two Lebanese suburbs: a stage between national and family allegiance' in R. Antoun and I. Harik (eds), *Rural Politics and Social Change in the Middle East* (Bloomington, 1972) p. 198f.

CHAPTER 13

1. Some biographical details in Bernard Wasserstein, *The British in Palestine: the Mandatory Government and the Arab-Jewish Conflict 1917-1929* (London, 1978) p. 182f.
2. George Antonius, *The Arab Awakening* (London, 1938) p. 250.
3. *Ibid*, pp. 182-3.
4. *Ibid*, pp. 321-2.
5. Richard Aldington, *Lawrence of Arabia, a Biographical Inquiry* (London, 1955); John E. Mack, *A Prince of our Disorder: the Life of T. E. Lawrence* (Boston, 1976).
6. Elizabeth Monroe, *Britain's Moment in the Middle East 1914-1956* (London, 1963).
7. Antonius Papers (Middle East Centre, St. Antony's College, Oxford): Antonius to W. S. Rogers, 15 February 1939.
8. Great Britain, Cmnd. 5974, *Report of a Committee set up to consider certain Correspondence between Sir Henry McMahon ... and the Sharif of Mecca in 1915 and 1916* (London, 1939) p. 10.
9. Thomas Naff, 'Reform and the conduct of Ottoman diplomacy in the reign of Selim III, 1789-1807' in *Journal of the American Oriental Society*, 83 (1963) p. 295; Allan Cunningham, 'Stratford Canning and the Tanzimat' in W. R. Polk and R. L. Chambers (eds), *Beginnings of Modernization in the Middle East: the Nineteenth Century* (Chicago, 1968) p. 245.
10. Lord Cromer, *Modern Egypt* (London, 1908); Afaf Lutfi al-Sayyid, *Egypt and Cromer* (London, 1968); Alexander Schölch, *Ägypten den Ägyptern! Die politische unde gesellschaftliche Krise der Jahre 1878-1882 in*

Ägypten (Zurich, 1972); Jacques Berque, *L'Egypte, impérialisme et révolution* (Paris, 1967).
11. Arnold J. Toynbee, *The Western Question in Greece and Turkey: a Study in the Contact of Civilizations* (London, 1922).
12. *Ibid*, pp. 61, 100.
13. Antonius Papers: Annual Report to the Institute of Current World Affairs, 1933-4 and 1934-5.
14. Amīn Saʿīd, *al-Thawra al-ʿarabiyya al-kubrā*, 3 vols (Cairo, 1934).
15. Antonius Papers: Antonius to W. S. Rogers 18 April 1933 and 16 May 1933.
16. Elie Kedourie, *England and the Middle East: the Destruction of the Ottoman Empire 1914-1921* (Cambridge, 1956) and *In the Anglo-Arab Labyrinth: the McMahon-Husayn Correspondence and its Interpretations 1914-1939* (Cambridge, 1976); Sylvia G. Haim, 'The Arab Awakening – a source for the historian?' in *Welt des Islams,* new series 2 (1953) p. 236; A.L. Tibawi, *A Modern History of Syria* (London, 1969) and *Anglo-Arab Relations and the Question of Palestine 1914-1922* (London, 1977); Z. N. Zeine, *The Emergence of Arab Nationalism* (Beirut, 1966); C. E. Dawn, *From Ottomanism to Arabism: Essays on the Origins of Arab Nationalism* (Urbana, 1973); R. I. Khalidi, *British Policy towards Syria and Palestine 1906-1914* (London, 1980).
17. Majid Khadduri, ' ʿAziz ʿAli al-Maṣrī and the Arab nationalist movement' in A. Hourani (ed), *Saint Antony's Papers 17, Middle Eastern Affairs 4* (London, 1965) p. 140.
18. Antonius, *The Arab Awakening,* p. 60.
19. *Ibid.,* p. 103.
20. C. E. Dawn, 'The Rise of Arabism in Syria' in *From Ottomanism to Arabism,* p. 148.
21. London, 1973.
22. André Raymond, *Artisans et commerçants au Caire au XVIIIe siècle,* 2 vols (Damascus, 1973-4); S. J. Shaw, *The Financial and Administrative Organization and Development of Ottoman Egypt 1517-1798* (Princeton, N.J., 1962); Abdel-Karim Rafeq, *The Province of Damascus 1723-1783* (Beirut, 1966); Karl Barbir, *Ottoman Rule in Damascus 1708-1758* (Princeton, N.J., 1962).
23. Barbir, ch. 1.
24. Antonius, *The Arab Awakening,* p. 13.
25. Robert N. Bellah, 'Civil religion in America' in *Beyond Belief: Essays on Religion in a Post-Traditional World* (New York, 1970).
26. Clifford Geertz, 'Ideology as a cultural system' in *The Interpretation of Cultures* (London, 1975) p. 218.
27. C. E. Dawn, 'The Amir of Mecca al-Ḥusayn ibn-ʿAli and the origin of the Arab Revolt' in *From Ottomanism to Arabism,* p. 1.
28. Antonius, *The Arab Awakening,* pp. 355-6.
29. *Ibid.* pp. 260-2.
30. Mayir Verité, 'The Balfour Declaration and its makers' in *Middle Eastern Studies,* 6 (1970) p. 48.
31. Sulaymān Mūsā, *al-Ḥaraka al-ʿarabiyya* (Beirut, 1970); Isaiah Friedman, *The Question of Palestine 1914-1918: British-Jewish-Arab Relations*

(London, 1973); Jukka Nevakivi, *Britain, France and the Arab Middle East 1914–1920* (London, 1969); Roger Adelson, *Mark Sykes: Portrait of an Amateur* (London, 1975); for Tibawi and Kedourie, see note 16.

32. Kedourie, *In the Anglo-Arab Labyrinth, passim*.
33. Friedman, *The Question of Palestine, passim*.
34. References to Nicolson, Toynbee and Grey in Kedourie, *In the Anglo-Arab Labyrinth*, pp. 207f, 209f, and 230f; references to Balfour and Lloyd George in review of Friedman's book in *Times Literary Supplement*, 2 November 1973.
35. Kedourie, *In the Anglo-Arab Labyrinth*, p. 163f.
36. *Ibid.*, p. 197.
37. Antonius, *The Arab Awakening*, pp. 274–5, 435–6.
38. 'Memorandum of a conference held on the 7 February 1917', p. 11, in Samuel Papers (Middle East Centre, St Antony's College, Oxford).
39. Kedourie, *In the Anglo-Arab Labyrinth*, p. 84.
40. *Ibid.*, p. 233f.
41. Gilbert Falkingham Clayton, *An Arabian Diary* (Berkeley, 1969) p. 120.
42. Antonius Papers: Antonius to W. S. Rogers, 12 February 1932, 9 April 1932, 23 April 1932, 13 May 1932, Annual Report to the Institute of Current World Affairs 1931–32.
43. Tom Bowden, 'The Politics of the Arab rebellion in Palestine 1936–39' in *Middle Eastern Studies*, 11 (1975) p. 147.
44. 'They ought to have thought' in *The Poems of C. P. Cafavy*, English trans. John Mavrogordato (London, 1952) p. 190.

Index

'Abbasids, 2, 4, 28
'Abduh, Shaykh Muhammad 70, 75, 91, 96, 98-100, 123, 184-5, 188
Abdülhamid II, Sultan, 15, 56-7, 62, 115, 119, 121-2
Abu Bakr al-Siddiq, 76, 77; Siddiqiyya, 77
Abu 'Izz al-Din, Sulayman, 159
Abu Shaqra, Husayn, 114, 161
Abyad, Georges, 118
Adams, C. C., *Islam and Modernism*, 90
Adams, Robert M., *Land behind Baghdad*, 3-4
Adelson, R., 208
Africa, North, 2, 6, 9, 12, 14-17, 20-2; notables, 37-8, 45, 51, 53, 65; Sufism, 76, 97-8, 101; nationalism, 182-3, 189-92, 197, 208
Ahdab, Khayr al-Din, 177
Aldington, Richard, 195
Aleppo, 6, 7, 13, 20, 23, 31; notables, 49-51, 57, 59, 65-7; and Egypt, 104-5, 115, 203
Algeria, 6, 12, 16-17, 65, 101, 190, 192
'Ali Bey, 69, 70, 107, 131
'Ammun, Salim, 135
Anaissi, T., *Bullarium Maronitarum*, 167
Anatolia, 46, 95
al-Alusi., Khayr al-din, 98
al-Ansari, 91
Antonius, George, *The Arab Awakening*, xiii, 165-6, 193-215; George Antonius Memorial Lecture, ix
Arab League, 18
Arabs, 1, 10-11, 16, 18; revolutions, 68, 71; culture, 163; nationalism, 166, 182, 186-7, 200-2, 204, 207, 210; 'Arabism', 206
Armenians, 9, 10, 16, 48, 50, 59, 112, 116, 148, 171, 183, 204
Arslan family, 126, 129
Ashtor-Strauss, E., 29
Asia, Central, 20, 77, 79, 95
Asia Minor, 9, 13, 20, 46, 56, 80, 87, 95, 198-9
'Assaf family, 125-6, 128
Assemani family: Joseph, *Bibliotheca Orientalis*; Joseph Aloysius; Simon, 151
Atatürk, Mustafa Kemal, 17, 95, 186-7
Aubin, J., 25, 31, 33
Austria, 111; Austria-Hungary, 195
'Awn, Bishop Tubiyya, 143
al-'Awra, Ibrahim, 82, 153, 167
Ayalon, D., 46
al-'Aynturini, Shaykh Antuniyus Abu Khattar, 152-3, 168
Ayyubids, 21, 29

Baban family (Sulaymaniyya), 60, 81-3, 86

Baer, G., 53
Baghdad, 2, 3, 13, 31-2, 48, 77, 83, 86-7
Bahri family, 110-11
Baktash, Hajji, Baktashiyya, 77, 79, 87
Balbas, L. Torrès, 34-5
Balfour, Arthur J., 208-9
Balkans, 2, 6, 9, 16, 46, 80, 183, 185, 202
al-Balkhi, Shaykh Sa'd, 80
Baqi Billah, Khwaja (India), 79
Baroja, C., 175
al-Barudi, Mahmud Sami, 54, 70
Barzani Shaykhs, 60, 86; Shaykh Ahmad, Mulla Mustafa, 87
Barzinji family, 60, 81, 83, 86; Ma'ruf, 81, 84-5; 'Abd al-Karim, 'Abd al-Rahim, 81; Shaykh Mahmud, 87
Basha, Fr. Q., 158, 167
Bashir II Shihab, 131-2, 153-5, 160-1, 167, 169
Ba'thist Revolution, Syria, 74
Batiniyya, 99
Bayhum family, Beirut, 169
Bayram, Muhammad, 39
Beduin, 2, 11, 45, 48, 51, 53, 59, 63, 84
Beirut, 59, 60, 104-5, 113, 115-6; politics, 126, 130-1, 134, 136-7, 139, 141, 143-4, 148, 172, 177
Bellah, Robert, 'The civil religion of America', 205
Berque, Jacques, *Egypt, Imperialism and Revolution*, xviii, xix, 36n, 197
Binder, Leonard (ed.), *Politics in Lebanon*, 170-2
al-Bistami, Abu Yazid Tayfur, 77
al-Bitar, 'A., 38, 40
Blunt, Wilfred Scawen, 70
Bowden, T., 214
Bowen, Harold (with H. A. R. Gibb), *Islamic Society and the West*, xvii
Bowring report (1837), 111
Boyle, Harry, 117
Britain, 14, 16-17, 54, 111, 116; Lebanon, 131-3, 140, 144, 146, 154, 157; occupation of Egypt, 183-4, 186; post World War I, 190, 193, 195-7, 199-200, 207-12
Brown, J. P., 80
Brunschvig, R., 34
Buhturi family, 126-8
Bulaq Press, Egypt, 110
al-Bustani, Butrus, 116, 120, 156-7, 204; Salim, 116
Bustani, F. A., 167-8
Butrus Ghali Pasha, 119
Byzantium, 6, 21, 26

Cahen, Claude, 24, 30, 33
Cairo, 2, 7, 13, 67, 69; Syrians in, 104, 106, 110-11, 115; nationalism, 182, 207
Caliphate, 2-4, 8, 20, 23, 28, 81, 181, 204
Carali, Fr. P. (Bulus Qar'ali), 158, 160, 164, 167
Cavafy, C. P., 214
Çelebi, Evliya, 80
Cevdet Pasha, 39
Chauvel, J., 213
Chebli, Michel, 164-5
Cheikho (Shaykhu), Fr. L., 163
Chevallier, Dominique, *La société du Mont Liban*, 66, 143, 149
Chiha, Michel, 138, 145, 164, 176
China, Sung dynasty, 3, 25-6
Chishtiyya, 83
Christians, 6, 9, 16; notables, 50, 52, 63, 65-6; in Egypt, 105-8, 110-11, 115-16, 118, 122; in Lebanon, 128, 134, 137, 143-4, 146-7, 150-1, 161,

173; nationalism, 182-3, 187, 201
Churchill, Colonel C., *Druzes and Maronites under Turkish Rule*, 144, 160-1
Clayton, Sir Gilbert, 200, 209, 213
Clot Bey, A. B., 111
Coles Pasha, 116
Constantinople, *see* Istanbul
Corm, Charles, 176
Crane, Charles, 193
Crete, 13
Cromer, Lord, *Modern Egypt*, 54, 117, 119, 197
Crusades, 12, 126-7, 150
Cunningham, Allan, 197
Cyprus, 10

Dabbas, Charles, 139
Dahir al-'Umar, 130, 153
Damascus, 7, 13, 23, 31; notables, 38, 49-51, 56-7, 59-61, 65-7, 70; Sufism, 80-2, 85, 87, 95; trade with Egypt, 103-23; relations with Lebanon, 127, 130, 134, 166; with Ottoman government, 203, 207
Darwish, Shaykh, 98
Dawn, C. E., 200-3, 207
al-Dayrani, Afram, 158
Derian (Daryan), Mgr., 158
Description de l'Egypte, 111
de Tarrazi, Vicomte Philippe, 158, 163
de Testa, *Recueil des Traités de la Porte Ottomane*, 162, 167
Dib, Mgr. P., 158
al-Dibs, Yusuf, 162-3
al-Dimashqi, Mikha'il, 159
d'Ohsson, M., 80
Druzes, 40, 60, 63, 65, 67, 115; Lebanon, 125-8, 130-4, 143-5, 147, 151-2, 157-61, 172, 174-5

al-Duwayhi, Patriarch Istifan, *Tarikh al-azmina*, 150-1, 158, 167-8, 173

Edmonds, C. J., 78, 84-5, 88
Education, 8, 16, 117-18, 121, 128, 135-6, 147
Egypt, 6-7, 9, 13, 15-17, 20-1; notables, 37-8, 40, 46-9, 51, 53-4, 57-8, 64-5; revolutions, 67-72, 74; Sufism, 98, 101; Syrian immigrants, 103-23; Lebanon, 131-2, 153-4; nationalism, 186-7, 189-90; Anglo-Egyptian relations, 195, 197, 202, 213
Egyptian Steam Navigation Company, 113
El-Ali, S., 31
Elisséeff, N., 24, 31
Emigration, 135-6, 139, 147-8, 175, 177
European intervention, xvi, xviii, 6, 13-16, 25-6, 38-9, 59, 62-6, 71-3; Lebanon, 133-5, 143-4, 146, 183

Fakhr al-Din II Ma'n, 11, 125, 127-9, 150-2, 160, 164-5, 167, 174
Far'awn family, 108, 110
Farhi family, 110
al-Faruqi, M. S., 207
Fatimids, 21
Faysal, Amir, 209, 211
Fertile Crescent, 49, 64-5
Financiers, 113-14, 171-2
Fitzgerald, Sir Gerald, 116
France: North Africa, 14, 16, 69, 95, 101, 106, 108-11; Lebanon, 129, 133, 136-7, 139-40, 144-6, 148, 156-7, 161, 164, 166; post-war policies, 183, 195, 207-12

Friedman, I., 208-9
Fuad Pasha, 70

al-Gaylani, 'Abd al-Qadir, 65-6, 87, 94, 101
Geertz, Clifford, *Islam Observed*, xviii, 205
Germany, 195, 207
Gernet, J., 25-6
al-Ghazali, *Ihya*, 97-8
al-Ghujdawani, 'Abd al-Khaliq, 77
Gibb, H. A. R., *Modern Trends in Islam*, (with H. Bowen) *Islamic Society and the West*, xiv-xvii, 142
Gilsenan, M., 101
Gökalp, Ziya, 185
Greeks, 9, 16, 21, 43, 112-13, 182, 198-9
Grey, Sir Edward, 209
Guys, H., 154

Haim, Sylvia, 165, 200
al-Hamadhani, Yusuf, 77
Hamada family, 128
Hamidiyya Shadhiliyya order, 101
Hanbalis, 94; neo-Hanbalism, 123
Harik, I. F., *Politics and Change in a Traditional Society*, 149
Hashimite family, 12, 200, 206-7, 211; see also Husayn, Sharif; Faysal, Amir
al-Hasibi, 40
Hasluck, F. W., 80, 87
al-Hattuni, Mansur Tannus, 159
Haydar Ahmad Shihab, Amir, 154-7, 161, 167, 174
al-Haydari, Shaykh 'Ubayd Allah, 87
Hegel, xv, 179-80
Heyd, U., 56
Hijaz, 6, 12, 14, 49, 57-9, 66, 82
Historians, 5, 37-9, 77, 144, 149-69, 202, 208

Hitti, Philip K., *Lebanon in History*, 165
Hittites, 2, 186
Hogarth, D. G., 200
Holt, P. M., 36n, 46
Holy cities, 6, 7, 13, 49, 61, 71, 81
Hourani, Albert, *Arabic Thought in the Liberal Age*, xv, 145
House, Colonel, 200
Hurgronje, C. Snouck, 87-8
Husayn, Sharif, 67, 71, 194, 207, 209-11

Ibn Abi Diyaf, 38
Ibn al-'Arabi, 97
Ibn al-Jawzi, 94, 98-9
Ibn al-Qila'i, 167
Ibn Khaldun, 5
Ibn Qayim al-Jawziyya, 91
Ibn Qudama, 94
Ibn Sa'ud, 'Abd al-'Aziz, 213
Ibn Sibat, 150, 152, 168
Ibn Taymiyya, 94, 98-9
Ibn Yahya, Salih, 142, 152
Ibrahim Pasha, 111, 131, 157, 168
Inalcik, Halil, *the Ottoman Empire*, 202
India, xv, 4, 11, 20, 26, 61, 63, 79-83, 95, 189, 195
Institute of Current World Affairs, 193
Iran/Persia, xv, 2, 4, 6, 8-9, 20-1, 47, 49, 77, 79, 83; nationalism, 186-7, 191-2, 197, 204
Iraq, 2, 6, 13, 16, 18, 20, 31-2, 38, 47, 57-60; political development, 67, 71, 95, 190, 192, 195, 201, 208, 210
Islam, xvii-xviii, 180-1, 183-9
'Islamic city', xvii, 19-35
Ismail, Adel, *Histoire du Liban*, 164-5, 174

Isma'il, Khedive, 54, 112-19
Isma'ilis, 22, 99
Istanbul (Constantinople), 6, 14, 38, 42-3, 49-50, 55-6, 65, 80, 86-7, 95, 105, 115-16, 129, 182, 203-4
Itzkowitz, N., 43
Italy, 16, 21-2, 95, 111-12, 129, 195

al-Jabarti, 'A., 38, 40, 103-4, 109
Jacobites, 127, 150-1, 158, 173
Jalal al-Din al-Rumi, *Mathnawi*, 91
Jalili family, 11, 13, 48-9
Jamal al-Din al-Afghani, 75-6, 98, 166, 184
Janissaries, 43-5, 49-51, 55, 58-9, 66, 109
al-Jazzar, Ahmad Pasha, 130-1, 153-6
Jessup, H. H., 144
Jesuits, *al-Mashriq* periodical, 167-8
Jews, 2, 6, 9-10, 16, 50, 52, 59, 63, 66, 81; in Egypt, 107, 110, 113; Lebanon, 128, 171; nationalism, 186, 190, 195-6, 199, 204, 207-8, 211-3
al-Jisr, Husayn, 98, 100
Jordan, 2, 66, 190
Jouplain, M. (B. Nujaym), *La Question du Liban*, 162
Journalism, 116, 118-19, 122, 163
al-Juburi, Shaykh Musa, 87
Jumayyil, Antun, *al-Ahram*, 123
Jumblat family, 12, 106, 130, 132, 144, 155
al-Junayd, 76, 91, 99

Kant, Immanuel, xv
Karam, Yusuf, 175
Karama, Butrus, 156
Kedourie, Élie, *In the Anglo-Arab Labyrinth*, 196, 200, 208-11

Khadduri, Majid, 201
Khalid, Mawlana (Abu'l-Baha Diya al-din Khalid al-Shahrizuri), 77, 81-9, 95
Khalidiyya, 77, 86-7
Khalil, Shaykh, 78
Khalwatiyya, 80
Khayr al-Din, 53
Khazin family, 128-31, 161, 169, 174
Khazin, Farid and Philippe, 167
Khojaganiyya, 77
Khurasan, Iran, 77
al-Khuri, Bishara, 139
Kitchener, H. H., 119
Kléber, J. B., 110
Kubrawiyya order, 83
Kurdistan, 10, 13, 51, 60, 66, 81, 83-6, 88, 149, 192
Kurds, 9, 16, 78, 81-2
al-Kuzbari, Shaykh Muhammad, 81, 85

Lambton, A. K. S., 39-40
Lammens, Fr. H., *La Syrie— précis historique*, 163
Lane, E. W., 111
Langer, W. L., xiii
Languages, 7, 11, 68, 77, 109, 114-16, 122, 126, 128, 130, 151-2, 162, 181, 186, 201, 205
Laoust, Henri, 90, 94
Lapidus, I. M., *Muslim Cities in the Later Middle Ages*, xx, 30
Lassner, J., 31
Lawrence, T. E., *Seven Pillars of Wisdom*, 194-5
Lebanon, 10, 11, 13; notables, 38, 40, 60, 63; revolutions, 67, 71; Sufism, 97-8; contacts with Egypt, 104, 106, 110, 115, 123; political development, 124-41; nation-

state, 142-8; national image, 149-69; civil war, 170-8; modern developments, 187, 190-1, 201, 204, 213
Levant, 112, 115
Lewis, Bernard, 3, 5
Libya, 12, 14, 16-17, 76, 97-8
Literature, 118-22, 163, 201
Lloyd, Lord, 213
Lloyd George, David, 209
Longrigg, S., 145
Lutfallah family, 114

Mack, John, 195
McMahon, Sir Henry, 209, 211
Makdisi, G., 94
Ma'luf, 'Isa Iskandar, 142, 159-60
Mamluks, 6, 13, 20-1, 30; notables, 46-7, 49, 51-3; revolutions, 68-9; trade, 106-8; Lebanon, 125-7, 130, 150-1, 153; Egypt and Syria, 181
Ma'n family, 126-7, 129, 142, 151, 154, 160-1; *and see* Fakhr al-Din II
Mandates, 62, 72-3, 136, 140, 163, 186, 193, 200
Marçais, George and William, 22-3
'Mardaites', 174
Mardam, J., 72
Mardin, S., 55
Maronites, 9, 40; in Egypt, 105-8, 110-11, 115, 118; in Lebanon, 125-38, 140-1, 143-7, 150-2, 157-8, 161, 173, 176
Marx, Karl, xv, 192
Masabki, Niqula, 110
Massignon, Louis, 22-4, 32, 91
Ma'sum, Shaykh Muhammad, 80
Mawlawiyya order, 96
Melkite families, 105, 113
Mengin, F., 106

Mishaqa, Mikha'il, 121-2, 144, 161
al-Misri, 'Aziz 'Ali, 71
Mogul Emperors, India, 4, 11, 20, 79, 95
Molé, M., 77
Mongols, 4, 21
Morocco, 23, 101, 191, 197
Mosul, 11, 13, 48-9, 58, 60, 66
Mountain, ideologies of the, 173
Mubarak, 'Ali, 38, 111
Muhammad 'Ali, 15, 17, 40, 51-6, 64, 69-70, 110-11, 115, 117, 131
Mujaddidiyya, 77, 80, 83
al-Munayyir, Hananiyya, 154, 168
Murad, Nicolas, 174
al-Muradi family, 80-1, 85, 95; 'Ali, 80; Husayn, 80-1, 85; Khalil, 80
Musa, Sulayman, 195, 208
Muslim Brotherhood, Egypt, 187
Mustafa II, Sultan, 80
Mu'tazilites, 96
Mutran, Khalil, 120
Mystics, Islamic, 8-9, 181-2, 184, 192

al-Nabulsi, 'Abd al-Ghani, 80
Nadim, 'A., 70
Naff, Thomas, 197
Nahhas, M., 72, 73
Najjar, Rose and Cécile, 118
Nallino, C., 213
Napoleon Bonaparte, 14, 108-10, 131, 153, 156
Napoleon III, 66
Naqqash, Marun, 118
Naqqash, Salim, 118
Naqshband, Baha al-Din Muhammad, 76-8
Naqshbandiyya, 75-80, 82-5, 87-8, 95-7, 99

Nation states, 14, 16-7, 182
Nationalism, 1-2, 16-17, 53-4, 62, 70-2, 121-2; Lebanon, 136-7, 140-8, 165-6, 174; modern developments, 179-92, 195, 198, 201-2, 207, 213
Nevakivi, J., 208
Newman, John Henry, *Lectures on the History of the Turks*, 2
Newspapers, 16, 56, 118-19, 121, 123
Nicolson, Harold, 209
Nimr, Faris, ed. *al Muqtataf* periodical, 119-22
Nomads, 5, 10, 15, 26-7, 34
Notables, 11, 29, 36-66, 68-71
Nubar Pasha, 54
Nujaym, B., *see* Jouplain, P.

Orthodox Christians, 9, 10, 16, 48; Syrians in Egypt, 105, 108, 111, 125; Lebanon, 134, 137, 154, 158-9, 166, 171, 213
Osman, 7, 55
Ottoman Turks, xix, xx, 1-18, 20-1; reform and notables, 36-66; Arab revolutions, 68-70; Lebanon, 126-9, 133-5, 143, 145, 150-1, 157, 177; modern developments, 181-2, 197, 200-5, 206
Owen, E. R. J., 36n

Pakistan, 189
Palestine, 2, 47-8, 63, 67; merchants in Egypt, 104, 111; refugees in Lebanon, 171-2; Jewish state, 193, 195-6, 199, 201, 208, 211-12
Pan-Islamism, 206
Pan-Turanism, 186, 204
Parti Populaire Syrien (Hizb al-Qawmi), 177
Pauty, E., 19-20

Periodicals, 119-23, 168
Persia, *see* Iran
Phoenicia, 1-2, 176, 186
Pilgrim routes, 7, 49, 61, 81-2
Plato, xv, 9
Porte, Sublime, 47, 144

Qadiri order, 81, 83, 85; Qadiriyya, 101
Qar'ali, Bulus, 174
Qays families, 129, 132
Qudsi, Iliya, 58
Quwwatli, S., 72

Rabbath, Fr. A., *Documents inédits*, 167
Rahim Allah, Mirza (Darwish Muhammad), 82
Raphael, Fr. P., 158
Rashid 'Ali, 67
Raymond, A., 32, 202
Revolutions, Arab, 67-74
Riaz Pasha, 54, 70, 117, 119
Rich, C. J., 84
Rida, Muhammad Rashid, 75-6, 88, 90-102, 120, 122-3, 184, 187, 201
Rogers, J. M., 32
Rondot, P., *Institutions politiques du Liban*, 145
Rousseau, J.-J., 2
Royal Institute of International Affairs, xiii-xiv, xvii
Russell, A., 37
Russia, 13-14, 16, 64, 87-8, 95, 183, 198, 204
Rustum, Asad, 160, 167-9

Sabbagh family: 'Abbud, 153; Mikha'il, 153, 167
al-Safadi, Ahmad al-Khalidi, 150, 152, 160, 167
Safavi dynasty, Iran, 4, 6, 8, 20
Sa'id, Amin, *al-Thawra al-'arabiyya al-kubra*, 200

Saʿid Pasha, 114-15
Sakakini Frères, 113
Salafiyya movement, 90, 94, 99, 101, 201, 204
Salibi, Ilya and Sulayman, 142-8
Salibi, K. S., *Maronite Historians of Mediaeval Lebanon, The Modern History of Lebanon*, 149
Sanusiyya, 76
Sarruf, Yaʿqub, ed. *al-Muqtataf*, 119, 121-3
Sassanian Empire, 22
Saudi Arabia, 190
Sauvaget, J., 20, 22-4, 31-4
al-Sayyid, Afaf Lutfi, 197
al-Sayyid, Ahmad Lutfi, 185
Scanlon, G. T., 33-4
Schimmel, A. M., 91
Schölch, Alexander, 197
Seljuq Empire, 6, 7, 21
Shahin, Tanyus, 175
Shamdinan family: Shaykh ʿUbeyd Allah, 87
Shammas, Fr., 158
Sharif Pasha, 54, 70
Shaw, Stanford J., 36n 37, 46, 202
al-Shaykh Ahmad, Sayyid, 100
Shaykhu, L.: see Cheikho, L.
al-Shidyaq family: Ahmad Faris, 110, 156, 204; Asʿad, 156; Tannus, 156-7, 163, 174
Shihab, Amir Maurice, 169
Shihab family, 12, 106, 126-7, 129-34, 142-3, 151-5, 160-1, 164, 174; see also Haydar Ahmad Shihab, Amir; Yusuf Shihab, Amir; Beshir II Shihab
Shumayyil, Shibli, 121-2
Sidnawi family, 113
Sidqi Pasha, 213
al-Sirhindi, Shaykh Ahmad, 77, 79-80, 88, 95

Spain, 20
Stern, Samuel, xv, xvii, 30
Sudan, 154, 190
Suez Canal, 52, 57, 61, 208
Sufism, 8-9, 75-89, 90-102; see also Mystics
Suhrawardiyya, 82
Sulayman Faʾiq, 38
Sulayman Pasha, 81, 87, 110, 153
Sultanates, 4-9
Sunnis, 5, 8, 46, 56; and Sufism, 77-8, 88, 99; in Lebanon, 125-7, 134-5, 137-8, 146-8, 159, 172, 205
Suwaydi family, 87
Sykes, Sir Mark, 194, 200, 210-11; Sykes-Picot Agreement, 209-10
Syria, xix, xxi, 2, 6-7, 13, 16, 18, 20-2; notables, 38, 40, 56-9, 61; revolutions, 67, 71-2, 74; Sufism, 95, 101; Egyptian relations, 103-23; Lebanon, 162, 166, 177; modern developments, 190, 195, 201-2, 207, 210-13; see also Aleppo, Beirut, Damascus
Syrian Desert tribes, 10, 13, 65

al-Tabari, 155
Tanukhi rulers, 126, 150, 152
Taqla family, *al-Ahram*, 118-19, 121, 123
al-Tarabulsi, Nawfal, *Kashf al-litham*, 159
Tayfuriyya, 77
Tibawi, A. L., 200-1, 208
al-Tijani, Ahmad, 96
Tijaniyya order, 96, 100-1, 187
Timurids, 79
Toynbee, Arnold, *Study of History, Survey of International Affairs, The Western Question in Greece*

and Turkey, xiii, xiv, xvii, 198, 209
Trade, 50, 103-7, 111-14, 123, 130-1, 133, 135, 139, 143, 148
Tripoli, 127, 130, 137, 151, 174
Tunisia, 2, 12, 15-17, 37-8, 51, 53, 182-3, 189-90
Tuqan family, 12
Turcoman families, 125-9
Turk, Niqula, 156
Turkey, 2-5, 16-18, 20-1, 57, 77, 157; post-Ottoman, 182, 186-7, 189-90, 202, 204

'Umar Makram, 40, 53, 70
'Umari family, 48
Uniates, 50, 105, 150-2, 173
United States of America, 193, 195, 197, 200
'Urabi Pasha, Ahmad, 54, 67, 70
Uways al-Qarani, Uwaysis, 78

Vereté, Mayir, 'The Balfour Declaration and its makers', 208

Wahhabis, 13, 82, 94, 98, 102, 184
Walzer, Richard, xv
Weber, Max, xvii-xviii, 23, 25, 41
Westermann, W. L., 200

William of Tyre, 150, 155
Wilson, Woodrow, 193
Wingate, Sir Reginald, 210
World War I, 18, 71, 73, 119, 122-3, 136, 167, 186, 193, 196, 203, 206-7
World War II, 12, 140, 168, 196

Yaman families, 129, 132
Yanni, Jirji, 162
al-Yasawi, Ahmad, Yasawiyya, 77
Yazbak, Yusuf, 132, 161
al-Yaziji, Shaykh Nasif, 154, 156, 159, 204
Yemen revolution (1962), 67, 190
Young Turks, 57, 62, 71-2, 121-2, 135, 183, 186, 201, 203
Yusuf Shihab, Amir, 153-5
Yusuf Genç Pasha, 81-2, 110

Zaghlul, Sa'd, 71, 72
Zakhar, Fr. Rufa'il Antun ('Don Raphael'), 109-10
Zaydan, Jurji, ed. *al-Hilal* periodical, 120-2, 163
al-Zayn, Shaykh 'Arif, 158-9, 168
Zayyat, H., 158
Zeine, Z. N., 200-1
Ziyada, May, 118
Zoroastrianism, 99
Zughayb family, 109